REX
AND THE
CITY

REX

A Woman,
a Man, and a
Dysfunctional
Dog

AND THE

CITY

Lee Harrington

VILLARD Ⓥ NEW YORK

Rex and the City is a work of nonfiction. Portions of the book have appeared in print, in somewhat different form, elsewhere. Some of the names and certain characteristics of the persons, dogs, and places involved—including the author's places of employment—have been altered. Any resulting resemblances to persons living or dead is entirely coincidental and unintentional.

Published in the United States by Villard Books,
an imprint of The Random House Publishing Group,
a division of Random House, Inc., New York.

VILLARD and "V" CIRCLED Design are registered
trademarks of Random House, Inc.

LIBRARY OF CONGRESS CATALOGING-IN-PUBLICATION DATA

Harrington, Lee.
  Rex and the city: a woman, a man, and a dysfunctional
  dog / Lee Harrington.
      p.   cm.
  ISBN 1-4000-6301-9
  1. Dogs—New York (State)—New York—Anecdotes.
2. Dog owners—Behavior—New York (State)—New York—
Anecdotes. 3. Human-animal relationships—New York
(State)—New York—Anecdotes.
SF426.2 .H35 2006
636.70974'71—dc22   2005045660

Printed in the United States of America on
acid-free paper

www.villard.com

9 8 7 6 5 4 3 2 1

First Edition

For my parents:
Jeanne-Amelia Duhart Harrington
Jane Palmer Harrington
Charles Francis Harrington, Jr.

And for

Sir Wallace Wagsalot,
Duke of Suffolk Street

I would like, to begin with, to say that though parents, husbands, children, lovers and friends are all very well, they are not dogs. In my day and turn having been each of the above,—except that instead of husbands I was wives,—I know what I am talking about, and am well acquainted with the ups and downs, the daily ups and downs, the sometimes almost hourly ones in the thin-skinned, which seem inevitably to accompany human loves.

Dogs are free from these fluctuations. Once they love, they love steadily, unchangingly, till their last breath.

That is how I like to be loved.

Therefore I will write of dogs.

— Elizabeth Von Arnim,
    from *All the Dogs of My Life* (1936)

What We Miss

Who says it's so easy to save a life? In the middle of an interview for the job you might get you see the cat from the window of the seventeenth floor just as he's crossing the street against traffic, just as you're answering a question about your worst character flaw and lying that you are too careful. What if you keep seeing the cat at every moment you are unable to save him? Failure is more like this than like duels and marathons. Everything can be saved, and bad timing prevents it. Every minute, you are answering the question and looking out the window of the church to see your one great love blinded by the glare, crossing the street, alone.

— Sarah Manguso, from her collection of poems,
    The Captain Lands in Paradise

Contents

REX
AND THE
CITY

CHAPTER 1

The Decision

I n New York City, on a daily basis, millions of women are faced with an existential conflict: what to wear. And on this particular day, on the last day of life as I knew it, meaning my last day of life without a dog, I too faced this conflict. It was the first Saturday of June 1997, and Ted and I had planned to take a day trip out to "the country" (which is what New York City people call the far reaches of Long Island). All week I had been planning to wear a pink linen dress from Paris, with a matching pink hat. To me, it was an outfit that suggested innocence and femininity, a certain je ne sais quoi. But when I pulled said dress out of the closet, I discovered that there was a big dark sticky stain on its backside. Gum or something. From the subway system, no doubt. One of the great risks you take, in New York City, is sitting down.

"Oh, no," I said to Ted. "Look!" I held up the dress to show him.

"Well, find something else to wear," Ted said. Ted was the live-in boyfriend: handsome, talented, responsible, and too smart for his own (or anyone else's) good.

"How many weeks have I been walking around with gum on my ass? The last time I wore this dress was to my interview at that literary magazine."

"I'm sure nobody noticed," Ted said. "Just find something else to wear. And hurry. We're supposed to be at Chip's by noon."

Chip was one of Ted's best friends from college, which was a place they called "New Haven." Chip had been promising for months to take us to the Lloyd Neck Country Club—one of the most exclusive country clubs in the entire Tri-State area, and perhaps the world. And today, finally, we were going! All week long I had looked forward to a day of grand food and fine wine, served to us on silver dishes by waiters with white gloves, followed by some late-afternoon sunbathing by the Italian-tiled pool, where more white-gloved waiters would bring us chilled mango daiquiris, and then perhaps a shirtless George Clooney (who was rumored to belong to Lloyd Neck) would stroll past our cabana and I could say to people that I had seen his naked chest.

But *what to wear?* I had no Plan B in the wardrobe department. And to top it all I was feeling fat. I had gained seven pounds since Ted moved in seven months ago, and there seemed no end in sight. To either predicament. I liked to blame the weight gain on love, however (rather than on the fact that Ted and I drank sangria practically every night). There is something about being in love—the cushion of it, the safety—that simply adds weight to my body, as if the very gravity of the emotion has a substance that grounds you to this earth.

Despite all that, I still wasn't willing to accept that the weight gain was permanent. Therefore I refused to buy anything in a size ten.

But all the dresses that hung in my closet were size eight or smaller. And Ted was breathing down my neck. So I went with the old standby: the little black dress. (An LBD never fails to de-emphasize the bulge and emphasize the legs, and what woman in New York doesn't have great legs?) *My* LBD had a square-cut neck and scooped sleeves and fell just above the knee. I paired it with a Wonderbra and a pair of hip Italian platform sandals and voilà! I was ready.

"Okay," I said to Ted. "I just have to brush my teeth and then we can go."

Ted came out of the bedroom and shook his head when he saw me. "You can't wear that."

We lived together for the same reason most young uncertain-about-each-other couples cohabited in New York: because separately we couldn't afford to rent a decent apartment. Marriage, I suppose, was a p-p-possibility, if only another M-word could enter the equation on my behalf: maturity.

"Why not?" I said.

"You can't wear black to Lloyd Neck." Ted was wearing a pair of khakis, loafers, and a crisp yellow Oxford shirt, buttoned one button too many at his neck.

I lifted my chin. "*I* can."

"No, I'm telling you, you can't. Why don't you just put on a polo shirt and those white Bermuda shorts we got for you at Brooks Brothers last week?"

"I don't want to look dowdy," I said. I was twenty-nine years old and already terrified of such things.

"Who's going to care?"

"I'll care," I said. "Besides, this dress is fine. It's *cute*." And then I set about the task of finding the right handbag to go with my black dress. Deep down, of course, I knew that Ted, having been groomed at some of the nation's finest country clubs himself, was probably right about my outfit. But something in me that day didn't want him to know I knew he was right. It was more important to look thin.

Ted stood right behind me as I opened my wardrobe. "What do you mean you have nothing to wear? You have a whole closet full of clothes."

"This dress is the only thing that *fits*!" I said. "This is what I'm wearing. This is what I *want to wear*!" My voice rose as I spoke, and cracked, and Ted must have sensed that I was on the edge of something, something they used to call female hysteria, and because of that—and because, perhaps, my dress displayed ample cleavage—he let me have my way.

"Well, let's hurry then," Ted said. "If we get to Chip's by noon, he and I might be able to get some golf in before lunch."

I smiled in triumph. Those Bermuda shorts, for the record, were a size ten.

My triumph was short lived. When we arrived at Chip's weekend house in Nassau County ninety minutes later, Chip took one look at my getup and announced that we wouldn't be going to the country club after all. "I know of a great place in Bayville," he said as he led us into the kitchen. "It's right on the water and they serve lobsters and crab. We can sit outside, drink a few beers. How's that sound?"

I was too stunned to answer.

Chip (or Charles Ingersoll Pingrey, as he was known in the Yale alumni magazine) was a benignly handsome, immensely likable man with a large frame and a kind smile.

"Aren't we going to golf?" Ted said.

"Nah," Chip answered. "I couldn't get a tee time."

"Did you even try?" Ted said. I could tell he was half-amused, half-irritated.

Chip answered with: "You guys want something to drink before we go?"

"No," Ted said. "Let's hurry. I'm starved. We didn't have time to eat before we left, because I thought we were going to *golf*."

"Okay then," Chip said. "I just need to find my keys."

After he'd left the room I gave Ted a look, which he knew meant: *Why aren't we going to Lloyd Neck?* "It's this dress, isn't it?" I whispered.

"Don't be paranoid," Ted said. "Chip is simply like that. He changes his mind at the drop of a hat."

And while it's probably true that Chip—who is uncomplicated and a pleasure seeker and above all good of heart—had had a sudden craving for beer and lobster, I thought I knew better. Some people have gay-dar; I have snob-dar. And when it comes to snobbery, LNCC takes first prize.

To cheer myself up, I began to snoop through the cabinets in Chip's kitchen. Whenever we went to Chip's house, which was technically his mother's, I liked to check out all the expensive All-Clad cookware, the two-thousand-dollar German knives, and the cabinets full of French mustards, champagne vinegars, and first-press olive oils from Spain. "Look!" I said to Ted. "An entire cabinet devoted solely to jam! Such beautiful jams! Can you imagine living in a house so big you had room for three different types of lemon curd?"

Ted hugged me and laughed. "That's one of Lee's goals in life," he explained as Chip returned to the kitchen. "To have a cabinet full of fancy jams."

Chip laughed, too, but in an uncertain way. The haves of this world don't always get the have-nots.

"So what's this restaurant we're going to in *lieu* of the club?" Ted asked. He had been an English major at New Haven, and he still loved to use all the uncommon funny-sounding words. "Is it any good?"

"Yeah, it's great," he said. "It's where the locals go."

"Are we going to at least drive past the club?" I said as we climbed into Chip's car.

"No," Chip said. "We're going in the opposite direction."

The opposite direction. My day, my life, clearly were not going as planned.

The Lloyd Neck Country Club is located on a tiny fist-shaped peninsula that juts into Lloyd Harbor. From the center of this fist extends another finger-shaped peninsula, and the club is situated at the very tip. And so, from an aerial point of view, one could say that this peninsula looks something like a hand giving the world the finger, and therefore one could call the Lloyd Neck Country Club the Fuck All of You Club. But nobody did. Because manners at LNCC were very important. And it costs like $350,000 just to join.

So we drove in the opposite direction. I stared out the window and sulked. Saturdays are precious to those of us who live in New York City, you see. Sometimes it's your only chance to get from life what the city, in all its bountiful cruelty, will never deliver: air, sky, space, parking spaces, and a sense of belonging and peace. You can pretend, for a few precious hours, that the clock isn't ticking, that your relationship is solid, that your apartment isn't really only three hundred square feet.

So imagine a Saturday in Lloyd Neck. We passed mansion after fabulous mansion. We passed stately oak trees and fine green lawns. The sky somehow seemed bluer out here than it did in the city, and the color of the grass was almost unearthly, surreal. Even the sunshine had an eternal quality to it; it was as if the inhabitants of what was known as Long Island's Gold Coast were simply entitled to more of it, all the time. They say F. Scott Fitzgerald set his novel *The Great Gatsby* out here, and Fitzgerald is by far my favorite author—one I try to emulate, less the alcoholism and the crack-up at the end of his life. So I put my window down and took a gulp of his epic, golden air, and it tasted of hope and promise. Some of the greatest wealth in the *world* could be found here on this slender, riotous island (one can't help but make Gatsby references on the Gold Coast), and the fact that

I was so close to and yet so far from all that wealth suddenly bothered me for reasons I can't even explain. I mean, I wasn't an *entirely* shallow person back then, before we got the dog. But I certainly did have shallow days. Especially on sunny Saturdays in Lloyd Neck. When you were *supposed* to go to the country club.

And couldn't one argue that every New York City woman has her shallow days? In New York, thousands of people spend hours each day trying to fill their voids with material possessions. The Fendi baguette makes up for your miserable childhood. The Ferrari replaces your low self-esteem. So maybe, on that fateful day, I had been hoping that three hours at the Lloyd Neck Country Club would lift me far above my own reality and carry me beyond my three-hundred-square-foot apartment, my noncommittal relationship, and my ho-hum job.

Lunch, needless to say, was a disappointment. The soft-shell crabs looked and tasted as if they had been soaking in formaldehyde for a few months before they reached our table, and a ratty-looking seagull kept flapping onto our table to beg for food. Above our heads was a giant banner that said: WET T-SHIRT CONTESTS EVERY THURSDAY NIGHT SPONSORED BY BUD LIGHT.

"I'll have champagne, please," I said wearily to the waitress. There was nary a George Clooney in sight.

"We don't have champagne," she said. "We got white, we got red."

I looked over at Ted, and he did a shrug/smile.

"Red, please," I said.

"Oh, let's have a pitcher of margarita instead," Ted said. Chip, subliminally seduced by the banner, perhaps, ordered a Bud Light.

When the waitress left, Ted said to Chip, "I thought you said this place was good," but he was laughing, because our table overlooked a boardwalk, and teenage girls kept Rollerblading by in bikini tops; plus we were the only customers in the restaurant, which meant we would get served right away.

Soon our food arrived, and our drinks, and we filled one another in on the past few months. I was still temping and trying to finish my first novel, which I wrote on the job (I only took jobs that required no actual work of me). Later that month, as I did every summer, I would teach a creative writing course at New York University. "I'm looking forward to it," I said. "It's my favorite part of the year." As for Ted, he was still enjoying that blissful state of existence called "between jobs." He had moved to New York last November and was looking for work in documentary film. But no one could ever have referred to Ted as a slacker, or even called him unemployed. He had worked hard at his previous production job, and had been diligent enough about saving money to live on those savings for a year. Plus he was talented and experienced enough in his field to be picky about where he would work next. "So I've signed up for a couple of classes at Film and Video Arts," he said. "Photography. Intro to Avid. I'm looking forward to that."

Chip worked in something called a holdings firm—whatever that was—and he told us everything was the same with him. Everything was always the same for Chip. He was the only person in our circle of friends who had an actual job. "I get a lot of golf in on weekends," he said. "Can't complain."

This conversation somehow, for Chip, segued into the Neil Young concert he had seen the previous weekend, and then he and Ted were on to their favorite subject: all the drugs they had taken at all those Grateful Dead concerts during their New Haven days. This could go on for hours, I realized. And, no matter how much I enjoyed these two males' company, there was only so much "And do you remember the way Jerry segued into 'Not Fade Away' from 'Space'?" I could take.

So I gazed across the street toward the harbor. A few small sailboats bucked in the water, trying to move forward in that anchored sort of way. It was almost officially summer, I realized, and a crisp anticipation began to move through my veins—or perhaps it was the grain alcohol with which they had spiked the margaritas. I became aware of the rare, wondrous feeling of direct sunlight upon my skin and the lap-lap-lapping sound of the water. I straightened in my seat. Maybe this summer would be the summer I had always dreamed of: with perfect weather, invitations every weekend to friends' beach houses in the Hamptons, and weekly gatherings with my girlfriends at the Bryant Park Café, where we would drink rummy, fruity concoctions, and wear elegant, jeweled shoes paired with fetching handbags, and talk about art and books. Maybe I would finish writing my novel, and Ted would get going on that travel documentary he wanted to produce. In June we could attend the polo matches in Southampton and in July we could see the horse races at Saratoga, and in August we could go sailing at Ted's friend's plantation in Beaufort, and by September, I could relax with a sense of accomplishment, as opposed to the usual Labor Day freak-out in which I agonized over all the things I did not do that I'd said I'd wanted to do.

I sighed. Who's to say any of that would make me happy?

"Remember that time they played that cover of 'Couldn't Get It Right'?" Ted said. "Saratoga '86."

"No, it was Hampton '88," Chip said. "I remember because Charlie took so much acid he took all his clothes off and ran into the street." He raised his sandwich to his mouth. There was a bluish-gray claw dangling out the side, like something from *Dawn of the Dead*.

Some customers arrived: a couple with a dog. They looked to be our age—late twenties—and she had her hair pulled back in a ponytail, in that casual, unattended, weekend way that I could never quite pull off. She also wore a platinum engagement ring and jeweled shoes. But I barely noticed the ring, or stopped to think how it might fill some void. I was more interested in the dog. He was a golden retriever, a great teddy bear of a dog, and I watched the way he curled himself under the table, sighing with ease as he positioned himself in a perfect patch of sun. Every moment is a summer moment for a dog.

The man whispered something into the woman's ear, and she gazed at him adoringly while the dog gazed adoringly at them. The way this couple kept their hands knitted together suggested that their lives were knitted too.

I looked over at Ted: smart, handsome, reliable Ted. He was now laughing about the time he and Chip were shrooming during history class. I thought of our own relationship. Sometimes it was rocky, other times solid as a rock. Sometimes I wanted to cling to that rock—your one chance at survival in a whitewater river. Sometimes I wanted to give up and let go, and float with the current, not caring where I might land. In this sense I didn't think our relationship was different from any other. And yet, all my life I had wanted to be knitted to someone. And I'd always wanted a dog who would sit under the table and gaze at my lover and me as we held hands.

"Ted, look at that cute dog!"

"He's handsome," Ted said.

We smiled at the couple, and they smiled back.

Getting a dog, it is important to note, was something Ted and I had talked about seriously but sporadically over the past few months, during those moments when we were getting along so well we could giddily envision a future together. I had been yearning for a dog since I was ten, when I lost my husky, Tasha. Ted, too, loved dogs, with the wounded, stubborn insistence of a boy who had never been allowed to have one. So here was something we actually agreed upon—that we both loved dogs, that we *wanted* a dog.

But in our two years as a unit, we'd also talked about traveling, and moving to a bigger apartment, and getting a new computer, a new mattress, new careers, new lives, and so far none of those things had materialized. We were always talking about the time not being "right." Plus, I think we both secretly enjoyed the slow, nonthreatening pace at which things were progressing in our relationship.

"Our relationship is like a French movie," I often said to my friend Tara. "There's a lot of interesting character development, but no plot."

I straightened up in my seat again. Suddenly I was tired of being an all-talk-no-action kind of person. I was tired of things not going as planned. I was tired of saying I wanted something and then, when I was faced with the real possibility of getting it, deciding that I didn't want it after all and retreating back into the comforting, safe zone of indecision. I was tired of having all my summer goals thwarted for stupid reasons, like a dress. I wanted to call myself on something and make it happen. And I wanted to call Ted on something, too.

And thus it was that I suggested we stop at the animal shelter on the way home. "Let's do it," I said to Ted after we'd left the restaurant and picked up our car at Chip's. "Let's stop and look at dogs." We were idling on the Long Island Expressway, which was backed up for miles. "We drove all the way out here," I reasoned. "We might as well do something productive with this day."

Ted was silent for a moment. The car behind us honked and honked every time a light turned green, even though it was clear that, with a hundred other cars also trying to beat the same light, we weren't going to get very far. Then Ted's face broke into a warm but cautious smile. "Okay," he said. "But we're just looking."

On the way down to Chip's, we had passed a giant billboard for the Nassau County Pet Rescue that showed a floppy-eared beagle puppy sitting alongside a cardboard pet carrier, with a caption that read: THINK OUTSIDE THE BOX. We now followed those signs and soon found ourselves pulling into the shelter's parking lot.

"JFK Junior got his dog here," I said to Ted as we walked toward the building. "They mention that in all their ads." I suddenly had an image of myself as Carolyn Bessette Kennedy (albeit several inches shorter and with red hair), sauntering down the cobblestoned streets of Tribeca with the leash of an Irish setter in one hand and a Birkin bag in the other, looking very chic in a trim wool coat and leather boots. I looked at Ted and smiled. "We're looking at doggie-dogs!" Ted had a John-John sort of look: tall, lean, with dark hair and intense eyes, and a cute-in-sweatpants butt. I could have a dog with a man like that, I thought.

"We're just looking," he reminded me, but in a playful way. He, too, seemed suddenly possessed by a kind of wanton excitement, and he took my hand as we entered the building.

"We can take the dog to the beach!" I said. "To Montauk! Southampton!"

Another young couple was coming out just as we were going in. Their ironic T-shirts and oil-paint-splattered jeans gave them away as East Village inhabitants. They carried a sleeping Dalmatian puppy, and the boyfriend had his arm wrapped around the woman's shoulders proudly and protectively, as if she had just given birth. There was an air of tenderness about them, and of togetherness, and of hope. "You two wait here," the boyfriend said, using his most adult voice. "I'll go get the car."

I couldn't contain myself. "Did you see that puppy?" I said to Ted as he held the door for me. "Did you see how cute she was?" For as long as I can remember, I have always preferred dogs over children. Place a friend's baby on my lap, and I'll give her a few perfunctory bounces and a pat on the bottom before I pass her on to the next person. But show me a puppy, anytime, anywhere, and I will be on my knees, blubbering in baby talk, asking the owners in a high-pitched squeaky voice how old the puppy is, and what kind of toys he likes to chew on, and what he eats. I will kiss puppy noses and tickle puppy bellies and writhe ecstatically on the floor well past the point of appropriateness (and therefore have repeatedly been ostracized at dinner parties and family gatherings). But what can I say? Puppies make me happy. And don't we all just want to be happy in a stupid, blubbering way?

"Yes, I saw the puppy," Ted said, again with that smile. "But remember we agreed we'd get an adult dog." The official agreement was that we would adopt rather than purchase a dog, and that said dog would be a needy adult. "This will help purify some of your negative karma," my Buddhist friend Anna had advised us several months ago, long before I had an understanding of what Buddhism was. Or karma for that matter. But I liked the idea of adopting a needy dog.

We entered an efficient, immaculate-looking hallway, with signs directing us toward either dogs or cats. The dog wing was designed in such a way that you had to walk through the adult section before you could get to the puppies, and obediently we funneled through. "The adult section," Ted said with amusement. "That makes it sound like the porn section of a video store."

"Well, as long as I get to kiss one—no, two or three puppies today I'll be satisfied."

I could tell right away that this was a well-run shelter. It felt clean and organized, and there was an air of militant optimism that suggested the dogs were well taken care of and they would all find homes. Ted and I walked slowly past the rows and rows of open-air pens and fell in and out of love a dozen times. We met Dudley, a droopy pit bull with an eye infection. And Scooter, a Harlequin Great Dane. Then there was poor, miserable Clarence, an arthritic old bloodhound who kept his head on his paw and his eyes raised skyward, like a martyred saint. "Can we get Clarence?" I said to Ted, but he said no, a bloodhound would be too big for our apartment. "That's true," I said. I was willing to be open minded, to go with the dog who pulled most at my heartstrings, and so was Ted.

Slowly, he and I separated, each of us in our own dog trance. I stood in front of beagles and bassets and every variety of shepherd mix and Lab. Some of them wagged their tails at me and barked and spun in circles. Some of them rested their heads on their paws and barely lifted their eyes, as if they were tired of being passed by. Each dog was appealing in his own special way, and I stopped thoughtfully in front of every one of them, waiting for my One True Dog to reveal himself. I looked, paused, listened. Nothing happened, though. Nothing within me stirred. I even walked past the dog who would become our dog, but all I noticed at first was that he had an interesting face: it was half white and half brown, with one ear in each color, and a sort of yin/yang marking on top of his head. I wish I could say there was a moment of Knowing, an instant bond between us, but for me at least this was not the case. When I tried to make eye contact with this dog, who was then named Chance, he turned his head away with a studied, practiced look of disinterest on his face, as if we had quarreled long ago and he was determined to never, ever forgive me. I knew that look. And so I moved on.

Ted, however, had a moment of Knowing with Chance. He knelt down in front of Chance's cage and said "Who's this?" in an inviting voice. I love Ted's voice, because it cracks with emotion on certain high notes, and whenever he talks to dogs. "Who's this handsome boy?"

I watched the way Ted interacted with the dog. There had been an unmistakable moment of Knowing when I met Ted two years earlier. I realize this might sound clichéd, but on our first date I sensed that I was in the presence of a person—*the* person, even—I might marry, even though I was not, by any means, the marrying kind. I had endured too many disappointments and failed relationships, too many liars and louses and cheats, and I was no longer so eager to commit to anyone. Or anything. And yet there was this *feeling* when I met Ted. A stirring. That I already knew him. That I was supposed to know him. That a part of him already existed in my blood. And he'd felt the same about me.

Now Ted was trying to get a response out of the dog. "Who are you?" he said to Chance. "What's a good-looking dog like you doing in a place like this?"

Chance eyed Ted suspiciously, then inched himself to the back of his pen and bared his teeth.

"He *is* handsome," I said. In fact, the more I looked at Chance, the more taken I was by his beauty. There was his face, of course. And his body was mostly white, with brown patches on his back and tail, and little spots on his legs like chips of chocolate. His fur looked soft and fine, with fringing on his legs, and he had a long, feathered tail. "In fact, he's absolutely regal," I said. "He looks like one of those high-bred sporting dogs you see in English paintings, or on the lawns of great hunt-country estates. What *is* he doing here?"

There was a clipboard attached to the front of the cage with the dog's statistics: name, approximate age, approximate breed. It said Chance was an approximately eleven-month-old "English Setter X."

"What's the X for?" I said to the dog, addressing him in a sing-songy voice. "Is that like Malcolm X? Is that your rapper name?" As I knelt down, the fur between his shoulder blades rose and bristled and he curled his lip.

"It means he's a mix," Ted said. "Chance is a setter mix."

"What a sad name to give a dog in a shelter," I said. "It's like Last Chance." I told Ted about a certain category of short story that I taught my students, called the "Last Chance to Change" story, in which a character is given one final opportunity to change the course of his life. In a classic short story, I explained, a character has to change by the end of the story. "But in a Last Chance to Change story," I said, "the main character doesn't change and the readers realize that he never, ever will."

"He doesn't look like a Chance," Ted said. "What do you think he's mixed with? Some kind of spaniel?"

"Who knows?" I said. "Can we go look at the puppies now?"

At that point we were intercepted by a volunteer. She carried a clipboard, and wanted to know if we were interested in adopting a dog. "Oh, we're kind of just looking around," I said. This woman wore a name tag that said HI, I'M MINDY with a smiley face on it. She seemed to be in her late teens or early twenties and struck me as a perky do-gooder who hoped someday to be a perky do-gooding vet. I began to pull Ted toward the puppy cages, but he stopped and asked the volunteer about Chance: How old was he? Where was he from?

She told us Chance had been rescued from a pound in Connecticut. He'd been at the pound two weeks and was about to be put down when the Pet Rescue saved him and brought him here. "He's only been here three days. Do you like him? Do you want to try him out?"

"Try him out?" I said.

"Walk him," Mindy said. "We have a walking room. We call it the bonding room."

"Not yet," I said. "We're going to look around a little bit more. But maybe later."

We continued to make our way through the adult section but now with Mindy in tow. She followed us and told us how we should feel about each dog before we'd even had a chance to shake paws with them. "Oh, you won't like her," she said of a sweet-looking border collie. "Too much work." "And that one," she said of the Great Pyrenees, "sheds much too much." I didn't care about shedding, and I'd heard Pyrenees were nice, but I held my tongue. I was starting to realize this girl had all the makings of a used car salesman and I wanted to ditch her fast. "You should meet Lucy," she said. She pulled me by the arm, away from Ted. "She's epileptic and she's everyone's favorite dog."

I didn't want to see Lucy but I went along anyway, not wanting to hurt Mindy's feelings.

"Lucy's owner absolutely loved her," she said, "but unfortunately she couldn't keep her because she was allergic. Here she is."

We stood outside the pen. Lucy wagged her tail and pressed her body against the gate. Then she whined softly and closed her eyes, as if she were trying to remember what it felt like to lean against a human leg.

"Isn't she adorable?" Mindy said.

I just stood there. She was a sweet dog, yes, a mixture of shepherd and Lab, but she had pointy ears. I didn't like dogs with pointy ears. Except huskies. And I didn't see why I had been singled out as her potential owner. The volunteer hadn't asked us any questions about our wants or needs, about our lifestyle. I was starting to think she had attended the "how to talk to customers" session but not the "how to listen" one.

"Isn't she sweet?" Mindy pressed. "Do you want to walk her?"

I looked around for Ted, who was kneeling in front of Chance's pen again. Chance was still cowering at the back of his cage and growling in a deep-throated sort of way. I muttered something about puppies and tried to move away from Mindy.

"Puppies are different," she said. "They're so much work. You can't bring them outside for eight weeks; they have weak immune systems, you have to be prepared."

"I know," I said.

"Lucy's only three years old, but she acts like a puppy. Don't you want to walk her?"

"No!" I finally said. I excused myself, and returned to Ted. "That woman is sales-pitching me! It's obnoxious. I don't have a good feeling about this place anymore. Maybe we should just leave."

"I have a good feeling about this dog," Ted said. "I don't know what it is, but I like him."

"He sure is cute," I said, suddenly willing to give Chance a chance. "Look at that face! Those mismatched ears make him look sort of goofy, but also dignified. Are you dignified?" I asked Chance, but he just paced back and forth, wolflike, a mixed expression of worry and violence on his face. "Poor boy," I said. "I wonder what happened to him. Why doesn't he even bark?"

"Maybe we can find out," Ted said. He went and got Mindy, who came back with a leash and opened up Chance's cage. She leashed him up, apparently against his will, and then led us into the walking area, a glassed-in room with a concrete floor. "You can spend as much time in here as you'd like," Mindy said as she closed the door on us. Chance became frantic, and suddenly I felt like a Christian left in a Roman arena with the lions. He panted and whined and scrambled across the slippery floor, clawing and scratching at the windows, as if he were looking for a means of escape. Ted, who held the leash, struggled to control him, and tried to calm him down by saying "Sit" and "Heel," but Chance didn't speak this language. He seemed to know only Fear. I tried to sweet-talk him and stroke his fur, but every time I went near him he scrambled away from me. Through the window, I saw Mindy write something on her pad. I motioned for her to come back in.

"He's so nervous and skittish," I said when she rushed in. "Is he okay?"

"All dogs are like that," she said. "This is unfamiliar to him."

"Let me try to walk him," I said to Ted. I've always had a rapport with animals and considered myself the kind of person all dogs instinctively know to trust.

Mindy raised her eyebrows at my dress and platform sandals. "Are you sure you know how to walk a dog?"

"Yes, I know how to *walk a dog*. During graduate school I was a dog walker. And I grew up with dogs. Huskies. Two litters were born at my house."

"Where are they now?" Mindy asked.

"What do you mean?"

"The dogs. What happened to the dogs?"

"My dog Tasha? My father's huskies from when I was a child?"

"Yes, yes. Where are the huskies? Is your father a *breeder*? A back-yard breeder?"

"No, he wasn't a *breeder*," I said. "Tasha had puppies. She was a champion sled dog. So many people wanted her offspring that my father had her bred." Ted started to pinch me. "And when I was ten we had to give Tasha away."

"Exactly what do you mean, you 'gave her away'?" Mindy said.

"My mother *died*," I said. "We had a newborn baby in the house. My poor father was overwhelmed. So we had to find our dog another home."

Mindy made yet another notation on her clipboard. "You need to state that on your application," she said. "You're required to let us know if you've had any history of getting rid of animals."

"A history?" I said. "Of getting rid? Look you have *no* idea what it was like—" Before I could finish, Ted pulled me away. "We need to talk privately," he explained to Mindy. And we left the volunteer with Chance.

"Don't piss her off!" Ted said outside the bonding room. "She could deny our application."

"Who trains these people?" I said. "That ninny! Here we are in a situation where lives and connections and feelings and major decisions are involved and she's treating me like a criminal. Has she asked us our *names*? Has she asked us where we live or what kind of dog we want? I would make a good dog parent! And I am tired of having my efforts thwarted!"

I shouted that last sentence and a woman who was coming down the hallway pressed herself against the wall when she passed us, as if my wrath were a disease she might catch.

"Look," Ted said, putting his hand on my shoulder. "Why don't we go see the puppies now? You'll feel better when you've had some puppy kisses."

And who can stay mad in the puppy room? Soon I was surrounded by dozens of warm, sweet, fuzzy, cuddly puppies. The air had a fecund, yeasty smell—the smell of new life, and helplessness, and promise—and the room was filled with the sounds of canine yipping and whimpering, and human oohing and aahing. I felt something ancient and maternal shift within me. I asked one of the attendants if I could hold a puppy. "That one, there," I said, pointing to a plump, squirmy female who looked like a black Lab. Her name was Niblet, I was told, and she was one of a twelve-pup litter that had just come into the Pet Rescue. "Someone just dumped them off," the attendant explained. "We have no idea who the parents are. But they look like Labs." I lifted the warm, squirming Niblet to my face and breathed in that puppy smell. My heart expanded, and I felt certain Ted's would too. Niblet had a white blaze on her chest and a tiny bit of white on the tip of her tail. She whimpered rhythmically and quieted a little when I brought her to my chest. "I can't believe someone would just dump them off," I said. "Believe it," the attendant said. "It's a cruel world, and dogs got it worst." I began to kiss Niblet and whisper all sorts of promises into her ears, how we would love and protect her, and honor and serve, and how she would never have to be scared again. She stopped and fell asleep against my chest. "Don't you want to hold her?" I said to Ted, but he shook his head. He kept glancing back in the direction of the adult section. "I really like Chance," he said thoughtfully. "I don't know what it is about him, but I'm drawn to him."

"But look at this little wittle cutie," I said.

And then, as if on cue, Mindy reappeared, her straight hair swinging pendulously as she hurried toward us. "Someone else is interested in Chance," she told us. "You need to make up your minds."

"We're still thinking," Ted said. "Can't you let us think?"

"You have three minutes," she said, and literally spun on her heels.

Ted and I looked at each other, and he opened his mouth as if to speak, and then he turned around and followed Mindy. I surrendered Niblet and followed Ted.

Another couple stood in front of Chance's cage, with their backs to the dog, discussing. When we approached they tactfully moved away. They were older than Ted and I, and looked much more responsible. She had a J. P. Tod's handbag and matching shoes, and the way he studied the adoption application—with fearless disdain—made me suspect he was a contracts lawyer. No doubt they had a cabinet devoted solely to jam.

Ted stopped Mindy before she could reach this couple. "Would it be okay," he asked Mindy, "if we decided we wanted Chance, to come back and pick him up on Wednesday? We'd like to get our apartment prepared and things like that."

"This is not a boardinghouse," Mindy snapped.

"We know it's not a boardinghouse," I said. "We're simply not familiar with the procedures. We're asking questions."

"Look." Mindy folded her arms. "Do you want him or not? A dog like him will be gone by Wednesday, so you need to decide now."

This time I was really going to tell Mindy to piss off when something happened. Chance started barking. It was a loud, insistent bark, as if he were trying to tell us something very important. He ran to the front of his cage, leapt up, paws on the rail. He took Ted's wrist in his mouth and gummed it.

Ted said kindly, "Don't chew." Then he turned to me. "Should we do it?" he said.

"I guess," and then I started to cry. Because it was so much like saying "I do."

Stunned and compliant, we were led into a processing center and told to wait in line to get our application. After we stood in that line for half an hour, we were told we had to wait in another line to verify our references. Then we had to fill out more forms, and swear on the Holy Bible that we were who we said we were and that we had no intentions of selling the dog, or using him for medical research, and then we had to stand at the counter while they confirmed our address and called our three references, all of whom attested to our honesty, stability, and integrity and then probably doubled over laughing once they got off the phone.

Having passed these tests, we were asked to sit in the waiting room for twenty minutes, ostensibly for them to fill out more paperwork, but really, we thought, to give everyone one last chance to change their mind. The waiting room was set up like an auditorium: rows of chairs facing a small television set that had a bouquet of flowers on top of it, as if it were a shrine. We could smell the worry in the room, and the second thoughts, and the fear.

"It's so clinical," I whispered to Ted.

"Shhh," he said.

A few rows beyond us sat a woman with Lloyd Neck written all over her—she had the silk blouse, the Lilly Pulitzer skirt, the Pappagallo espadrilles. I watched with interest as this woman was called back to the interview area. As she stood, her bracelets clinked and a cloud of expensive perfume rose along with her. You could tell she got whatever she wanted and that she always demanded the best. But minutes later she came out screaming in rage. "I'm a donor!" she shouted to the volunteer who escorted her. "How dare you refuse me that cat? I've given hundreds, no, *thousands* of dollars to this place. How dare you!" She told her husband to get his coat. "We're leaving. They're not letting us take the cat. They think it's *my* fault Tuna got hit by a car! You'll hear about this!" she shouted to the room in parting. And she left us all with the sickening feeling that we, too, would be denied.

"I wish I hadn't told Mindy about those huskies," I said.

Ted said: "Should we go back and tell them we want that little black puppy you liked?"

On the television was a nature program in which two hideous giant lizards gnashed at each other's throats. Their hides were tough and textured, but they still bled red when their flesh was torn off. I shifted in my seat. "Should we go find that contracts lawyer and tell him he can have Chance?"

"We could at least get their names, I guess," Ted said. "In case they take him home and change their minds." But neither of us moved.

Another person's name was called and a lone young woman rose and disappeared. My heart pounded. We could still back out, I thought, as we had backed out before.

But then they were calling our names and delivering the good news—we had been accepted! We passed! And then they were giving us Chance, along with a pamphlet and some exit papers and a new blue leash, and then they wished us luck and pointed us toward the exit, and Chance, sensing a way out, yanked us through the doors and into the parking lot, and when he saw the woods beyond he headed in that direction. He was a medium-sized dog—fifty-five pounds according to his exit papers—yet he pulled with the force of a steam engine. We struggled and struggled to pull him toward our car, and he resisted, oh, how he resisted. God knew where he'd be taken this time, his resistance implied, but he would not have it. No, he would not. *No, no, no!* As we wrestled him into the car, he literally howled the word—*Noooooo!!*—and threw himself against the windows. I got in the back-seat with him, thinking that would help calm him down, but still he howled and scratched and hurled himself against the doors and windows, desperate to escape.

Ted put the car into reverse and we screeched out of the parking lot as if we were racing against time. He drove with control and precision, his jaw set. As we pulled onto the Long Island Expressway and headed for New York, Chance's brays got louder, more intense, as if he were saying: *Don't take me to the city! Don't take me to where I'll find glass on the sidewalks and needles in the park! Don't take me to your studio apartment—you don't have enough space! Your windows look out onto air shafts! You're not a real couple! You never follow through! NO! NO! NOOOOOO!!*

I put my arms around the dog and tried to hold him still, but he continued to squirm and scratch. I could feel his little heart pounding and the heat of his breath as he panted and yowled. He smelled like shampoo. He finally got loose and hurled himself against the door.

Ted looked at us in the rearview mirror. His eyes were disbelieving and glazed. "Are you okay back there?"

Chance cried, *No, no, no, noooooo!*

Eventually we reached that point on the Brooklyn-Queens Expressway where you can see all of Manhattan displayed before you like a postcard. A million office windows twinkled and winked, their height reflected in the river. Usually, whenever I beheld this sight my heart would surge and the first few bars of Frank Sinatra's rendition of "New York, New York" would start playing in my head. This time, however, my little black dress was being clawed to shreds by a psycho-setter. I felt like Tippi Hedren in *The Birds.*

"What have we done?" I said to Ted.

"We adopted a dog," Ted said. It helped, for a second, to hear him narrow it down to the essentials like that. The moment felt existential.

"We took a Chance!" I said.

The Chance tried to ram his way bodily into the front seat, like a Great White Shark attacking a diver's cage.

"Get him off me!" Ted said. "We're going to crash!"

"I'm trying. I'm afraid he's going to scratch my eyeballs out."

"Tell him we'll be home in about half an hour," Ted said. "Can you make it till then?"

"I think so," I said. Our eyes met again in the rearview mirror, and for a moment, I saw the real Ted. The eternal Ted. I felt that Knowing again, and trusted that we're in this together, for better or for worse.

So I put my arms around Chance and held him. I had to use all my strength to keep him still. "You're going to be all right," I told him. "We're going to take care of you."

"Yes, we're going to take care of you," Ted said. "You have nothing to be scared of."

But even as I said this, I didn't quite believe it. There is plenty to be scared of in New York. And in life. Especially when you make a major change.

"Let's rename him," I said. "It will symbolize his new life with us."

"Good idea," Ted said. "He's English, so it should be an Anglican name. Something dignified but also cute, like his face."

Back and forth, Ted and I called out goofy yet dignified names for the dog: Clarence? Watkins? Percival?

Chance cried, *Noooooo!*

Darcy? Bingley? Wickham?

Noooooo!

"How about Wallace?" Ted said.

I noticed that the dog's white ear had little specks of brown on it. "That's cute."

"We could name him after Wallace Stevens," Ted said. "Did I ever tell you I did my senior thesis on the poems of Wallace Stevens as compared to the lyrics of Robert Hunter?"

"Who is Robert Hunter?" I asked. The dog struggled to squirm out of my lap.

"He wrote most of the lyrics for the Grateful Dead. He and"—Ted's eyes widened—"Jerry."

"We're not naming him *Jerry*," I said. The dog was still howling and scratching at my arms, so I let him go. He leapt away and pressed himself against the opposite door, staring at me with terror. His little ribs heaved up and down.

"I like the name Wallace," Ted said.

"So do I. It's a good name to grow into."

The dog did not howl *noooooo*, so we took this as a yes.

And thus our dog had a new name, a new beginning, and a new life. And although he was really named after a great and complex poet, in these pages he shall henceforth be known as Rex. Rex of the City.

CHAPTER 2

The Indecision

One of the first things I did after we brought the dog home was call my beloved sister MJ.

"We got a dog!" I said. I felt excited, bemused, incredulous, and freaked out. MJ knew how much I had always wanted a dog—she'd heard me talking about getting one for years. And now I could prove to my family that I was no longer an all-talk-no-action person.

But my sister's response froze all my emotions.

"In the city?" she said.

"Well, yes, *in the city*," I said. "And you should see him, he's really cute."

"*Him?* You got a male? Oh, I would never get a male dog. They're much too aggressive." And as she went on, talking about how territorial males can be, and how unmanageable they are, and how New York City could not possibly offer any dog an appropriate quality of life, tears sprang to my eyes. I gazed out my kitchen window, which faced an air shaft, and then watched a cockroach skitter across the floor.

I love my older sister. I have always wished I could be more like her. But she has this thing about always facing reality. And encouraging me to face reality, too.

This is what I had to face: the first thing Rex did when we led him across the proverbial threshold of our apartment Saturday was growl at us. And then snap. No blood was drawn (not yet, anyway), but he snapped in such a way as to let us know that he would not tolerate close human proximity and that from now on *he* ruled this roost. Then he tried to wedge his fifty-five-pound body underneath our futon frame. But he couldn't fit under there, because in a tenement apartment on the Lower East Side one cannot expect such a thing as unused space. We're talking a three-hundred-square-foot studio here, with crates of winter clothing shoehorned under sofas and dozens of photo boxes crammed like a Rubik's Cube inside a large trunk, which doubled as a coffee table and tripled as a dining table if we ever had guests. Which we didn't. Because we were too embarrassed about the size of our apartment.

So our new dog found refuge under our tiny computer table (which doubled as an ironing board, and tripled as a pedicure station when Ted wasn't around). The look on his face—suspicious, vengeful, feral (but with such cute ears!)—suggested he would stay hunkered there, without food or drink, for days. And he would not let us come within three feet of his bunker without showing his teeth.

"Um, I have, like, work to do on that computer."

"I think it's going to have to wait," Ted said.

In the meantime, there was dog food to purchase. And choke-chain collars and a doggie bed. We had to gather up all the breakable things in the apartment—Ted's guitars, Ted's photo lamps, the collection of teacups that had belonged to my mother. (We later learned these actions are called dog-proofing.) The dog, of course, needed to be walked and fed and watered, and Ted and I scrambled to do these things with the harried cluelessness of new parents, both of us trying to apply all that we knew, to date, of dogs. We knew that dogs were pack animals. We knew that they liked to eat and sleep and chase balls. We knew that they pooped and you had to pick it up. But Rex was unlike any dog we had ever known. He wasn't romping around and playing like the yellow Labs in the Alpo commercials. He wasn't slobbering over us with exuberance or wagging his tail. He didn't even bark, this dog. No, he was completely silent, in an eerie, almost defiant way, as if we were his wartime captors and he the I-vill-tell-you-nothing prisoner of war.

We looked over the exit papers and pamphlet we'd received. "Your new dog"—and here there was a space on which someone had written his prison number: A4601—"is very sweet. He is . . ." and then there was a list of options, some of them checked off, some not. Here's what was checked off: house-trained, neutered, vaccinated, and sick. At the bottom of the page, someone had handwritten: "Your dog has diarrhea."

"The poor thing!" I said. "I bet it's stress related."

"Let's walk him right away."

And so we grabbed our new leash and took him around the block so that Rex could relieve himself, but he had clearly never been walked on a leash before. Picture a large hill with an unmanned SUV resting at its top. Now, release the parking brake and allow said SUV to begin rolling down the hill. Next, try to stop the SUV from rolling by attaching a six-foot leash of nylon to the bumper. That's what trying to walk Rex was like. On that very first walk he pulled and panted and wheezed on the choke collar, and at the other end of the leash, we pulled and panted and wheezed as well.

When we returned to the apartment, Rex bunkered himself under the table. He stayed alert, looking grave and serious. He seemed to frown, tight-lipped. Most dogs keep their mouths half open in a relaxed smile. But not Rex. This dog wasn't talking. Not without a lawyer, it seemed.

Ted and I stared at each other like two college students who have just taken psychedelic mushrooms and are waiting for the jubilation to arrive. "We should have thought this through," Ted said. "We should have at least waited until Wednesday, so that we could get the apartment prepared."

"Well, he's here," I said. "But we'll be okay," I added. "He doesn't know us yet. He'll come around in a few days. I have a good feeling about this."

And why wouldn't he come around? We had rescued this poor dog from a life of concrete and cages. We had snatched him willingly from the jaws of death. This was the first couply thing we had done as a couple, and frankly we were proud of ourselves and full of hope. We had done the right thing.

So we took him out again a few hours later—the way my father had encouraged me to get back into the car and drive after my first accident—and a few hours later we took him out a third time. It's hard to witness a dog's diarrhea—not to go into too much detail, but Rex looked pained as he squatted. He looked confused. And the mess we had to pick up seemed emblematic of too many things. "Things have not gotten off to a good start," Ted said as the dog bulldozed his way down the sidewalk again. By the time the sun had set that evening, our backs and shoulders and knees ached from all that pulling, and Ted's left eye had begun to twitch.

It was hard to sleep that night. For hours the dog panted and paced, and paced and panted, his nails click-clacking on the floor. Ted and I huddled on the bed, like castaways on a raft surrounded by sharks. It's funny—you get so used to sirens in the city that you can sleep right through them. But we couldn't fall asleep until the dog fell asleep, which he did finally, I think, at about four. Later we were awakened by an odd cracking sound, and Ted turned the light on, and we realized the poor dog was grinding his teeth in his sleep.

"I used to grind my teeth at night," Ted said, his voice quiet and hoarse. "But that's when I was so stressed at work."

"Poor boy," I said. We snuggled again, in a clingy, frightened kind of way, and finally dozed off. Two hours later the sun started to rise, and the early-morning trash trucks rumbled down our street, crashing and booming and grinding up barrels of glass. And then a foreign sound—panting—and it wasn't Ted, and I sat up, disoriented, not really knowing where I was, or who I was, and then I recognized the panting, and I remembered that we had a dog. Good Lord—a dog! It all came rushing back—the shelter, the walks, the diarrhea.

"We'd better take him out now," I said to Ted.

And so we rose dutifully and groggily, going through the motions we didn't quite have down yet. Outside, the sun had fully risen, and there were schoolchildren skipping down the sidewalks, and people with jobs heading off to work, and Rex barked at all of them. Furiously. He barked at a construction worker carrying a two-by-four into an old matzo factory that they were converting into condos. He barked at the club kids who were just arriving home, wearing their fishnets and glittery eyelashes. (And that was just the boys.) At all these denizens of our neighborhood, Rex barked and lunged and growled. Later we would learn that this behavior was called "fear aggression," but for now we saw it as just plain aggression. And this filled *us* with fear. He barked at the sculptor who lived down the block and liked to dress in Edwardian clothes. He barked at the Hasids who owned all the wholesale shops on Orchard Street. He even barked at the naked mannequin in the window of an abandoned girdle store.

Back inside the apartment, we could tell he wanted to bark at us. But he seemed too afraid. If we ventured in his direction, or even looked at him and said his name, he'd wince, as if expecting a blow. And then growl.

"This is your home," I told him in the singsong voice, with a big fake smile. "This is your new house. We are your friends." I smiled and smiled. We would later learn that shelter dogs often interpret a human smile as a threat—a baring of teeth. But for now Rex retreated farther under the table. He snarled.

"He looks like a stuffed animal from FAO Schwartz," Ted said.

"An FAO Schwartz dog with fangs."

Sunday night we decided the best thing to do would be to cancel all our social engagements and rearrange our work schedules for the next few weeks. I would not return to my current temp job on Monday, and Ted would postpone taking that photography class. That way, we reasoned, we could both offer full-time support to each other and to the dog. Plus in three weeks I was supposed to begin my full-time teaching gig at New York University, and that amount of time, we figured, would be enough for the dog to adjust.

But this dog didn't seem willing to wait three weeks. He seemed to want to get out of his present situation right away. Out on our walks, he kept trying to lunge out of his collar, rearing up like a horse. He strained at every intersection, his pupils reduced to pinpoints, making choking sounds. People on the sidewalks would back away, their faces aghast, and the less fearful ones would say things like, "Hey, who's walking who?" I could not even look at these well-meaning jokesters. Because this wasn't a joke. There was nothing funny, or even fun, about this dog. When we passed a storefront or an apartment building, which was like every second, he'd jump on the windowsills and howl and scratch, as if within those buildings was an escape route, or a paradise we could not provide. The bottoms of his paws were already black. At the shelter they had been pink.

"Maybe taking him to the park will soothe him," I said Monday morning. "All dogs like parks."

Believe it or not, we had never been to East River Park before, even though it was ten blocks away. It was one of those New York things—you were always looking ahead and beyond, and so never saw what was right in your face. East River Park was not, at that time, one of the crown jewels of the New York City parks system. Instead, like many of the smaller city parks that were located on the outskirts of the poorer neighborhoods, East River Park had been sorely neglected. Tourists didn't go there. Therefore, neither did funding. Broken glass littered virtually all of the paved walkways, while the nonpaved portions of the park (which one could not really call grass) were land-mined with heroin needles and chicken bones. Stroll along the riverfront promenade, and you would pass abandoned lots, broken park benches, and soccer fields that seemed to have been imported from some southwestern desert.

We had to cross over FDR Drive to get there, and as we did so Rex jumped up on the railing with his forelegs, his eyes frantic, as if prepared to leap to his death. "Be careful!" Ted shouted. I held the leash at the time. "I can't steer him!" I said. "He's like a car out of control."

"Well, give him to me," Ted said. Rex heaved and hoed and zigged and zagged, past the derelict tennis courts, past the drug dealers, past the gangs of boys. The dog struggled for breath as the choke collar choked him. He seemed to think the harder he pulled the more likely he would get away from us, to someplace safe.

Out in one of the abandoned soccer fields, some teenage boys were "training" their pit bull by beating it with a belt.

"Yo," one of these boys called out to us. "How much you pay for that thing?" He was referring to Rex, not Ted.

"How much did we *pay*?" I said. "For that *thing*? A dog is not a *thing*!"

"Quiet," Ted said, pulling me roughly by the arm. "Do you want to get us killed?" A breeze from the river brought to us the smell of human urine. We turned around and headed back.

"So not all dogs like parks," I said on the way home.

"Well, he's not really like a dog," Ted said. "And that really isn't a park."

Rex came to a sudden halt and squatted—more for us to clean up. Then he tried to scramble away.

Poor dog. I have since heard many stories of newly adopted dogs acting like this, always panicked, always trying to run away. So many that I now wonder if wanderlust isn't part of these particular dogs' personalities to begin with—if they, in human form, would have been the artists, the poets, the tortured souls? (All the humans, come to think of it, who gravitate to the Lower East Side.) But where would they go, these runaway dogs? Is there a community they know of in India, run for and by dogs? Is there a Doggie Guru waiting for them, a wise old schnauzer who could offer Rex and his imbalanced cronies the meaning of Dog Life? Oh, I wanted so badly to help this dog, to help him find his Mecca, his inner peace. Because he was driving us nuts.

That Monday we decided to call the shelter and find out more specifically what Rex's history was. If we knew where he had come from, we thought, and where he had been, and what kind of parenting he had had, we might be better able to work with him. Why, for instance, did Rex freak out when he saw a UPS truck, but not Federal Express? Why did he hate motorcycles, and men with hats? Why was he so deathly afraid of sudden movements? And of our hands? And why was he always trying to run away from us? To escape?

But the people at the shelter wouldn't tell us anything. Policy, they said. "People tend not to adopt an animal if they know its history," the woman on the phone told me.

"But we already adopted him," I said. "We want to know what his history is so that we can know what to do with him. He's a really difficult dog. We think he may have been abused or abandoned, and it would really help to know."

"Sorry, ma'am," she said. She spoke atonally, and I could tell she was checking her e-mail at the same time as she talked to me.

"Could I speak with someone else?" I said.

"Sorry, ma'am."

"Could you not call me ma'am?" If you're under thirty, that is a four-letter word.

"No need to get snippy, ma'am," the woman said.

I hung up.

Later that day, the dog got snippy. He was lying on the floor, staying still for once, and Ted and I sat on the sofa and watched him, enjoying the moment of rest. When I reached over to pet him he growled at me, then snapped at the air near my hand. Ted seized the dog by the collar and threw him onto his back, shouting "No! No! Bad dog! You bad dog!"

The dog lay completely still, his chest heaving, a terrified look on his face.

"Maybe you shouldn't be so rough with him," I said.

I saw that Ted's eyes were bloodshot. He was starting to look like an American Werewolf. Usually he was so polished and kempt.

"Look, I'm sorry to yell," Ted said. "I just don't think we can handle him. Maybe he's damaged beyond repair."

On Tuesday, we decided to take Rex to the vet, to see if perhaps he had some physical problem that was compounding his emotional distress. Ted and the vet struggled to get him up on the stainless-steel inspection table, and Rex resisted, so she called in an assistant to help hold him still. While the assistant held Rex, the vet felt his ribs, inspected his ears, shined a light into his eyeballs, and stuck one finger into his butt. Rex reared around at the latter offense and growled.

"Easy boy," she said, snapping off her surgeon's glove. "You have a healthy pup. The diarrhea is stress-related. A lot of shelter dogs get it. It goes away in a few days. We can give you some medication for that." She was already bringing out the file for her next patient and taking off her mask as she spoke. "But all in all you've got a strong boy. He's a hunting dog. Hunting dogs are active breeds. They need to keep busy. Especially at his age—I'd put it at six months."

"They told us at the shelter he was about a year."

"No, he's a puppy. You can tell by his teeth."

"We're no strangers to his teeth," Ted said.

"You can wait in the waiting room for the medication and your bill," she said.

That's when Ted asked her the question that had been nagging us for days. "How long do you think it will take for this sort of dog to calm down?"

The vet answered, without irony, "About ten years."

"Ten *years?*" I said on the way home. "Can we do this for ten years? We haven't even been in this apartment for ten months."

Ted was a few paces ahead of me, being dragged down Delancey Street by the dog. The last barber he'd visited, I noticed, had failed to shave a straight line at the back of his neck. It made him look imbalanced and out of sorts.

"It's like that line from that Talking Heads song," he said. " 'Well, how did I get here?' "

And of course we knew how we got there. We had been saying for *months* that we wanted a dog. I personally had been saying that, in various degrees of seriousness, my entire adult life. But I guess what I meant was I wanted the dog of my childhood: a loving, jolly husky who would eat my unwanted brussels sprouts and allow me to dress her up in my brother's hockey uniform. Tasha was an independent, sturdy dog who slept outside in a wooden doghouse (something that I now consider a form of abuse), walked herself (dogs could do that in those days), and pooped in *other* people's yards. So maybe what I really wanted all this time was the joy of dog companionship, with none of the effort, none of the strain. And I realized, at a deeper level, that I also wanted—ravenously, with the stubborn illogic of a lonely child—some good old, nonstop unconditional love. I wanted to live in wonderful, rejuvenating proximity to a high-spirited being. How then had I ended up with the only dog on the planet whose love was conditional? Who thought people sucked?

Rex would not let us pet him. He would not even let us look at him. Every day, every walk, Rex continued to lunge at any passing dog or human who came too close. On Wednesday morning, he lunged at a large, good-natured black sanitation worker who put his hands up and said, "Whoa!" ("Rex hates large dark-skinned men," I later wrote in my Rex log). Wednesday afternoon, he lunged at a slight white male in a baseball cap ("He hates light-skinned men in baseball caps"). Early in the evening it was a poor woman carrying a small red handbag, perhaps because she was *swinging* the red handbag, the way Mary Tyler Moore did when she first beheld the city of her dreams ("He hates Mary Tyler Moores"). And that night, he even lunged at our neighbor Stephanie, a sweet, gentle librarian who is barely five feet tall in heels.

"Okay," I said to Ted. "He just officially snarled at the nicest person in the world. She's a Jane Austen fanatic. She *knits*. She volunteers at a nursing home! What possible threatening vibe could he have gotten from her?"

"Who the fuck knows?" Ted said. "Maybe he hates Jane Austen. Maybe there's a weird vibe he's picking up on. Those librarians are full of latent sexual fantasies, after all. They're all into S and M."

"That's a stereotype," I said.

Stephanie, for the record, *was* going to give my manuscript, when I completed it, to her husband, a literary agent, but she always avoided me after that.

"Why didn't he lunge at us at the pound?" Ted said. "Why did he bark at us like he wanted us to take him home?"

"I'd like to think he liked us," I said. "I thought he felt connected or something."

Usually I believed in that sort of thing—I believed that people came together, not by chance, but by subconscious intentions; I believed that paths crossed for reasons that you had to stick around to understand. Good Ted had come into my life, you may recall, at a time when I felt I had officially sworn off all dysfunctional relationships, all poets and rock musicians, all drug addicts and assholes. I thought I was done with all that; I thought I had done my time and could walk down Easy Street from now on. So why then had this *asshole* of a dog chosen me?

"It's *your* fault!" Ted began to say. By Friday we had begun to argue. Hatefully. "You're the one who insisted on going to the shelter," Ted said. "You're the one who insisted we get a dog!"

"You picked him out!" I'd say. "I wanted a puppy."

"Oh, sure," Ted said. "A puppy that wasn't house-trained?"

Rex, to his credit, at least had the house-trained thing going for him. But when he peed, it was like a girl dog, squatting right outside our apartment building with a frightened look on his face, his eyes darting around and all his muscles tense, as if prepared for attack. Then, relaxing only his bladder muscle, he would eliminate all at once, as if uncertain he would ever have another chance to go.

"You couldn't handle an un-house-trained puppy!" Ted continued. "You couldn't handle the responsibility!"

"Well, I'd take an un-house-trained dog over an *asshole* any day!"

"Well, why do you keep him?" my friend Tara said. "He seems so
messed up. Why don't you bring him back and take home that little
black puppy you liked?"

"The consensus here on Garrison Drive," my father pronounced,
"was that you should not have gotten a dog. You should have gotten
a full-time job."

"Do you guys want to come out to the country club next weekend?"
Chip said. "We can have lunch, hang by the pool, play a little golf."

So why did we keep him? What were the advantages for us? I mean,
every morning we had to wake up at an ungodly hour, and there was
this dog there—this terrible, hateful dog—and we had to go out and
walk him, an activity he seemed to despise, and then we had to feed
him, and he seemed to take no real pleasure in food, and then we kind
of had to avoid him until the next walk, for fear that, in an Ozzy Os-
bourne moment, he might bite off our heads. So how was this better
than drinking sangria every night? How was this better than teaching, or temping, or taking a photography class?

I don't think, at that point, Ted or I even knew why we should
keep Rex. Was it enough to say you'd keep a dog because he was so
cute and goofy-looking, and because the spots on his legs looked like
chips of chocolate? Was it enough to say that you'd keep him because
he peed like a girl dog, and you wanted to teach him how to act like a
boy? Was it enough that, when he actually ate the canned food you
fed him, you felt like a provider? A provider who has gone out and
shot down that can yourself? I mean, how do you explain to a non-
dog-lover that you might be willing to love a dog simply because he
smells like one? How do you explain that you are willing to love him
because his previous owners didn't, simple as that?

"But pity and love are two different things," Tara said. Who, for the record, does not even own houseplants. "You're always confusing the two. I think you should bring him back."

"We've only had him a few days," I said. "It's not always going to be like this. He'll adjust. It's like any new relationship. It'll change. He'll change."

"Like boyfriends?" Tara said.

I didn't answer.

On our one-week anniversary the diarrhea disappeared. We started our new day with a solid poop, which Ted picked up like a gentleman. "Who'd have thought we could get so much joy from a solid poop?" he said.

"It means he's not so stressed!" I said.

Was it possible? Sure, for, oh, 161 of the past 168 hours he had been impossible. But sometimes, in this past week, he had yawned, sometimes he slept, sometimes he scratched himself behind the ear. As he scratched, his eyes would half close and his lips would flap about, and he looked like a normal happy dog. Sometimes he'd put his head between his paws, looking at us with his serious, amber eyes. He yawned twice in a row on Sunday, which suggested that in less than ten years, perhaps, he would actually get tired.

We researched dog breeds on the Internet. Side by side, we scrolled through all the setter and spaniel sites we could find. I felt a certain solidarity, sitting there next to Ted, and believed, once again, that together we would make it through this. I put my arm around him. But then we came across a setter site that stated: *It is cruel to keep this type of exuberant hunting dog in a city apartment.*

I looked at Ted. His face glowed blue before the screen, which in the world of auras is the color of someone who is in a highly agitated emotional state.

Then I looked over at Rex, whose worried eyes blinked from underneath the table. The word *cruel* really stuck with me. Rex had no more hair around his neck because his choke collar had pinched it all off from his pulling so hard (think Epilady). He had to walk *backward* out of the bathroom, because there wasn't enough room for the poor dog to turn his body around. And not even sleep gave him solace, as he spent most nights growling and battling invisible demons in his dreams, and crack-crack-cracking his teeth.

"All this time I've been thinking it would be cruel to bring him back to the shelter," Ted said. "But maybe that would be better for him. He could go live with some couple in Greenwich with a huge estate."

I thought about this. The sidewalks of our neighborhood were littered with chicken bones and broken glass. Trash collected in soggy piles in the storm drains. There was nothing in the way of prey to offer a hunting dog except cockroaches and pigeons and rats. And then there was the *noise* of the city. They say dogs can hear four times better than humans, so I winced every time a horn honked, or a trash truck crushed up its barrels of glass. I winced as the police cars and ambulances blared past us, sirens wailing, and each time one of our neighbors screamed out the window, "Fuck you, you fucking bastard!"

This poor confused dog! The Lower East Side must have seemed like an assault to him, a place under siege. Our street—Suffolk Street—was just off a truck route leading onto the Williamsburg Bridge. And this meant that at all hours, every day, giant semis barreled up the bridge ramp, accelerating with their great heaving engines, rising and crashing over potholes, which would result in a thundering boom, which would set off all the car alarms, and thus, at four o'clock in the morning, Ted and I would be serenaded by dozens of alarms, all out of sync. Why, I hadn't had a decent night's sleep in the past seven years. Could you blame me for being edgy? Could you blame Ted? Could you blame the dog? The noise, the madness! Even the smallest details must have been loud to Rex. The rats sifting through the trash cans outside our building; the cockroaches skittering through the walls. Ted watching *The Simpsons* and startling both me and the dog with a sudden, uproarious Simpson-laugh. Me tap-tap-tapping away on computer keys. No wonder the poor dog ground his teeth! No wonder he kept trying to escape!

Two days later, Rex finally did escape. He somehow slipped out of his collar as we were trying to get into our building. We weren't quite sure how he did it. All we saw was the aftermath: the dog bolting up Suffolk Street. He disappeared between two parked cars and reappeared right in the midst of the traffic, and we watched in horror as one car skidded and another swerved. Horns honked, someone shouted "Catch that dog!" and then Ted was running into traffic, shouting both "Chance!" and "Rex!" For some reason I could only stand there, holding the empty collar in my hand, so much like a noose. For a second I wished that Rex *would* get hit by a car, because then our time with him would be over, and we could say we tried. And failed. But at least all the failure and all the tension and all the violence would come to an end.

But Ted, alas, returned with the panting dog in his arms and asked me to open the door for him. "Could you get the keys out for me? They're in my front pocket."

I found that I couldn't look at him. Or at Rex. What if they knew what I had been thinking? As I put my hand into Ted's shorts to fish the keys out, I felt shy and indecent, as if I were fondling a stranger. When I'd promised the dog we'd stick with him for better or for worse, I had no idea the emphasis would be on the worse.

Inside the apartment, I offered the dog some fresh water, but Rex was not thirsty. He turned his back to us, positioned himself dominantly above his doggie bed, and began to hump it. He humped it savagely, muttering all kinds of threats and curses, as if he bore this bed a deep-seated grudge. Ted and I both slumped into the two wooden chairs at the little breakfast table and watched. It seemed that Rex was trying to erase something within himself, trying to dull some undullable pain. I understood his motive. But what had caused this pain? And what could we do to take it away?

"This was not in the Alpo commercials," I said. Rex had now seized the bed between his forepaws with remarkable strength and was grunting and gyrating in an obscene way. "Maybe I should go look this up in the shelter book. But this is more like those stories I hear about back-alley men violating hollowed-out cuts of meat."

Ted looked at me and smiled a little. "Where do you hear stories like that?" he said. And then he started to cry. I had seen him get teary eyed once before—on our first date, in fact, when he told me how much regret he felt at not being able to say goodbye to his grandmother before she died. Such undisguised sentimentality has always endeared Ted to me, for I have a soft spot for softies.

"Oh, honey," I said. I moved over to him and put my arms around him and sat on his lap. "What should we do? Should we take him back?"

"I knew it was going to be a lot of work," Ted said. "But not like this." A friend of his, he said, had to be hospitalized for clinical depression after his second child was born. "He said he realized it was too much responsibility, having two kids, and he didn't realize he didn't want the responsibility until *after* their second child. That realization sent him over the edge." Ted looked toward the ceiling and his eyes welled. "Until it was too late, in other words. I feel like my freedom has been taken away."

Rex, having proven something at last to the bed, went into the kitchen to lap up some water. The sound was that of any normal dog.

"I feel like my freedom has been taken away, too," I said. "Freedom I didn't even realize I had. Now we can't even do something so simple as read a magazine."

I gestured toward the storage-trunk-that-doubled-as-a-coffee-table. There loomed a stack of unread *New Yorkers* that I planned to read once I finished reading all the *New York Times Magazines*. Beyond that stood a filing cabinet that contained an unfinished novel, and an unfinished screenplay, and pages and pages of journals from an unfinished life, and beyond *that*, on the other side of our tenement wall, New York City itself pulsed and gyrated, a city full of movers and shakers who were making movies, *finishing* novels, saving lives. For God's sake, if you sat still for a second in New York you might as well move to the Midwest. Were we being forced to make a choice between all the bounty and promise the city had to offer—and this madly humping dog?

I sat back and folded my arms. Why did I not recognize, those few days ago, just how easy and dazzling my life had been? How *effortless* it would be to finish a novel without a dog to walk? How easy it would be to travel, and go to all the gallery openings in our neighborhood, and listen to music at night at the local bars? Oh, God, here I was yearning for a life that, two weeks ago, I had felt wasn't good enough. Because it wasn't perfect. Because I seemed to focus only on what I hadn't accomplished, rather than what I had.

But maybe it wasn't too late to accomplish these things. I could meet Pete Townshend. I could paddle a kayak through the waters of Patagonia and hike Machu Picchu under a full moon. I could find a guru, get published in *The New Yorker,* pay off my student loan. I could lose those seven pounds and get back into my Thin Jeans, and put everything right. And what of the Pulitzer, the Nobel, the National Book Award? Wait! Didn't I always say I wanted to take up painting again, and horseback riding, and brush up on my French? In France?

And what of Ted? He talked of making quality documentaries about architecture and travel and art. He talked of traveling to China, Japan, and the South Seas. He wanted us to go to Mexico and drink real tequila. He wanted to learn how to fly-fish and take that Avid editing class. He talked of buying some land in New Mexico, and building a house. Sometimes, at night, he drew sketches of the house on drafting paper, and showed me his ideas. Sometimes I wondered whether we'd live in that house together or not.

"Can we do it?" I said to Ted. "Can we take him back?"

"I think we're going to have to," he said.

I nodded and hugged him tighter and then, together, we cried. We cried because we were tired and overwhelmed. We cried because we felt like failures and perhaps it was time to admit it. Perhaps it was time to admit that we were the type of people who, if pressed, would not meet challenges head on, or embrace them; no, we were the types who would back off, tails between our legs, and run away. We had done it before; we could do it again.

"I just wish there were a sign," I said. "Some sign, some guarantee that it's not always going to be like this. If he'll love us some day. That there will be some reward."

Rex was lying on the floor as I said this, and he had begun to lick his privates in a loud and rather lewd way. Rex glanced at me suspiciously and belched. Then he went back to licking himself.

"There's your sign," Ted said. "Nothing comes between a male and his dick."

"If we do this," I said, "if we take him back, we'll be bad people, and everyone will know."

Ted nodded.

"What will I tell my parents?" I stood up and gazed out the window. Which faced straight into our neighbor's window. In New York, you can't escape coming face-to-face with other people's better lives. I beheld a pretty young woman who was talking on her cordless to her girlfriend, discussing where they'd meet for dinner that night.

"I guess I could just lie to them and tell them Rex got hit by a car," I said.

"You can't do that," Ted said. "Talk about bad karma."

"It's better than admitting we're failures."

I saw the Adam's apple move up and down along Ted's throat.

That night, in bed, Ted and I lay entwined at the center of the mattress. Neither of us slept. Rex was grinding his teeth. The window was open and I listened to the layers of summer sounds. There was the wind chime on our fire escape. Then, beyond that, the meows of feral cats. Farther beyond: the traffic on Delancey Street, and farther still, the faint pulse of Spanish music, a tink-a-tink-a-tink that matched the rhythm of the dog's swift pants. Inside I felt the still internal quiet of having made a decision. And also, in my gut, a churning knot of guilt.

In the morning, we awoke in a kind of self-conscious silence, and made coffee, and geared up to take out the dog. We were very aware of all these steps, how robotic they felt, and remained self-conscious all the way to the park. It's easy to stay in the moment when you know something is about to end. As we walked along, I waited for Ted to bring up taking the dog back, and he, I imagine, expected the same of me.

On Clinton Street, we passed an old man walking an old Dalmatian. The dog was arthritic, laboring with every step, skin and bones, with fur missing in some places, exposing pink spotted skin. But we could tell the dog was well cared-for. The man walked alongside her, holding up her hips, encouraging her along. He too, had an arthritic limp, and you could tell they had been together for a long time. I welled up—the man had found someone to grow old with.

And then Rex did his pee-like-a-girl-dog thing, looking from side to side with that worried look, and I filled once again with doubt and pity. It was not his fault that he did not know how to pee correctly. It was not his fault that he was confused and frightened and mean. The world of faulty human beings had made him this way. And we had an opportunity to correct this.

"He's gender confused," I said. "No one taught him how to be a dog."

"Plus," Ted said, "beneath all that fur he's pink. How could someone who's pink be truly bad?"

"Let's bring him home," I said.

We had a decent day that day, dogwise. Ted was able to sit and read the paper. I checked my e-mail. Rex ventured from beneath the table and sat for a few seconds near Ted's feet. He yawned. He rose and stretched—the Downward-Facing Dog pose that I did in yoga. Then he turned in circles, sat again, and scratched himself behind the ear. Ted and I watched him and smiled. Next, he sniffed the sofa and studied it, as if expecting it to make the first move. "You can go up there," I said to Rex of the sofa. "It's okay." (Ted and I both felt dogs should be allowed on furniture, except the bed.)

"Hop up," Ted said. "It's comfy. It's a comfy place."

Rex hopped and circled and settled, and he looked surprised, because he had probably never known softness. "Good boy!" Ted said, and reached out to pet him, but the dog jumped up and darted to the back room. We heard him hop onto the bed.

"That's not allowed," Ted said. "You can sit anywhere but the bed." He went into the bedroom. "No. Noooooo." Ted reached for the dog's collar to pull him off, and Rex took this as a threat and lunged. And then dog and man were engaged in a battle reminiscent of St. George and the Serpent, until Rex finally gave in, and recoiled, and made himself small, and Ted swatted him on the nose one last time and said, "No!"

"He bit me!" Ted said. He showed me his hand. "I can't believe he bit me!"

I took his palm. "It doesn't look like he broke the skin."

"I hope he doesn't have rabies," Ted said.

"He was vaccinated."

"Rabies would explain his personality disorders at least."

Rex crawled back underneath the desk. Ted watched him with a solemn look on his face. I couldn't tell if he was thinking of the past or the future.

"I'm glad we're doing this together," Ted said. "I don't think I could handle this by myself."

I tried calling the shelter again, because I was still convinced that we weren't going to have any true breakthroughs with this dog until we knew his past. In fact, unless we knew his history, I felt it might be pointless to keep trying. But we went through the same rigmarole, in which I explained that Rex was really difficult, that he kept trying to escape, that it would help to know what had happened to him before we got him, and the Ma'am-er said that it wasn't their policy to release files. "Just give him some time," she said. "He's probably just getting to know you, checking things out. You gotta give him some time."

"How much time?" I said. "Do you mean like ten years?"

"Ma'am, I just told you, you gotta give him some time." Then she added, in a manner that seemed as practiced as it was snide: "If you can't handle him, then why don't you just bring him back?"

"Bring him *back*?" I said. Of course *bringing him back* was by that time our theme song, but to hear someone else voice this option was another matter. Suddenly I was insulted. This shelter worker was lumping me in with all the other inadequate, ill-prepared, selfish, clueless people who callously adopt an animal, thinking only of their own shallow, selfish needs, only to find, a few days later, that Little Miss Muffet has to go to the bathroom all the time, and she sheds buckets, and she chews up cell phones and paintbrushes with her pointy little teeth.

"He's just—really difficult," I said to the stranger on the phone. "I don't think you understand."

"Oh, I understand all right. You can't handle having a dog. Well, you all bring her back then. You know the address."

"Him," I said. "He's a male. His name was Chance."

"Sorry. *Him*. We're open until eight P.M. every night. Sunday noon till six."

I was in tears after I hung up the phone. "Even they think we can't handle it," I said. "Everyone thinks we should just take him back."

Ted nodded. There was my father's consensus and my sister's doubt. There was the website's pronouncement that keeping a hunting dog in the city was cruel. So far, only his mother had expressed delight and enthusiasm at our decision. She had already ordered a

Christmas stocking for the dog, from some needlepoint company that would personalize the stocking with Rex's name.

"But I love him," Ted said.

I had been lifting a handkerchief to my eyes, but I stopped. "You do?"

Ted had been the first to say "I love you" back when we first began dating. A bunch of us had driven out to Brighton Beach in Queens to get some authentic Russian food, and on the way back, giddy from all that dill-flavored vodka, Ted and I snuggled together happily in the front seat. I sat on Ted's lap. The car was crowded—there were seven of us, I think, including Tara, who rode in the back, and everyone was singing made-up versions of the Soviet national anthem. It was at that point that Ted whispered, "I love you." I kept silent for a second, processing these words, but then Tara said, in her most sarcastic voice, "Oh *God.*" She had killed the moment. Sometimes Tara wasn't very nice.

Now, Ted said again that he loved the dog. "Already, I do. Look at him, he knows we're talking about him." Rex had been panting as Ted said this, and sure enough, he stopped. He blinked. He looked away—a sad, sideways glance.

"I don't know what to do," Ted said. "I don't know if I'm capable of taking him back. Maybe if we just try harder he'll come around. If we turned him in I don't know if I'd forgive myself."

Here's something Ted didn't know about me: I *was* capable of bringing a dog back. The truth is, there had been one dog between Tasha and Chance. His name was Stinky Townshend (after my idol, Pete), and my alcoholic carry-over-from-college boyfriend had brought him over to my apartment after a binge. I was twenty-two. And Stinky was too young to be taken from his mother, which we didn't know was bad, and the alcoholic boyfriend was feeding him French fries, which he didn't know was bad, and I had a job as a waitress at the time and left the poor puppy home alone, even though he was sick, and lonesome, and puking up all those fries. Bad, bad, bad. We had to give him away eventually. I can't even remember how long I had that dear sweet pup. I just remember the look the new people gave me as we handed him off, in a cardboard box. They were dog people. They understood how irresponsible and cold we were being. But I did not. Oh, Stinky, wherever you are, please forgive me.

I couldn't tell Ted that I had already heartlessly given one dog up. I could barely admit it to myself. "No, I don't think we could forgive ourselves," I finally said.

So, once again, we decided to "give it some time." On Friday nights, it was our habit to order from Two Boots Pizzeria, and we always took great pleasure in the fried eggplant topping with smoked mozzarella cheese, but this time, as we lifted the slices to our mouths, Rex glared at us, and began to snarl. I offered him a piece of crust—because if anything can resolve an issue, pizza can—but Rex leapt back as if I had brandished a weapon, then lunged at my outstretched hand. "Goddammit!" Ted shouted, leaping from his chair. "That is enough!" And he seized the dog by his collar, pushed him to the floor, and then dragged him bodily into the bedroom, slamming the door before Rex could even think of trying to escape.

"Goddamn dog," Ted said, returning to the table.

We finished our pizza in silence. It was hard to swallow anything with Rex pacing and grumbling and muttering all kinds of threats on the other side of the door. It felt, in many ways, like that last meal they serve you on death row. I was about to share this observation with Ted, when I realized he was on the verge of crying again. "I just want to be able to eat in peace," he said. "I just want to be able to eat my pizza and drink a beer and not have to have it be a fucking battle all the time. I can't sleep anymore," Ted said. "I have these crying fits. And my appetite is poor."

"Do you want to see a doctor?" I said. "My therapist is—"

"No, I don't want to see a doctor," Ted said. There was a blue vein throbbing at the center of his forehead that hadn't been there a week before. "This is clearly related to the dog."

"We'll bring him back, then," I said. "Tomorrow. I'll call the shelter again and tell them we're bringing him back."

We watched Rex through the French doors. He was humping his bed again.

"The poor boy."

"He's dangerous," Ted said. "He bit me."

I nodded.

"And he's tried to bite you. I have to protect you, don't I?"

"Couldn't we just get a different dog?" I said. "Another needy adult?"

"No, I don't think I could handle another adult dog. Or any dog. At least not right now. Maybe someday in the future, when we're more settled and are more financially secure, but definitely not now."

I sat down, suddenly exhausted. I'd heard these words before. I looked over at the calendar, and saw that it was the twenty-first of June—the longest day of the year. How sad it was, how unfair, to have only this one long day and then have everything get shorter again.

I must have looked bitter, and disappointed, because Ted changed his mind again. "I'll tell you what," he said. "We'll give him a month, okay? Thirty days. And if he doesn't show any progress by then, well, we tried."

Thus, we finally made a decision. And sure, it was technically a decision to put off the decision; but it felt like a step. And whether this was a step forward or backward we still didn't know.

CHAPTER 3

The Trial Period

J ust one week had passed since we adopted our dog. And now he was officially on trial.

"Like an electronic hedge clipper you buy from an infomercial," Ted said. "Satisfaction guaranteed or a full refund within thirty days."

I said: "Like a coffee maker from Gevalia Kaffe."

We weren't quite laughing as we said this, but at least we tried. It's easier to be flip, after all, than to face the truth. Which was that a dog on a leash is like a ball on a chain.

"Waiter, there's a dog in my apartment," Ted said.

But our decision to put off the decision was a good one for us. It freed us somehow—it made all the challenges and obstacles seem temporary, a simple phase to pass through.

In the spirit of a fair trial, Ted and I decided to better educate ourselves on the world of dogs. That instruction manual, *How to Care for Your Shelter Dog*, had been helpful up to a point, stating that dogs needed to be fed and exercised and house-trained, but we were looking for something more.

And in New York, if you are looking for something more, if you find yourself at an impasse and need advice, there are hundreds of options. There are 764 churches, 157 synagogues, and 46 Buddhist temples in Manhattan alone. There are also 21 Barnes & Nobles, which is where all the clueless new dog owners go for information, comfort, and advice.

We didn't have a Barnes & Noble in our neighborhood—the Lower East Side wasn't that gentrified yet. But at Astor Place, eleven blocks away, we had our choice of two Barnes & Nobles, each of which you could see from the café of the other.

Rex howled as Ted and I left for our neighborhood Barnes & Noble that Saturday. It was the first time we'd left him alone in the apartment and this made him frantic. He howled and scratched at the door as it shut behind us, and as we made our way down the stairs he emitted a primal scream on par with Roger Daltrey's last yaaaaaaahhhhhhh at the end of "Won't Get Fooled Again."

"I don't get it," I said to Ted as we hurried out of the foyer. "First he doesn't want to live with us, but now he doesn't want to live without us? Is he just playing hard to get?"

At the bookstore, we ordered coffee and carrot cake, brought a few dog books to our table, and settled down to read.

"This place is full of humans!" I said excitedly. "Reading! No one is talking about dogs."

Ted said, "This cake is delicious. Try some." It felt good to be back in the world.

We focused on our books. I started with a collection of photographs taken by the famous dog photographer Elliot Erwitt, and Ted chose a manual from the American Sporting Dog Club, and within half an hour we were in love with the idea of having a dog again. This is easy if all you're doing is looking at pictures. "Look at these setters," Ted said. He pushed his book toward me. "Such handsome dogs. It says they're easy to train. They're smart."

"And look," I said. "Here's a picture of a spaniel *in a city*. She's on a leash, on a sidewalk, and her humans are window-shopping, and she looks *fine*. And look, here's a picture of a woman walking *three* Afghans. And she's smiling. And she's wearing heels and a little Chanel suit."

"Look at this man snuggling with his setter at the campground after a hike," Ted said.

We bought five books to start with that day, and wrote down the titles of fourteen more. Back at home, after we had taken the dog out, we ordered those fourteen books on Amazon, and for every one we ordered a little message would pop up on the computer suggesting, *"If you liked this book, you may like _____ and _____."* Then they'd list an additional seventy-five training books to read as well. And because we wanted to be good caretakers, because we didn't know any better, and because we never knew which book was going to be *the* book—the one that would crack Rex's code—we ordered all of them. To the tune of several hundred dollars.

Every night, for days upon days, Ted and I stayed up late, reading in bed side by side, poring over training guides and veterinary manuals. We'd make all kinds of notes, hoping in the meantime that the foreign four-legged creature who paced our bedroom would not kill us before we reached that Final Book—the book that would save our lives.

And so, every morning we'd take him to the East River Park and situate ourselves in an enclosed baseball field, and try to apply whatever training methods we had learned from the books of the night before. We started out working on the basic commands of Sit, Stay, Heel, and Come, and sometimes Rex would look at us when we spoke, and cock his head, as if he were trying to figure out our language. Sometimes he tried to bolt. But we kept trying. Oh, how we tried. Every morning, we'd get up with that alarm clock, experience that momentary daze, remember that we had a dog, and then head on out to the park with our latest book. Ted and I both *believed* in the written word. But the thing was, not all these books offered the same advice. "Buy a good choke collar," one book advised, and suggested a metal one that would snap quickly and efficiently around the dog's neck. If his attention strayed even for one second while you were training him, you were supposed to give the collar a "pop" and repeat the command. Another book, however, stressed that "popping the choke" was unnecessary; that it was better to keep a dog's attention with treats. And yet another book would come along that said treats were for idiots. You want your dog to love you for *you*, in other words. Not your Liver Snacks.

And because we didn't know what to believe, we kept blindly following along. We were the blind leading the blind.

"Always reward your shelter dog with a toy when he obeys a command," we read. "A good game of tug-of-war for five minutes at the end of each training session will condition the dog to associate training with play."

"Never play tug-of-war with a shelter dog," the next book warned.

"If an aggressive dog is allowed to win—even just once—he will begin to think he is the leader of the pack."

"Oh, great," Ted said. He'd been playing tug with the dog for the past few days. "So now Rex is going to kill us in our sleep."

I had a friend who had taught her terrier to ring a little bell every time he had to go to the bathroom. Another friend had a Newfoundland who was so in love with her he slept with his leg draped over her midriff at night. Our neighbor's malamute was so well trained she knew to never, ever step off a sidewalk or cross a street without permission. One time, when the dog got loose, another neighbor found her sitting at the sidewalk across from our apartment building, waiting to be told she could go home. Each time Rex reared up like a horse with fangs bared I thought of these people with yearning and jealousy—the same feelings I had whenever some twenty-four-year-old author made the *New York Times* bestseller list despite his wooden prose.

Rex really had no interest in treats. And most toys—other than that tug-a-rope, which he seemed to see as a Weapon of Mass Destruction—frightened him. The first time I waved a rawhide bone in his face, he leapt backward and crouched low, with his teeth bared. The first time I tossed a tennis ball toward him, he scrambled away. This odd reaction had not been described in any of the books we'd read, for some reason. It seemed we were going to learn by trial and error. Mostly error.

And of course, both Ted and I were on trial as committed dog owners, too. No one took into consideration how hard it would be for us non-prey-animals to keep the attention of a hunting dog, or, for that matter, how hard it would be for me to stay focused at that early hour myself. I'd always said I wanted to be a morning person—out there at dawn with the joggers, the go-getters, the high-strung Wall Street freaks who made eight hundred thousand a month. But now that I was required to get up every day before seven—at an hour when most of the club kids in our neighborhood hadn't even come down from their K highs yet—and stand in the middle of an abandoned baseball field, I wished I were still in bed. While Ted talked about, say, the importance of always heeling the dog on his right side versus his left ("They need rules; they need consistency"), I'd find my attention drifting off toward the other dog people, who passed beyond the fence with their well-trained dogs.

There was the tall, sleek Icelandic woman gliding by on Rollerblades with her ice-blue Weimaraner. There was the hipster East Village dude racing his unstoppable Ridgeback on his bike. And then there was the perfect blond yuppie couple with their perfect blond baby and a matching yellow Lab. Every day they would appear through the morning mist like aliens from Planet Future with their high-tech stroller and their crisp, ironed clothes. The Lab trotted alongside them happily with a ball in his mouth, his leash slack, his focus on them. They would park the stroller under a willow tree and throw the ball for the dog exactly thirty times. The baby never cried; the dog never pooped. Then they were off again, disappearing into the mist, off to their bright, promising days. I would stare after them in wonder. How did she manage to push the stroller, drink a Starbucks Caramel Macchiato, *and* hold the dog's leash all at the same time? How did she find the time to have a dog *and* a baby? Or even just a dog?

Ted would yank on my sleeve and say, "Pay attention!"

At about this point, the Icelandic woman would be gliding by in the other direction, her sleek body now glistening with sweat. She was tall enough and long legged enough as it was, but on Rollerblades she was otherworldly. Her proportions were that of a Barbie Doll and her daily uniform consisted of a silver jogging bra and tiny matching shorts. And of course she was one of those careless Aryan beauties who never wore makeup and barely combed her short blond hair. Who needed to, with such a bod?

"We should get Rollerblades," Ted would say dreamily.

And then it would be my turn to say: "Pay attention!"

Life is so much easier when you stay in bed.

Our bodies were on trial. Ted read that it was easier to keep a dog's attention if you stayed in motion and talked to the dog the entire time, so we each bought a pair of running shoes, and we each remembered, with a swell of pride, those bygone days when we had been runners ourselves. I too used to exercise in hot pink sports bras and silver running shorts. Ted, in prep school had run track. So the next morning, as we laced up our new shoes and leashed up the dog, it was with a renewed sense of hope. We could be people who jogged again! Who jogged with our dog! We could become young and healthy and buff!

But when you take up exercise after a long spell of nonexercise, you quickly remember why you gave it up. Within two days of running alongside the dog on the promenade, reeling him in beside us and shouting encouraging words, I had damaged something in my knee my doctor called a patella. I was told to keep ice on that knee and "lay off the jogging." Then I had to purchase a geriatric knee brace, which meant the end of my summer dream of wearing short, flirty skirts. I was walking like Frankenstein.

"You look bionic," Ted said when I came home from the doctor's office sporting the brace.

"I look like my father," I said. "Only he pairs his knee braces with black socks and madras shorts."

So that was the end of jogging. I decided to take up smoking instead.

"You bought cigarettes?" Ted said when he caught me. "What's wrong with you? How many years ago did you quit?"

"I don't know. About three? There's something about self-destruction I find reassuring, I guess."

"You shouldn't be smoking."

"It helps in times of stress," I said.

Ted raised his eyebrows. "Give me one," he said.

Our sense of time was on trial. All our books stressed that dogs need consistency. A consistent schedule gives a newly adopted dog a sense of safety and security. In fact, many behavioral problems in newly adopted dogs, we were told, result from the dog not having had a routine. Life in a shelter or in a series of foster homes can be very stressful. So simply establishing a routine and sticking to it can help resolve all kinds of problems, from excessive barking to chewing to separation anxiety.

"But what's a routine?" I said. I was only half kidding. I thought of Daisy Buchanan saying, "What do people plan?"

Side by side, Ted and I read the sample schedule of a woman we'll call Mrs. Flint.

6:00 A.M.	All rise. Mrs. Flint lets dog into yard.
6:30 A.M.	Mrs. Flint prepares breakfast for husband and children.
7:00 A.M.	Mrs. Flint clears the breakfast dishes and feeds dog.
7:30 A.M.	Mrs. Flint and the dog accompany children to school bus.
8:00 A.M.	Daily dog grooming: Mrs. Flint inspects teeth, anal glands, and ears.
8:30 A.M.	Mrs. Flint commences daily household chores while dog naps.
12:00 P.M.	Lunch break.
12:30 P.M.	Dog into yard for "relief" and fifteen-minute training session, followed by five minutes of play.
12:45 P.M.	More household chores.
1:30 P.M.	Walk to mailbox with dog. Socialize dog with mailman and neighbors.
3:00 P.M.	Meet children at school bus. After snack, children play with dog.
4:00 P.M.	Mrs. Flint supervises children's homework; dog naps.
5:00 P.M.	Mr. Flint returns; dinner for humans.
6:30 P.M.	Dinner for dog.
6:45 P.M.	Let dog out.
7:00 P.M.	Dog to bed.
8:00 P.M.	Kids to bed.
11:00 P.M.	Parents to bed.

When we finished reading, I said, "Where's the part where it says: Have a life?"

This was our life before we got the dog:

On weekends, we slept in and then spent at least an hour at a local place we called Café Caucasian, where we discussed whether to go to the warehouse sale at Barney's or the flea market on Twenty-sixth.

For lunch, we might walk up to Little India for chicken tandoori, and later that afternoon meet friends for mojitos at a Brazilian café. After a dinner in Chinatown, we might go to the Anthology Film Archives to see *Jules et Jim*. Sitting there in the dark theater, holding hands, eating imported Swedish gummi bears, reading the English words while listening to the French, we would feel as if we had been to four different countries in the span of three hours, and there was something exhilarating and magical about that.

Could there be magic with a *plan?* If I asked Ted on Thursday what he wanted to do on Saturday, he said: "I don't know yet. We'll see." Sure, this could be frustrating at times, but also liberating. We allowed ourselves to be lulled by whim and fancy, or by the music coming from within that Brazilian bar, or by a marquee. So how did you put a schedule like that down on paper?

We tried:

6:00 A.M.	Are you kidding?
7:30 A.M.	Open one eyelid, peek at clock, groan.
8:00 A.M.	Open other eyelid; repeat groan.
9:00 A.M.	Open both eyelids, stare aghast at clock, say "Fuck! We overslept!" and jump out of bed.
9: 30 A.M.	Coffee, shower, discuss what to do with the day. . . .

I put the pen down. "And after that it's never really consistent. Not day by day. I don't suppose I've ever really done anything 'like clockwork.' Have you?" I always thought my inability to plan meant I was spontaneous, and free spirited, and fun. But maybe it just meant I was a lump.

"This will be good for us," Ted said. "The dog will help us keep a schedule."

We *had* been taking out the dog daily. But not with Mrs. Flint's precision. So we tried to start getting up at exactly 6:35 and leaving the apartment at exactly 6:50 to get to the park precisely at 7:10, give or take a few minutes for the amount of time it took Rex to pee. And such precision for some reason made us grouchy. Lying in bed at 6:29, we'd waste a few precious minutes arguing over whose turn it was to get up and make the coffee, and then we'd complain about the fact that we didn't have one of those machines that made the coffee for you while you slept, and then we'd squabble over whose fault that was. And then the second alarm would go off and we'd *both* have to get up, neither one of us able to gain the satisfaction of having won some stupid argument. I found myself filling up with resentment. At Ted for being the one to have to remind me that I had to get up. And at the dog, simply for being in my life. "We're making all this effort to accommodate his needs," I'd say to Ted on the way to the park in the mornings. "But shouldn't this dog be trying to learn how to accommodate *us*?"

I began to calculate the number of hours I was "losing" by walking this unappreciative dog. I resented devoting all my mornings now to *him* rather than to my writing. I resented not being obeyed and listened to. I resented having someone else's schedule to think of in addition to my own. I resented having to clean dog hair, daily, off my clothing and the floors. As I walked behind him on the sidewalk, this dog who didn't even really seem to know I was there, I would list all the things I resented in my head. It took *time* to purchase that dog food. It took time to open the cans, then rinse those cans for recycling, and then clean out the dish. It took *hours* to read all those dog books.

Then he'd stop and pee like a girl dog, or flinch when I lifted my hand to brush back my hair, and the guilt would come. The same guilt, the probably permanent and latent guilt, that all parents of human children seem to have, which consisted of the loathing I felt for myself for resenting this guileless creature, who did not ask to be born, who did not ask to come into my life, who had suffered unthinkable atrocities as a puppy, and who now simply wanted to be free. What kind of monster was I to resent this wish of his? They were exhausting, these internal monologues. I would then conclude that I had no business having a dog, or anyone or anything else in my life, because I was not a nurturer. I could not give. I was just too mean and selfish. It was time to just go off and be a nun, I decided. Just not at one of those monasteries that raise dogs.

"So how's the writing going?" my father asked in his weekly Consensus from Garrison Drive.

"Oh, it's great," I said. This was an untruth. I hadn't written a sentence since we got the dog. I hadn't even written an exclamation point. But I'd *thought* about writing, as we know, albeit in a backward-glancing sort of way. "I finished another story this week and am ready to send it out."

"Good, good, I'm glad to hear that."

"Oh, and I got that reading job at the literary magazine that I interviewed for weeks ago."

"Good, good. How much do they pay?"

"Um, it's kind of a volunteer position. One day a week. And this position will lead to a paying position, I'm sure. In the meantime, my temp agency says they can find me a four-day-a-week gig. I'll start in a few weeks, once we feel comfortable leaving the dog. We decided to get back to our work when we feel it's safe to leave the dog alone for eight hours. Ted thinks it should be five hours, but I keep saying every other dog in this city stays home alone for at least eight. So we'll do that."

My father paused, as if trying to figure out the moment in his parenting life where it all went wrong. "Well, don't let that dog take up too much of your time," he said. "Although according to that picture you sent he seems very cute."

Our sanity was on trial. Twenty-two more dog-training books arrived via UPS. Some were addressed to me; some to Ted. And therein lay the beginning of a Great Divide. The books I favored encouraged a positive, gentle approach to training, whereas most of Ted's favorites advocated brute force. Take Ted's favorite book, for instance: *How to Be Your Dog's Best Friend* by the Monks of New Skete. Now, there is a reason why this worthy book has become a staple of every new dog-guardian's shelf—the Monks encourage you to establish a sensitive, trusting relationship with your dog, and they believe in honoring a dog's dogness. But the Monks also favor harsh "corrections" such as shaking, hitting, and administering the famous "alpha roll," in which you are supposed to roll your dog onto his back and pin him down with your knees, all the while shouting "No! Bad Dog!" into his face.

The Monks even offered four pages of delicately written instructions on the proper way to hit your dog. Do not use newspaper or a stick, they cautioned. A conscientious owner must use his own hand. "The dog should be anchored in the sitting position," they wrote. "Your fingers meet the underside of the dog's mouth in an upward motion . . . and your fingers should be closed together, your palm flat."

"That sounds like a volleyball serve," I said as I read the book over Ted's shoulder.

"Stop reading my book," he said. "Read your own."

"*My* book says all you have to do is show your teeth when the dog has done something you don't approve of," I said. "Like a mother wolf. She never hurts her pups. She just shows them who's boss. Like this." I bared my teeth at Ted and gave a little growl. "See?"

"Yes, yes, very frightening," he said. "You have a poppy seed stuck between your two front teeth."

Aghast, I limped to the mirror. I'd last eaten a poppy-seed bagel three days ago.

I attempted to administer the alpha roll the very next morning, out in the ball field, after I tried to pull Rex's forelegs into a Down position and he growled. Just like a Monk, I flipped him and wedged my knee onto his chest and held him by the throat and said "Bad dog!" But my heart just wasn't in it. I didn't see submission on Rex's face so much as fear. Terror. I could feel his little heart pounding. He flopped his head to the side and held his breath—as if waiting for me to plunge in the knife. I burst into tears.

"Here," Ted said. He held out his hand to help me up. The dog lay there, motionless. Poor confused thing. Oh, he *had* to have been abused—I could see it in the way he tried to hide under the table any time we raised our voices. I could see it in the way he bristled and cowered any time we raised our hands. And of course I saw it in those serious, amber eyes, which, after two weeks, were still dull and unresponsive. Whoever had had this dog before us had not only abused Rex physically; this person must have killed something else in him as well.

"Do you think he spent his entire puppyhood locked in a basement?" I asked Ted. "Do you think he was ever exercised?"

"I don't know, honey," Ted said. "They don't get all that much exercise at the shelters."

We tied Rex's leash to a chain-link fence and tried to let him howl himself out like an infant in a crib. We watched him and flopped onto the grass.

"Can you imagine how cute he must have been as a puppy?" I said. "With the one white ear and the one brown ear? And a pink spotted belly? And those big floppy spotted paws?"

"He was the cutest puppy in the world," Ted said, hugging me.

"Who could have been mean to such a cute puppy? Now he'll never trust anyone again. As far as he's concerned, we're just another pair of abusers as well." I explained to Ted that all this neck snapping and choking, these shakedowns and alpha rolls—all of this seemed somewhat abusive. Because it conflicted with my idea of love. Love was not harsh or punitive or depriving. Anger and aggression did not seal the loving bond.

"It's not abuse," Ted said. "It's dominance." He said he trusted the process, and he knew it was for the best—that a hierarchy needed to be established, that Rex could not continue to dominate, that he needed to know who was boss.

"Don't you worry that if you hit him, he's going to think you hate him?" I said.

"Dogs are tough," Ted said. "Even your books say puppies are used to getting cuffed by their mothers. That's how she teaches them what's right and wrong. This is about control. Dogs need authority. Rex wants a leader. He wants someone he can trust. There's even some trainer out in California whose motto is, 'Leadership, Not Love.'"

Rex was suddenly quiet. We turned to see him sitting down, his head cocked toward the sky. I followed his gaze and saw a flock of Canada geese flying south in formation. They were four months ahead of schedule.

I turned back to Ted. "Are you talking about that guy who calls people like me humaniacs?" (This particular trainer encouraged you to pick your dog up by the collar and suspend him in the air until he nearly choked to death. If that wasn't enough to "teach the dog a lesson," you were then supposed to swing him around by the chain, further choking and frightening him into eternal damn submission, a method called "helicoptering." And if *that* wasn't enough, you were supposed to submerge your dog's head in a big bucket of water, until he nearly drowned.)

"No, I'm not talking about him, come on!"

"It sounds like what that guy wants you to do is break the dog's spirit," I said. "I don't want to do that to Rex. He doesn't even seem to have a spirit yet."

"But we're not breaking his spirit," Ted said. "Trust me. We're training him. We're giving him a sense of who's in charge."

But who *was* in charge?

Unless I am remembering incorrectly, it seems to me that, until we got the dog, we had had more of an equal partnership as far as cohabiting was concerned. We both did the dishes, we both shopped for groceries, we each paid our separate bills. Household decisions, such as what mop to buy—or even what restaurant to go to—were made diplomatically, without much incident. With a dog, of course, there is much more at stake than a choice between Chinese or Italian. And any parent wants what is best for his child. But who's best was better?

Inside the apartment, I tried to teach Rex how to fetch a tennis ball, and Ted announced that ball playing was not allowed in the bedroom. "But, look, he's not so afraid of the ball," I said. I rolled it toward Rex, and he stood there, stock-still, eyeing the ball suspiciously. Ted said: "The Monks say the bedroom is supposed to be a peaceful place and that the dog will learn to respect that." Outside, on the sidewalks, I'd give Rex a little leeway on his leash so that he could sniff a little, and I could give my arm a rest, and Ted would say: "Don't let him get so far ahead of you." Another time, I gave Rex a pair of my freshly ruined nylons to chew on, thinking that he might enjoy having something to annihilate, but then Ted said: "You're not supposed to give them shoes or socks. They'll start to think that all of your clothing is fair game."

"But Monks don't wear nylons," I said. "If they did, they'd know how quickly a pair gets ruined."

Ted said, "Look, just don't give him clothing to chew."

I began to call the Monks of New Skete the "Monks of Steel."

Ted got a kick out of some of the Monks' more bombastic statements, and he went around the apartment quoting them, half in jest. "Stay away from cute toys at the pet store!" he'd announce when I tried to entice Rex with a stuffed animal. "All he needs is a block of wood."

Or: "Leash biting should not be tolerated!"

"Never kiss a dog on the nose!"

"Teach the dog that nothing is free! Even a pet must be earned!"

"And never let a dog initiate play. Keep their toys hidden in a toy box, and let them see that you decide what they can play with, and when!"

"Good Lord," I said. "That's how I grew up."

Soon Ted had a new nickname: Alpha.

"Don't call me that," he said.

"Alpha."

"Don't *call* me that."

"But you look so cute and stern, strutting around with your leash and your choke chain."

"Yes, yes, very funny. Who's Beta then?"

We both looked at the dog.

"Well, what's the Greek word for the one who's third in rank?" I said.

The good news is there were some things Ted and I agreed on about training the dog. We agreed that Rex should be taught to sit at every street corner; we agreed that he could not sleep on the bed. We agreed that we had to say "Do your business" every time he went to the bathroom outside. We agreed that he had to remain in a Down/Stay position while Ted and I ate our dinner and that Rex would be fed only after we had put away the dishes, which he was not allowed to lick.

"Why not?" I said. "It will help clean all the food off."

"I'm not even going to answer that," Ted said.

It was the agreed-upon rules that Rex responded to most quickly. He began to sit more readily at intersections, allowing us to push down his rump, as long as he could see what we were doing. He watched. We pushed. He sat. "He's learning!" I said on Day Fifteen. "He's changing!"

But he was still on trial. He still refused to look at us when we said his name. We tried talking to him in high, buoyant voices, or in low, authoritative ones. We tried speaking to him in French and Spanish. Ted once even mooed like a cow, to see if Rex would look at him. But Rex did not want to be a Rex in the City. All he wanted to do, it seemed, was leave.

On Day Sixteen, Rex tried to escape again. This incident occurred inside a fenced-in playground at the end of our street. We were trying to get Rex interested in a tennis ball. Ted and I first bounced the ball to each other, talking in loud, baby voices about how *fun* it was, and then we tried it out on Rex. We unsnapped his leash, bounced the ball up and down in front of his face, and said "Good boy!" as he followed the ball with his eyes. Ted then threw the ball into the center of the lot and said, "Go get it!" Rex sprinted in the direction of the ball, and I remember thinking, with excitement, He's being a dog! But then, I swear, he cut away at a ninety-degree angle and made for a hole in the fence. We hadn't noticed that hole, and were astounded that Rex had. "Rex, come!" Ted shouted.

Rex was already a full block ahead. After a complicated, death-defying chase, which involved lots of shouting and hurtling ourselves over hydrants and parked cars, Ted tackled Rex in front of an abandoned bodega and alpha-rolled the dog right there on the street.

"Look at me!" Ted was yelling at Rex when I reached them. "You look at me when I'm talking to you." Ted had his hand clamped around the dog's throat. "Don't *ever* do that again! Do you hear me? Don't. Ever. Do that. Again. Look at me when I'm talking to you!"

Poor Rex was terrified. He had his tail tucked high between his legs and his gaze averted. I could see his chest heaving up and down.

"Don't scare him like that!" I said. "He's not going to look at you. He's upset."

"You!" Ted said. "Why did you let go of his leash back there? He could have gotten killed!"

"You *told me* to let go of his leash," I said. "Don't try to turn this around and blame me! Now leave the poor boy alone."

"You baby him too much!"

"Well, *you* bully him," I said. "And he's not going to look at you because dogs don't like eye contact."

"Says who?" Ted said.

"Says my book. Mother Knows Best."

"Well, *my* book says you're supposed to stare them down to show them who's boss. Whether they like it or not. Damn dog." Ted got up off his knees and yanked the dog into a standing position. "Your book sounds like it was written by a twit." Ted positioned the choke collar around Rex's neck and gave it a sharp pop.

"Don't hurt him."

"Don't tell me what to do!" Ted said. "I'm sick of both of you. Let's go!"

Plastered to the wall right behind Ted's head was a poster for the Broadway musical *Jekyll & Hyde*. I was starting to wish I could hop that fence myself.

"And *why* do you keep him?" Tara said on the phone that night.

"I just hate to think we'd be causing this dog further trauma by bringing him back to that prison again. They'll probably just put him to sleep."

"What's wrong with a little sleep?" Tara said. Then she added, "Kidding."

Tara, for the record, was a famous insomniac, and in New York insomnia can translate into a hip, high-paying job, such as deejaying at nightclubs, which is what Tara did.

"I cannot play a part in this dog's death," I said. "It's not fair. He's already been through so much. He has feelings, just like anyone else. We adopted him, and I feel like it's our duty to follow through. In fact, it's like both Ted and I have to prove that we can follow through."

I paused. I could hear Ted in the other room laughing uproariously at *The Simpsons*, as if he had not, one hour earlier, flipped his lid.

"It's a very volatile environment right now," I said. "I just want him to love me. To trust me. It's too unsettling to think that he could freak out without warning at any given moment."

"You should date a wax sculpture then," Tara said.

"I'm talking about the dog!"

I went out to the fire escape to smoke. It was a Saturday night, and the sun had set, and the air had cooled ever so slightly, and all the hipsters and trendsters from all five boroughs were about to descend on our neighborhood bars to drink and laugh and discuss their bright futures. I could feel them closing in, the way a horse trapped in a stall can sense a storm coming.

I took a drag of that first heavenly, hellish cigarette. Down below, a jogger jogged past, her ponytail bobbing. Everything felt like it was unraveling: my body, my self. Why did Rex want so badly to leave us? *Was* our environment too volatile? Did he sense that we had no idea what we wanted, or what we were doing, and that he could do better with someone else?

One thing we never considered, in all that time, was Rex's point of view. Few humans do. How must it feel to be adopted by a different species? How must it feel to be taken away from your mother, after just six weeks, your eyes barely open, and then trucked off, cold and lonely, to a pet store, or a shelter, from one barred cage to another, with no explanation at all? How must it feel to then enter a world of humans, who expect you to listen, to understand what they are saying, and to obey them because they say so; to obey simply *because*. How confusing it must be to suddenly learn that all that comes naturally to a dog—eating when hungry, seeking a warm place to sleep when tired, and eliminating when the need arises—has no place in the human world. We expect dogs to grasp the English language, we expect dogs to grasp the workings of our human universe, with its own sets of laws and quirks. And Ted and I expected Rex to understand New York City, where all the rules had exceptions, and everyone broke the laws. Was it fair to put Rex through all this, and to expect him to know how to cohabit with humans, with New Yorkers, when clearly he didn't even know yet how to be a dog?

Back inside the apartment, Ted was still prostrated in front of his deity of choice: the television set. I could tell by the set of his jaw that he still wasn't speaking to me. I questioned at that moment whether Ted and I knew how to be human beings.

"I'll take the dog out for his night walk," I said to the back of Ted's head. But he kept his eyes on the television set, his face glowing alternately green and yellow, which in the world of auras are the colors of a complete jerk.

I had already changed into a short, silky nightgown with spaghetti straps and was about to change back into a dog-walking outfit when I realized that would mean having to walk past Ted again. Slip dresses were in that season, and I decided my nightie looked enough like a slip dress to pass for one. Or at least a knockoff of one. And who really cared about authenticity when you were showing that much leg? I put on some sandals and leashed up the dog.

In the past few months, our neighborhood had become a hot spot, and every day a new bar or boutique appeared almost magically, occupying, in full force, what had been an abandoned, graffiti-scrawled storefront only the week before. It was as if these bars had been airlifted in their entirety, in medias res, from another planet—a planet full of beautiful people with beautiful clothing, purple martinis, the latest cell phones, and straight white teeth—and plopped down onto Ludlow Street without anyone spilling a drop.

That week, all the hippest bars in the city suddenly seemed to be on Orchard Street, which used to be a merchants' row for Jewish wholesalers back when this was a garment district. Rex and I walked up Orchard, with him lurching in all directions and me trying to hold him back. I felt like a water-skier, struggling to manage my own emotions, my arms getting stretched as I flopped around in this dog's wake.

Soon we were passing a bar that the locals called the Dark Night of the Sole. Apparently it had been a wholesale shoe store in its day. Now it was full of fun-loving, skinny women and the rich men who circled them, wolflike, on the prowl for sex.

This bar had floor-to-ceiling windows that opened out to the street. As Rex and I walked past, I felt a sharp cool current of air-conditioning stream out over the sidewalk. All at once I could feel a man staring at me—first at my legs; then at my breasts. Suddenly I understood why some women preferred wearing burkas. "Beautiful dog," he said. He had the dark, arrogant looks of a polo player. "He must love you."

"No," I confessed. "He doesn't. He's mean."

He exhaled smoke through both nostrils like a dragon. "I can't believe that. A pretty girl like you."

Rex chose this moment to squat down and take a dump.

I turned my back on the bar and got my plastic bag out. As Rex did his business, he glanced at me guiltily, as if worried that I might get mad at him for taking up so much time. "It's okay," I said. "I'm not mad." *Poor Rex*, I thought. Sometimes it seemed as if he really was trying—I realized that. But were we trying? As best we could?

We continued on, confused dog, confused human, past an abandoned store: graffitied, gated shut, with giant impenetrable locks, like something that could never be. Rex yanked me toward another bar, this one so hip it didn't have a name. There was just a blue neon sign on the outside that said BAR. A limousine glided up and deposited a new shift of beautiful people: tall, slender, reedlike women wearing slip dresses and gorgeous, teetering shoes. One blond woman said "Excuse me" and motioned to brush past, but then we locked eyes. She was on to my pajamas, her look told me. And I was on to the possibility that, at my core, I would never live her life, and that I was unwilling and unable to offer unconditional love.

We both looked away, ashamed.

Ted was asleep when Rex and I returned. I hung the leash on the door while Rex went up to sniff Ted tentatively, as if he were a corpse. I tiptoed into the bedroom, touching one of the shelves in the dark. Our shelves were bowed with dog books. Our shelves were on the verge of collapse. And I felt like I hadn't learned a thing.

I crawled into bed, next to Ted. He was curled into the shape of a question mark, his face to the wall. I curled into a question mark, too, facing opposite.

CHAPTER 4

The Last Chance to Change

My sister called the next morning to check in.

"I wanted to see how you were doing with your new dog," she said kindly.

"Oh, he's great!" My eyes were puffy from crying and I was lying flat on my back, because my spine seemed to have gone out of alignment from trying to catch Rex the day before. "Best dog you could ever want." I told her how much time we spent "acclimating" him to the apartment, how much money we had already spent on his "grooming needs." "Yesterday Ted bought him a ninety-dollar Neoprene coat for when it gets cold."

"Oh, I'm so glad to hear you're taking such good care of him," she said with true relief. "When you first told me you got a dog I didn't think you realized how much work it was."

"I didn't. But now I do. And they say it's a lot more work with a shelter dog."

"That's why I'd *never* get a dog from a shelter. There's too much about them you don't know. And the males can be so aggressive and too difficult to control."

For the record: My sister was a superwoman. Older sisters always are. She'd raised two spectacular children, tended to a husband who worked long hours, held down a full-time job teaching disabled children, and, on weekends, she built her own stone walls. She herself had a dog, a perfect yellow Lab named Bailey, who had come from Cape Cod's most reputable breeder. Bailey was a zero on the integer scale between passiveness and aggression. It was my sister who did the crate training, the scruff shaking, the little puppy alpha rolls, and within days the new pup knew not to bark unnecessarily, not to stray from the property borders, not to sit on furniture, and not to beg for food. This was last April, I think. My sister had finished all her Christmas shopping by the end of May.

After we hung up, I continued to lie there in a state of paralysis. I wished I could find a way to be more like my sister. If I had half her stamina, I could have built the Great Wall of China by now. If I had half her common sense, I would have thought this all through.

"Are you okay?" Ted said when he returned to the apartment and found me lying there.

I stared at him. His eyebrows were curved in such a way that he looked perpetually angry and frustrated. I thought of my sister's earlier warning about males: aggressive. Impossible to control. "I wish we wouldn't fight so much," I said. "We didn't fight like this before we got the dog."

Ted nodded in understanding. He had offered to take the dog out that morning, which was his way of saying "sorry about last night."

"I'll tell you what," he said. "Why don't we go camping this weekend? Up in the Catskills. I think a little time away from the city will do us all good."

Ted always took me to fun places after an argument. Ted was at his best at a campsite. He loved nature, he loved hiking, and he loved to show off his wilderness-cooking skills on his tiny tin stove. I liked camping well enough, too—I loved the sound of crickets, and the size of the country sky. Camping was fine with me as long as I didn't have to do any of the manual labor. "When should we leave?" I said.

"Today."

It was about eight hundred degrees when we left our apartment Friday morning—the kind of heat that slams into you the second you walk out the door, seizes you up, and makes you feel as if you have just passed through a sound barrier. Rex began to howl and clamber and scratch as soon as we got him into the car. On Canal Street, Ted cranked up the AC and pressed a button that slowly closed all the windows. Rex shouted *Noooooo!* and tried to thrust his body through the gradually decreasing crack.

"He *hates* riding in the car," I said. "Maybe his previous owners just dumped him and sped off."

"We'll never know," Ted said, as Rex slammed his body against the other window, howling. "But this is going to be a loooong trip."

And indeed it was.

It took forty-five minutes to cross Canal Street and as soon as we emerged from the Lincoln Tunnel into the Other Side (a.k.a. New Jersey), we missed our exit. Ted blamed me for not reading the map correctly, so I told him he could read the map himself. We screeched into a rest area and Ted did just that—he read the map. We got lost again, however, and Ted then declared that the map was all wrong.

Meanwhile, Rex continued to howl in protest the entire way. He hurled himself against the backseat and clawed at the windows, calling out in desperation to the birds overhead and the passing cars: *Save me! Can't you see I'm being kidnapped? Poliiiice!* It was like traveling with your own personal mosh pit, and by the time we actually reached the mountains our ears were shot, our jaws were tight, and my crisp linen skirt was as crumpled and dirty as an old dollar bill.

I wanted to howl when I saw our campsite. First of all, there was the unfortunate location: between the outhouse and a group of about five dozen English rugby players who drank gallons of beer and kept announcing that they had to "take a piss." Then there was the realization that the entire lower half of Manhattan seemed to have arrived at the very same campground just hours earlier, and they had already set up generators and full-system stereos and—I swear—a genuine New York City streetlight that warded off any trace of darkness.

"Did they bring a parking meter, too?" I said.

"I hope you plan on keeping that dog on a leash," came a voice from the lightness.

"I'll go back to the check-in booth and see if we can get a better site," Ted said.

Mercifully, we were allotted a new campsite, one that was more remote, and much closer to the lake. And as we drove in that direction, the smell of lake came through the windows and we were mesmerized. It was as if each of us beheld in that shimmering water the solution to all our needs: the need to be cool, the need to relax and float, the need to be cleansed. I could already feel the calming sensation on my skin and I imagined myself swimming next to Rex, his wet doggie head bobbing along the surface. My face relaxed into a smile. Ted was smiling too. I managed to convince myself that maybe it was the heat that prevented us from thinking clearly. In fact, if the temperature weren't so oppressive, maybe we wouldn't be having any problems at all. And Rex's final trial would certainly be fairer in a more forgiving court: the Catskill Mountains.

We headed to this lake as soon as we had set up the campsite—Ted and I in flip-flops, Rex on his Epilady leash. His great plumed tail shimmied in the sun as he trotted. Two fishermen in a rowboat were just coming in from a day's outing, and when they saw us at the shoreline they touched their caps. "Good-looking dog you got there," one of them said. I smiled and thanked them. Rex's coat was shining and blinding white. His body was tense in the stance of a hunting dog. The sun beamed off the water electrically, each flash of light like a musical note.

"Are you supposed to thank people who compliment your dog?" I whispered to Ted. "Because it wasn't like we birthed him." But Ted was already busy trying to coax the dog into the water. Rex seemed nervous as we waded in. He lifted one paw out of the water, then another, as if trying to figure out a way to lift all four at the same time. Ted tugged gently on his leash. "Come on, boy," he said. "Come! Come!"

"Maybe he can't swim," I said.

"All dogs can swim."

"Where did you read that?"

"It's just a fact," Ted said.

I decided to let him have that one, even though it was *not* a fact. My husky didn't swim. Granted, my family didn't have a lake, but no matter. I just wanted to believe that Rex could swim. This would prove that he could be doglike. There seemed to be so much resting on this moment. Ted waded farther into the water and said, "Come, Rex. Come." Then he started to say *come* in an authoritative voice, the way the Monks of Steel said to do it, so I joined in using a happy, lilting voice, in the manner of Mother Knows Best.

We backed deeper into the water and splashed playfully at the dog, pulling him in farther. Rex seemed to be in some form of emergency-brake pose: feet planted, tail between legs, body set in reverse. "I don't get it," Ted said. "Why doesn't he want to swim?" But then a duck flew overhead, and Rex's mouth flew open in a look of surprise—or perhaps even ancient recognition, as if somewhere, back in the reaches of his fear-plagued brain, there still lurked within him the instincts of a bird dog. Soundlessly, he plunged forward, in the direction of the duck. His body made lovely, acrobatic arcs, like a dolphin, until he found himself immersed. Then, he looked around, confused. He moved his legs slowly, then more quickly as he realized that paddling would propel him forth. He seemed both alarmed and impressed by his newfound abilities, and he kept jerking his head around as if to get a bearing on his surroundings. Or perhaps to find the duck. This gesture made him swim in circles, and I laughed.

"Look at him swimming!" I said. "Isn't that cute?"

All at once, Rex seemed to realize he could steer himself. So he dog-paddled to the shore and, as they say, hit the ground running.

"Really cute," Ted said.

We scrambled out of the water to pursue him, but in flip-flops this was going to be hard. And I was not about to bounce through the woods in a bikini. So Ted ran off ahead of me while I threw on my clothes. Alone on the lakeshore, I tried to slip my dirty wet feet into the legs of my shorts (yes, the Bermuda shorts) without mucking them up. I lost my balance and fell. Suddenly Ted ran up to me. "What are you doing?" he said. "Get up! I need you to help me find this dog!"

I stood, dusted the sand off my shorts, and began to walk in the direction Ted had just come from. "Why are you walking?" Ted shouted. "Run!"

"I can't run in flip-flops. Plus, my knees."

"Well, you go get the car, then. I'll look for him in those woods. Damn dog!"

I hurried as fast as I could toward the parking lot while Ted ran in the other direction. He screeched Rex's name hatefully, at full force. I had all sorts of thoughts going through my head: Rex getting lost. Rex getting hit by a car. Ted blaming me, as he always did, for everything. And as Ted's angry voice faded farther and farther away, I had to ask myself: Why had we gotten a dog? I seriously could no longer remember. The answer seemed as elusive and impenetrable as Rex himself.

I began to walk, thinking: What was the use? Then I had the impulse to look for Rex on the wooded hillside, a few yards away from the road. And sure enough, there, galloping down the hill, was Rex, a brilliant, jubilant streak of white. He ran down toward a creek, stopped for a quick drink, and then went up the bank on the other side. I kicked off my flip-flops and ran after him. Rex zigged, I zagged. Barefoot, I felt like a brave Indian. The earth was surprisingly soft and giving beneath my feet and my knees stayed strong. Rex zigged down again, toward me. And it was then I saw, on his face, a look I had not seen before. It was a smile. A doggie smile. He stopped in his tracks when he spotted me, his chest heaving. But not, for once, in fear. He was happily inhaling fresh air into his lungs.

"Stay!" I shouted. "Rex, stay!"

I knew he knew this word. We'd been practicing it on him every day for the past ten days. Panting, and happy for once, he stayed.

I leashed him up and led him back up the hill. He and I walked side by side. I noticed all at once that our environment was beautiful: moss carpeted the forest and sunlight trickled through the trees. "Good boy," I told him. "You're a good, good boy. But you can't keep running away like this."

Back on the road, Ted spotted us from a distance and ran up to meet us.

"How did you find him?" he said.

"I listened," I said with disgust. "I listened instead of yelling my head off."

Ted started to say something, but I cut him off. "When something like this happens you don't alienate me by yelling at me. We have to work together to find him."

We glared at each other. Then something snapped in us both. It was as if all the fears and setbacks and frustrations of the past few weeks had finally burst in each of us, like an overstretched balloon. It was a stupid fight. We stood there in the boiling sun, pointing fingers, each of us accusing the other of not trying enough, of not doing his/her share, of being *impossible* to live with, of *always* having to be *right*, and then came the third-grade insults: "It's your fault he escaped." "No it's not, it's yours." "No it's not." "Is too." And then the dog was barking, and Ted said, "Look, now you're upsetting him!" And I screeched "*You* are!" and I grabbed the dog and yanked him off in the direction of the car, with Ted saying, "Where are you going? Tell me where you're going!"

"I'm going to the *car*!" I said. "Rex, heel!"

The dog trotted alongside me, and stayed close, perhaps because I had him choked up on such a short leash. We stepped through a puddle full of tadpoles—some of them squirming, most of them still and dead. Hundreds of eggs had been laid. Why, then, did so few grow into frogs and escape?

I was sobbing by the time Rex and I reached the car, but we couldn't get in because Ted had the keys, so we had to wait for him. Rex kept lifting his feet, perhaps because the pavement was too hot.

"Thanks for waiting," Ted said when he arrived a few minutes later.

I would not speak to him.

Today, I had seen Ted's darkest side. He, I assume, felt the same of me. And could we blame it all on the heat, or the hunger, or the metal trap of domesticity that was slowly clamping around both our throats? Could we blame it all on the dog? Whatever the reason, it seemed that something primordial and dark had been unleashed in Ted. And that some ancient, timeless resentment had been released in me. Our core issues here in the light, out and raw and exposed. Would taking the dog back be enough to return us to our original selves? Or was it like Pandora's Box, impossible to rein it all back in?

Ted opened the passenger door for me, but I climbed into the backseat with Rex. He curled himself into the nap position, for once truly tired, country tired. With his snout tucked into the crook of his back leg, he looked like any old dog on a Saturday. But this one made sure that our bodies didn't touch. On this, our seventeenth day, our seventeenth date.

If this attempted escape weren't enough to lose points with the judges, Rex tried escaping again, later that same day. It was dinnertime, and Ted had made an omelette, and the way he cut it in half and silently served me my portion felt like an attempt at a truce. When it was time to eat we tried to transfer Rex from his leash to a long rope we had tied to the picnic bench. In an instant, Rex sprinted off, and Ted, shirtless, threw down his spatula and gave chase. I was left staring at the burning firewood, wondering if I should douse it quickly or let it exhaust itself. Then Ted reappeared. He had tackled the dog and was now carrying him in his arms the way a farmer carries a lamb to slaughter. As they got closer, I could see that Rex looked distinctly embarrassed by his capture and by being carried like this. He actually looked emasculated (e-dogulated?), and he didn't protest when Ted set him down on top of the picnic table. He remained there, stiff, like that statue of the husky Balto in Central Park, like something to be sacrificed.

"Get the camera out," Ted said. He was so agitated his voice shook. "I want to take some pictures to remember him by, because on Monday we're taking him back."

I nodded. So here it was. The moment. Again. But at least we might be able to get our relationship back.

"You're limping," I said.

Ted nodded. "That last chase reactivated an old ski injury, I think."

"So now we're both limping," I said.

He nodded. "Just get the camera out, would you? Please?"

"Okay," I said. I kept thinking of Rex's dog-smile, back when he was galloping gleefully up that hill. I started to think that maybe he knew what was best for him more clearly than we ever would. We were only human after all. He was Dog.

And so, sadly, we took pictures—one with Rex and Ted, one with Rex and me, and then a family shot, automatically timed. Looking at those pictures now, you can see how exhausted and unhappy we all were. We were like the three angry members of a grunge band on an album cover. We're all looking in opposite directions. Our faces are in shadow. The sky is gray.

That night, in our tent, we laid out separate sleeping bags. Ted kept his back to me, his body a question mark again. It was impossible to sleep. Rex was outside, tied up, and he paced around like, well, like a wild animal. We had invited the dog to sleep inside the tent for his last night, but he did that emergency-brake thing when we tried to pull him in. So I lay there, listening to his footsteps, listening to my own heart. Was it fair to ask this dog to be perfect when we ourselves weren't perfect?

Ted turned over to face me. "Maybe I have been too hard on him," he said. He put his arm out—an invitation.

I crawled into his sleeping bag. "Maybe I've been too soft."

As we dozed off, Rex continued his pacing. It was as if he, too, had some serious thinking to do. Or perhaps he had simply sensed the weight of our thoughts. I could only hope that Rex, in some moment of clarity, would recognize that we kept chasing him down because we wanted to help him, not because we wanted to hold him back.

In the morning, as the sunlight sieved through the tent screens and the swallows chirped, I felt a strange weight on the right side of my body. I thought for a moment that half my body was asleep, but then I realized that the pressure came from outside the tent—and that it was something large and warm. Rex, at some point in the evening, had gotten cold or lonely or even repentant, and had spread himself against me. We were separated by only a thin wall of nylon, human and canine, but we no longer felt worlds apart.

"Ted," I whispered. "Give me your hand."

Sleepily he complied, and as I took his hand and pressed it against the warm flank of Rex's body, he opened his eyes. "What's this?" he said. And I answered: "I think it's a dog." We smiled hugely. "It's a dog!"

On the way home from the Catskills that fateful weekend, we stopped at a small-town diner for some sandwiches and left Rex in the car. He howled, of course, and everyone in the restaurant (a waitress and three customers lined up at the counter) turned around to see what all the ruckus was about.

"That a bird dog you got there?" one of the men at the counter asked. He wore jeans and a plaid shirt and a John Deere baseball cap, which made me think he must shoot deer for sport.

"Yes," we said sheepishly. We explained that Rex, as far as we knew, was some sort of setter or spaniel, a handsome hunting dog with a great plumed tail. We then went into our now-familiar spiel about how we had gotten him from a shelter just weeks ago, and that we suspected he had been abused because he was so hard to deal with, and that he tried to run away from us and menace us *all the time,* but that we loved him despite all that. The latter part was true. We loved him now. And he kind of liked us back.

The waitress, one of those gruff, big-bosomed, grandmotherly types, smiled at us and said, "Yep. Dogs is harder than kids. But you gotta love 'em."

She walked over to the window and tapped on it and began to coo. "Aw, what a sweetheart!" she said. "Look at that face! Look at that brown and white puppy-wuppy face!" This sent Rex into a froth of snarls and barking and backseat twists.

"Looks like you got a live one there," another man said. He had one of those beards that I thought had gone out of fashion during the Civil War.

"That we do," we said, but when Ted and I turned to each other to exchange a look, I saw that something had changed in our attitude. Yes, we had a live one, but he was *our* live one and we knew we were going to keep him, for better or for worse. Emphasis on the better. We hoped.

CHAPTER 5

Leadership and Love

Once the three of us returned to New York City, Ted and I recommitted ourselves to working together to turn Rex into a normal dog. The first thing we did was hire a personal dog trainer—an eager young woman from neutral Switzerland with a tiny voice and short, butchy hair. Her method was to yank violently on the dog's choke collar when he went in the wrong direction, screech at him, and *then* offer praise. And because Ted and I didn't know any better at the time, because we didn't recognize this as a rather questionable and contradictory training method, we agreed to sign Greta on. She was inexpensive, she had flexible working hours, and, as we saw it, she managed to strike a workable balance between my coddle-and-nurture methods and Ted's sock-it-to-'em New Skete. We were all about truces now.

And so, for the next several days, we met Greta out in East River Park, and there Ted and I ran the length of the baseball field, alternately screeching at Rex, shouting encouraging words, and yanking on his leash. He had no choice but to follow alongside us, looking a little confused, a little insulted, and mostly searching for the gate. We continued to work on the same five basic commands: Sit, Stay, Down, Heel, Come. We weren't sure why—perhaps because Greta was there, a third party watching—but Rex seemed more responsive. Perhaps he thought she was a talent scout, his sure ticket to Hollywood; perhaps he simply sensed that something had shifted in our attitude—that we actually wanted him to stay with us. He began to come. Greta taught Ted and me to crouch on the ground forty feet from each other, and hold open our arms, and call Rex to us by shouting a happy "Come!" And Rex, attached to a forty-foot lead, came bounding toward each of us, as we waited with our arms outstretched in a welcoming embrace. Sometimes he would run right past us, as if we were mere traffic cones, and sometimes he would allow us to reel him in like a swordfish, grab him, and give him a hug. He would squirm away, of course—for Rex still did not like physical affection—but Ted and I saw those moments as sure triumphs. He hadn't tried to kill us, after all. No; he came to us! What a joy! What progress we were making, out there in the ball field! In those moments, when Rex ran from me to Ted, he was like a link between us, bringing us closer and closer together, like a giant needle on a thread.

"Now move farther apart!" Greta shouted. "See if he'll answer to you from sixty feet."

Ted and I looked at each other yearningly. We didn't want to move apart anymore.

All in all, Rex caught on quickly to the neutral Swiss training sessions. In one short week, he learned that for one hour every morning we would take him to a certain spot on a certain leash in the presence of a certain short-haired woman and require him to be obedient. The rest of the time he pulled on his leash as much as ever. But it felt like a different kind of pulling. He seemed to have begun to acknowledge and accept that we were behind him now; that we weren't just some cumbersome ball at the end of his chain. In fact, he was pulling us *with* him now, as opposed to trying to get away from us. And we, in turn, were more willing to be dragged along. To go along for the ride.

But this is not to say we were living the days of wine and roses. Sometimes it was more like the Days of Whining and Pee on the Roses. And I was the one doing most of the whining. Sometimes I still had moments when I felt that I was getting sucked into something from which there would be no turning back: responsibility, domesticity, change. I loved Ted. And now, because of that one moment of physical contact, I loved Rex. We had signed a contract. Yet whenever I saw a couple walking with a happy, squirming, friendly puppy; or better yet, whenever I saw a chic, confident-looking woman walking alone, I'd start to second-guess myself. Should I have waited until I had a husband and a family and a house? Should I have waited until I felt more certain about Ted? And what was "certain"? (She said uncertainly.) All I could think of was those tire shredders they put at the entrance of parking garages to prevent you from backing up.

Another dynamic was forming, you see. Which was that Rex wasn't really responding to me as well as he responded to Ted.

"Rex, sit," I'd say in the mornings, out on the training field, with both Greta and Ted looking on. "Rex, *sit*."

Rex would choke and pant and wheeze in his choke collar, straining his whole body in the direction of the fence.

"Sit!"

"You're only supposed to give the command once," Greta said.

"Do the hand gesture," Ted said.

"Now snap on his choke," Greta said.

"Push down his rump."

Some birds chirped in the distance, and it sounded like my cell phone ringing, so I looked over at my bag on the ground a few feet away.

"Pay attention," Ted said.

"Lower your voice," Greta suggested. "Try to make yourself sound more forceful and more male."

"Sit," I said in baritone.

Then Ted took over. "Rex, sit!" he commanded, and the dog sat instantly, and looked up at Ted, an expression of perfect obedience on his face.

"He knows you're a pushover," Ted teased on our way home. "He knows I'm the one in control."

I kept my eyes on the sidewalk. It had rained the night before and, ahead of us, a broken umbrella lay in the gutter, flapping in the wind like an injured crow.

"I'm just teasing," Ted said. "It's my deep, masculine voice. You know it's just the voice. All our dog books tell us that."

And we could joke all we wanted, but Ted and I both knew it was true. I was a wimp. A pushover. And now Rex knew this too. There I was, in the spotlight, exposed.

Now it was time to face another glaring spotlight: teaching college freshmen at NYU. This was my third year teaching this particular creative writing course, which meant that every day, for four weeks, fifteen or so intelligent, driven, and privileged teens from all over the country would gather in my classroom and listen to me and my team of co-teachers talk about poetry, drama, screenwriting, and fiction. It was a wonderful job, and I loved working with teenagers, who seemed to be on the cusp of so many things—self-knowledge, self-discipline, sex—but I was still, in that third summer, plagued with crippling insecurities about my abilities as a teacher. "I'm not smart enough," I'd tell my colleague Joy. "I have not lived a fraction of the lives these kids have lived." Already, these young go-getters spoke four languages, already they had safaried in Africa and spent the previous summer trekking through Nepal. Already, because their parents were media moguls or Wall Street scions or diplomats at the UN, they had met the Dalai Lama and Sai Baba; they had spent weekends at Mick Jagger's daughter's house in Martinique, they had tasted the finest Beluga caviar and port from the seventeenth century and had decided with a shrug, *Ah, it's okay.* And all of this made for wonderful writing, of course. I had come to them from a tenement apartment on the Lower East Side, by way of a rather unexciting town in Massachusetts, and I hadn't even succeeded in getting my own dog to lick my face. Thus, for these silly reasons alone, I entered the workshop each morning certain that my students would pin me as a fraud.

One of my most intimidating students that summer was a bespectacled, bearded, eternally thoughtful eighteen-year-old who had all the makings of a philosophy professor—he carried a tattered notebook in an old leather briefcase, and he had that insatiable hunger for understanding, plus a three-dimensional intelligence and a hyphenated name. This boy was so brilliant and so inquisitive, he'd bring up references to Schopenhauer and Kant and Odysseus all in one breath. One look at him—at his confident, adorable face—and I decided I had no business teaching at all.

"I'm just not as well educated as they are," I told Joy during lunch. Joy was a poet—with a profound intelligence, talent, and sensitivity not often found on this planet—and she and I were on our way to becoming cherished friends. Every day, after class, we would meet at the White Horse Tavern for a beer or two and agonize over all our seeming inadequacies and gaffes. We were like each other's shrinks in that regard, with the added bonus that in these therapy sessions you could get drunk.

"I mean, I was an *art* major as an undergrad," I said. "I majored in *painting*. Where does that get you in life? I haven't read Schopenhauer, I haven't even read *Ulysses*, and I don't even really like Shakespeare, because it's too much like poetry, and trying to figure out poetry is too much work. Besides, all I really did in college was drink."

"No one cares about that," Joy said. "You were hired because you are a writer. A working, published writer. Don't be too hard on yourself. They look up to you, I can tell. Plus you're so beautiful and talented, and I bet half the boys in that class have crushes on you."

But I just wasn't able to hear these words. Always, the feelings I had that summer at the end of the workshop, as I gathered up my books and papers, my empty water bottle and the last of my pride, were feelings of defeat.

And it was the same feeling, I realized, that I had out in the training field with Rex. I tried to get him to sit, stay, come, heel. At school, I tried to get my students to look, listen, think, feel. But whenever I told Rex to sit he'd remain standing; when I told him to come he'd sit and scratch his ears. Each time this happened, a great and ancient fear awoke within me: that I wasn't worth listening to. That I was not an authority figure. I was inadequate, unworthy, incapable of being in charge. So I should just give up, stop trying, stop kidding myself, because it was always going to be me, standing alone in the middle of a rat-infested park on the East River (or a brat-infested classroom in the Village) being ridiculed and humiliated by the very beings I was trying to help.

"I still feel like I can't do this," I said to Tara on the phone. "He still growls at other dogs and strangers, and this makes me feel like a failure. I feel like a failure when he tries to escape. I feel like a failure when he doesn't eat his food, or when I forget to fill his water dish. He doesn't even wag his tail when I come into the room. I'm tired of feeling like a failure. The only thing I've ever succeeded at is shopping."

"You're not a failure," Tara said. "Good God. You live in New York—you always said you wanted to live in New York. And you've got this great boyfriend who's good looking and well mannered and highly evolved, and you can get into Bowery Bar without having to stand in line behind those ropes."

"Come on. None of those things matter—the dog has eclipsed all that."

"You're taking this way too seriously," Tara said. "It's just a dog."

Just a dog? Why, I was responsible for feeding him, for keeping him bathed and sheltered and exercised. I was responsible for both his emotional and his physical well-being. Everything this dog was going to learn in the world would be learned from me. I was responsible for keeping him safe and secure and alive. "If I didn't take this seriously," I said to Tara, "if I didn't take care of him the way he deserves to be taken care of, what kind of person would I be?"

Tara paused, and I heard the distinct whir of a Jacuzzi kicking into motion, which told me she was over in Soho having a pedicure. "A cat person?" Tara said.

Out in the training field, Greta showed me ways to become more dominant. She instructed me to kneel down next to him and put him in a Down, then roll him over, gently, and lean over his neck. "This is how wolves and their domestic descendants establish rank," she said. Sometimes Greta sounded just like a textbook. Only later did Ted and I learn that she hadn't yet graduated from veterinary college, and that Rex was the first "client" she had trained.

I practiced this technique of establishing rank twice a day—once in the morning in the park, and again in the apartment. In an ideal world, one in which the human had true, innate, indomitable authority, the dog was supposed to stay still after he was rolled over. He was supposed to look away. This was the signal, in the dog world, that he had conceded submission. But my little Rex put up a fight. He thrashed around, and kicked his legs in the air like an overturned beetle. A break-dancer with fangs. Then I'd have to put my knee on his chest and my hand around his throat—the full-fledged alpha roll—and growl, "No!"

"Lower your voice," Ted would say, for he always observed our sessions, like a shrink. "Be more assertive."

"I'm trying. Can't you just leave me alone?"

And at those moments, when Rex thrashed and shimmied across the floor, I hated him. I hated having him in my life. He had no respect for me. He was arrogant and impossible to control. A flash of fury and resentment rose through me and got caught in my chest and throat, like heat. He knew, deep down, that I was a softie, that I would never have control. He would take advantage of me for the *rest of my life*. Finally, late one evening, I screamed at him, "No! No! You asshole! Stay still!" Then we all stayed still—Rex, me, Ted. Rex curled his tail between his legs and panted—both signs of fear. Ted's eyes were wide. "Are you all right?" Ted said. "Do you have PMS?"

I took my hand off Rex's throat. I knelt before him and began to cry. I felt certain he felt this hatred. Certain that he smelled that sulfuric vibe, as readily as he could smell his liver treats from a mile away, before I had even opened the package. And then would come the guilt. The conviction that I was vile and loathsome. That Rex would be much better off with someone else—a loving, caring mother who wouldn't freak out.

According to the Monks of Steel, you were supposed to ignore the dog for half an hour after a battle of wills such as this. Not paying attention to the dog was part of the punishment.

But how could I not offer comfort when I had just flipped out on the poor dog? How else could I say I was sorry? I'd sneak peeks at him while Ted and I "ignored him" by reading magazines or watching TV, and Ted would sneak a peek at me and say, "Don't look at him. Not paying attention to him is part of the punishment. Paying attention is a reward. You're just sending him mixed messages when you coddle him like that."

So then I'd wait until Ted went to the bathroom. "You're a good boy," I'd whisper. "Don't be sad."

"I heard that!" Ted would say.

We'd already concluded that Ted was too hard and I was too soft. But maybe that wasn't such a bad thing. If ours is indeed a balanced universe, there was a place for softies and a place for hardies too. Ted could provide the leadership. And I could provide the love.

With the balance of the Leadership and the Love, Rex became more balanced. He showed signs of liking New York, too. Or at least accepting it. He developed his own routine. He figured out which delis placed buckets of water out front for the dogs, and he figured out which of these delis contained cats. He knew where all the pet stores were located, because he could smell them a mile away. And he knew, if he pulled me in that direction, I would have no choice but to take him in. The clever pet-store owners kept treats in baskets on the floor—rawhide and piggy ears and smokehouse bones. Rex liked to steal a big pig ear and race to the door, his tail held high, his eyes stretched into a huge, goofy smile around the treat. He seemed to know that he was doing something illicit, which he found funny, and I found it funny, too.

He figured out which streets led to Krispy Kreme (a good thing) and which street led to the vet's (very bad). He figured out which street we lived on and which ones led to the park. He learned that on Clinton Street people dumped chicken bones by the bucketload, and that if he was quick enough he could scarf one or two. And then he learned that Ted would stick his fingers down his throat and try to extract the bone, shouting at Rex the whole time, "No! No! No!" He knew the more quickly he swallowed this gift from the heavens, the less likely Ted could take it away. And he knew that a few blocks beyond the school stood a tiny ice-cream stand that sold human and canine slushies in such gourmet flavors as Mango Nasturtium and Beef Consommé.

"Everyone hates New York when they first move here," Ted said. "Let's face it, sometimes New York sucks. It's expensive, it's noisy, you can never have a decent quality of life. But then you start to find all these little things to like about it. The architecture. Those guys playing the saxophones under bridges. The food. Now I wouldn't want to live anywhere else. Except maybe Marin County."

Truthfully I did not want to live in Marin County, despite its beauty. New York is the only place I've ever truly felt at home. (Probably because everyone in New York is insane.) Plus it looked like my dog was starting to feel at home here, too. And why not? Life here wasn't always cruel. In fact, as we were all slowly discovering, there were dozens of advantages to canine living in New York City. A city dog is never chained to a doghouse in a backyard, left to ponder his bleak existence, left to brave the elements and to spend long, cold nights alone, while the folks inside the bright warm house crack open Bud Lights and watch reality TV. A city dog does not have to *brave* the elements, thank you very much, because a city dog (at least on the Upper East Side) wears clothes. From Barney's, no less. And as for being chained to a doghouse, please. A New York City dog is too busy having his coat deep-conditioned and his toenails pedicured at the Pampered Pooch Pet Spa, or going for a quick dip in the temperature-controlled pool at the country's only dog athletic facility, City of Dogs; or window-shopping on Madison Avenue (where dogs are welcome in all the chicest stores, but people in jeans are not), after which he can enjoy a bowl of warm chicken stew at the Regency while a waiter in white gloves fills his silver water dish with Evian. And besides, don't you know dog chains are *out?*

So yes, a city dog could lead an exciting life. In fact, the more time I spent with Rex in the city, the more I realized that most of the suburban dogs I knew (I shall not name names), most of those Labs and goldens certain acquaintances of mine got "for the kids," seemed comparatively bored. With their cute puppyhoods long forgotten, these dogs were left to languish at home alone for hours, while the kids and parents went off to work and school. Twice a day, at most, they were walked on-leash along a bland suburban block, past *ranch* houses for God's sake, with nary a drag queen or a Tasti D-Lite in sight, by some harried parent whose mind was on dinner. And not even the dog's mind was on dinner anymore, because he had been eating the same processed dried kibble for thirty years. Oh, the horror, the horror.

I thought of all this whenever anyone said to us: You have a hunting dog *in the city?* Or whenever my father delivered his weekly Consensus from Garrison Drive. I thought of this when Rex dined on premium organic dog food, or the free-range buffalo jerky treats that cost more than a pair of new shoes. They say New York is the City of Gods. It is also the City of Dogs.

There are something like one and a half million dogs in New York City. There are dogs at the Greenmarket, dogs riding elevators, dogs catching Frisbees in the park. You can spot them resting peacefully under café tables, or waiting for taxicabs, or sniffing the base of the cosmetics counters at Bloomingdale's while the humans above dabbed their wrists. They are everywhere in New York City; I just really hadn't noticed them all before. But, in the same way you notice all the people wearing glasses once you need them yourself, or notice people's wedding bands when you yourself are married, I suddenly had a new radar for dogs: dog-dar. And all of the other dogs were better behaved than Rex.

Overnight, we became dog people. It was as if our new truce brought us up a notch, into the strange world of other dog people. Suddenly our neighbors—the very same people who might have hip-checked us out of the line at Bryant Park Café—wanted to know us. They asked us our names. They wanted to know all about Rex. All at once, all these dogs and their people started gravitating toward us, to say hello on the sidewalks, to share raising-a-dog stories, to give advice. They'd address Rex first, of course, saying, "Who's this?" And after he'd recoiled from their outstretched hands and barked at them or their dogs and/or lunged at their throats, we would go into the He's-a-rescue-dog spiel, telling these strangers all about our savaged pizzas, our dark nights of the soul, our desires to take him back. They'd nod their heads in understanding, for nine times out of ten it would turn out their dog was a rescue, too. The lady down the street had liberated three shepherds from a junkyard. The couple two doors down found their pit bull abandoned on the streets. It was a relief to have found an entire support group of people young and old, right in our own neighborhood, who had gone through what we were going through. And it was a relief to see that their dogs all seemed kind of normal now. They were collected, cool, calm. Even the couple with the pit bull told us that although Farley had been a fighting dog, he was a cream puff now. So that was encouraging. What alarmed me, however, was that the dog people were for the most part visibly insane.

It's easy to spot a dog person from a distance. They walk in a jerky, zigzag fashion, like those scary circus clowns, chit-chattering all the while—to themselves and to their dogs. They carry in their pockets all manner of strange foodstuffs, from liver treats to raw chicken, and they carry bags of poop. Because of the foodstuffs, their pockets bulge, and because of the bulging pockets many of them wear pleats. Pleated *pants*. From the eighties.

Which leads me to the scariest thing about dog people: Dog Lady Fashion. Dog Ladies wear baggy cotton clothing and sensible shoes. Gum on the ass? Not an issue. They wear putty-colored natural fibers—material that can stand up to roast beef in the pockets and dog drool and muddy paws. And if a Dog Lady occasionally gets a smear of dog shit on her fingers—no problem! She can wipe it off on her 100 percent hemp-fiber, machine-washable, no-iron carpenter pants! We lived in a city where even the woman who paints your toenails spends two hundred dollars on a haircut. Yet the Dog Ladies did not even bother to wash their hair. They simply threw on dirty baseball caps, gathered up their bloody roast beef and their plastic *New York Times* bags, snapped on the fanny pack, laced up the Aerosoles, and *voila!*—they were ready.

"I am being sucked into a club in which all the members smell like kennels," I said to Tara.

"Hey, at least it's free," she said. She had just put herself on the waiting list for Soho House, which wasn't supposed to open for another two years, but would set her back thirteen hundred bucks.

"Well, if I ever start to sport a fanny pack, or pleated pants," I said, "shoot me. Or at least organize an intervention and send me off to Betty Ford." A truck on Delancey Street smashed through a pothole and set off dozens of alarms. "I wonder if Betty Ford allows dogs."

Still, it was nice to recognize people in the city, and be recognized. It felt, for the first time, as if I lived in a real neighborhood. That I had an identity, a name: Rex's Mom. Ted was Rex's Dad. No one asked if we were married. All that mattered was how we took care of Rex. Everyone in the dog world had an opinion, you see; this was New York, after all. If you don't have an opinion in New York, they'll ship you straight to the Midwest. So out on the sidewalks, these opinionated dog people would tell us what kind of leashes to use, what kind of dog food to buy, and how to brush his teeth. "He's aggressive, you say? Dominant? Here's what you do." We'd come home from our walks with dozens of business cards—for trainers and vets, day care centers and the dog-friendly restaurants. We learned which car services would pick you up if you had a dog with you and which wouldn't. The dog people had opinions on spaying and neutering and off-leash recreation and the regulation of breeds, and Ted and I, eager to learn, listened to all of them. One neighbor even told me how I should wear my hair. "You should get a Josephine Baker," he said the day he first met me. "Darling, with those cheekbones and those eyes? Fab-u-lous. Otherwise you're just another redhead with a ponytail. *Bor*-ing!"

Meet the Marching Band Man—one of our favorite dog neighbors on the Lower East Side. He was a weathered man in his fifties who wore marching band jackets and painted his fingernails pink. His voice was gravelly from years of smoking and his arms were covered with soft, faded tattoos (of Jesus, Mary, and Joe DiMaggio). He rejoiced every time Rex barked at him. "What a wonderful dog!" he would shout from across the street. His three dogs—whom he called his children—would then bark back at us, and everyone would have to shout to continue the conversation. "My children bark at everybody and Mother of Mary I prefer it that way," our neighbor would say. "I got mugged back in the seventies when this place was a festering drug pit, and then I got my children and, thank the Blessed Mother, that was the end of that. Dogs are *wonderful*. They transform your life. I feel blessed—*blessed*—to have them." At this point he would be teary eyed and somewhat out of breath. "Your dog was definitely abused."

"How can you tell?" I said.

"Look at him! He has no hair around his neck. I don't even want to know what *that* is all about."

Ted and I looked at each other guiltily. "We did that," I said. "It's from his choke collar. He pulls so much when we walk him that all his hair gets pulled out."

"Well then, by God, get a new collar!" He paused to wheeze. "It took one of my children *three years* to figure out this leash. Patience is all it takes. Patience and a no-pull harness. Trust me. You're good people, I can tell."

Ted and I smiled as we walked away. His compliment had touched something deep within us, something we hadn't truly felt until this stranger spelled it out. "We *are* good people," Ted said. "Aren't we?"

"We are," I said.

I felt giddy for a moment. Our lives were changing so rapidly. Up until then we had been rabidly pursuing our careers and following what we thought was our bliss. Now we were following some mad dog's rump. And I loved his little wiggling rump. I loved the *word* rump. It was one of those words that made me smile.

"Buy that dog collar!" the Marching Band Man called after us. "I'm telling you it will change your liiiiiiiives."

The next day we got ourselves a Gentle Leader collar (a head harness shaped much like a horse's bridle), and the results were nothing short of miraculous. I could now walk Rex by holding his leash in the crook of my pinky finger, as if he were the slightest Yorkie, and in my other hand I could hold a latte or a cute handbag or a handgun or anything else I damn well pleased.

But many people in our largely pit-bull neighborhood mistook the Gentle Leader for a muzzle, and as we crossed their paths women and children literally began to leap out of the way. Or freeze in terror. I felt bad, of course, and tried to explain that it was just a Gentle Leader, and that Rex wasn't vicious, but the latter wasn't exactly true. And no one would have understood me anyway, because most of the people who were afraid of dogs in my neighborhood couldn't speak English. Rex seemed a bit perplexed by people backing up against walls as he passed, holding their breath, but people were still a mystery to him, so he just trotted along. Without pulling! And with me walking easily behind him. We were like Moses parting the Red Sea. There was only one problem with the Gentle Leader, and that was that Rex *hated* wearing it. If we stopped walking for even two seconds (which occurred at every street corner) he would dive straight at me, plant his nose between my legs, and start to rub. This was not your basic crotch sniffing (which, by the way, Rex never did); no, this was Rex trying to rub the Gentle Leader off. And how does one remove a madly wiggling dog snout from one's crotch if one is carrying a latte and a cute sequined handbag? One does not. One seethes in embarrassment (while some man inevitably calls out, "Hey, can I be your dog?"), shouts vile things at the spaniel, and threatens once again to take him back.

Ted thought this was all hilarious. Because of course Rex never did that with *him*. Ted was the authority figure—the alpha. I was the maidservant who didn't even get paid.

After one of our evening walks, I stopped in our lobby to check the mail. I struggled to insert a tiny key into the lock of our battered aluminum mailbox. Meanwhile, Rex struggled to get his Gentle Leader off by inserting his snout between my legs. From behind.

Enter Waylon. Our superintendent. On whom I had a secret crush.

"Can I help you out there?" he said.

"What?" I looked up at him. He was naked except for a pair of cargo pants and a tight white tank top and Doc Martens boots.

"Can I help with that key? Or with the dog?"

"Oh, here." I stood, and tried to toss my hair back like they did in the Pantene commercials, but it didn't quite work. I handed him the key and watched him work his magic. Rex, as if he, too, were awestruck by this human's beauty, settled down under the stairway.

Our super was not your ordinary gray-haired Mr. Fixit, you see. You would not find, on his person, eight hundred keys attached to his belt, or stained workman's pants. No; our super was a hot young poet/playwright/Marxist with a Jimmy Dean haircut and his own printing press. He kept a piano in his kitchen and held poetry readings in his bedroom and was so handsome and über-cool that in his presence even Lou Reed might shake in his combat boots. He lived one floor below us, in the tiniest apartment in the building. But as the super he got free rent. And of course, as a hipster he loved the irony of being a superintendent. He called himself Da Supah and had business cards printed up with just that, DA SUPAH, plus his phone number in a sexy script. "I intend," he now said, "to get you a new mailbox key tomorrow. It is my intention, as Da Supah Intendent, to get you that key." He handed me our stack of mail.

I never knew what to do with this crush. I was approaching thirty and sporting knee braces, and he was fresh out of college with a buff waxed chest. In his presence, I got tongue-tied and turned red. In his presence Rex always took gigantic poops on the sidewalk, which I then had to stoop down and pick up. With our telltale blue *New York Times* bag no less—a paper that Waylon dismissed as not genuinely left.

"Anything good?" he said.

"What?" I knew I had a huge dumb smile on my face.

"In the mail."

"Oh, the usual. Dog catalogs. Bills. We don't lead very exciting lives I'm afraid." I thought I could be cool in Waylon's eyes if I went out of my way to be nonchalantly uncool.

"Who's the best dog in the world?" Waylon said to Rex. "Who? You?"

Rex raised his lip and showed a bit of teeth.

"Sorry," I said. "He still isn't quite used to strangers."

"Well, then, I'll try not to act so strange." Waylon gave me an ironic smile. Rex took another nosedive between my legs.

❧ ❧

"You saw Waylon, didn't you?" Ted teased as I entered the apartment, because I was still red in the face. He was sitting on the sofa, looking at a collection of photographs by Leni Riefenstahl, whom they say had been Hitler's lover. Ted had wanted to look at these photographs for weeks, and he seemed happy and relaxed. The dog rushed over and nudged Ted's hand off the book, so that it rested on top of his head.

"Hey!" Ted said.

"We need to get a different type of collar," I said. "One of those prongs. They say it's less inhumane than a choke. And that it's good for strong pullers."

"They also say anyone who resorts to a choke collar or a prong is an idiot who's just too lazy to train his dog," Ted said.

"We're training him. We're doing well. But I still insist on a different collar. That Gentle Leader is going to ruin my reputation."

❧ ❧

It was time, Greta said on the training field the following week, for Level II. She encouraged us to praise Rex constantly—more so than we had been doing to date—on and off the field. Whatever he did that we wanted to reinforce, she said, name it and praise it. So when he peed it was "Good pee!" And when he pooped, "Good poop!" We praised him for eating and sleeping and drinking, for licking his paws, for not lunging at other dogs' throats. We praised him when he shook himself after rising ("Good shake!"); we praised him when he did a Downward-Facing Dog ("Good stretch!"). We praised his good looks, of course, which were beyond reproach. (So handsome! Such a good handsome boy!) Anything this dog did was of Olympian stature. So of course I wanted to share this news with the world.

"We had a big breakthrough with the dog," I said to Tara. "He's finally figured out how to pee like a boy. He marks, as they call it. And marking is serious business." I told her how he stopped to sniff more often on our walks through the neighborhood, as if he finally realized walking could be done in a leisurely way. I told her how Rex would evaluate each potential spot, his brown nose quivering studiously like a sommelier comparing wines, and then finally, after about twenty minutes, he would back his butt toward the chosen spot at various angles, until he finally found the perfect pose. I told her how Ted always said "To pee or not to pee" as we waited for Rex to do his business. "That is the question."

"I saw Leonardo DiCaprio at Moomba last night," Tara said.

"Did you see him pee?" I said.

"I have to get off the phone now," she said.

Tara had only heard the half of it. She did not learn that pooping was serious business with this new dog, too. He couldn't go just anywhere, but had to choose the spots for his deposit carefully, as if he were divining water for a spring. And I learned that, if and when he finally did make a deposit, he would try at once to run away from it, despite the fact that he was attached to a human by a leash. This human had to pick up the poop, of course, using one hand, while trying to hold, with the other hand, the leash of the fleeing dog, who by now had wrapped himself once or twice around the human's ankles. And thus I learned it was impossible to carry a Grande Iced Skim Mocha *and* hold a leash, *and* try to squat down with a plastic bag in my leash-holding hand, *and* keep my balance while I held the Starbucks cup aloft, trying to save it at all costs from spilling. For inevitably Rex would pull on the leash-holding hand, and as I tried to grasp the poop with the plastic bag it became a clash of wills. Then I would lose my balance, and my patience, and set the coffee down, and Rex would wrap himself around my ankles one more time and knock over the coffee. Near tears, I would tie up Rex to the nearest street sign, grab the coffee cup, seize the disgusting poop, still warm, in my plastic bag, and march off petulantly to the nearest trash can, usually two or three yards away. From this, I learned that city dogs, especially shelter dogs like Rex, do not like to be left tied to street signs. They will throw tantrums on par with a prisoner on a rack having his limbs dislodged. And then I learned that Ted didn't like my tying the dog to a pole either, and he would remind me that all our books said you should never leave a dog unattended, and that dogs in this neighborhood got stolen all the time. "I see flyers on basically every single telephone pole," Ted said. "You have to be careful. You can't leave him tied to a pole."

"How do you get to be one of those Hindu goddesses with like eight hundred arms?" I asked my Buddhist friend Anna. "Because that's how many arms I need to walk this dog."

"It takes several lifetimes," Anna said. Without irony.

"Okay," I said to Ted. "I promise not to tie him to any more poles. You're right."

"Did you just say I'm *right?*" Ted said, grinning.

Things were on an upswing. With all this dog praising going on, Ted and I seemed to find more and more things to praise about each other, and the world.

"You look good today," Ted would say on our way to the park. "Healthy. Awake."

"Thanks," I would say, blushing, almost shy. "So do you. This is good for us, being outside." The East River on those mornings would smell like an actual river; the grass would give off the scent of actual grass, and we wouldn't think of the drone of traffic on nearby FDR Drive as a cacophony of horns and sirens, but rather the sound of progress, of people moving forward with their days.

We began to come home from those walks strangely exhilarated. The dog still pulled as much as ever—but maybe that would never change. Maybe we should focus instead on all the good things about this shelter dog. And how uplifting to have a dog who tolerated us! How good it felt to care for something other than ourselves! "Look!" I said to Ted on one of these walks home. "Look how shiny his coat is! It's sparkling in the sun. And look—he has little muscles on the backs of his legs."

"You're right," Ted said. "He's getting buff."

"He's ripped. And look at the way he's trotting! Look at his happy little spotted rump!"

Sure, our backs still ached and our knees still smarted and our arms got stretched a few centimeters longer every day; but still, we were glad to have a dog.

And one might say Rex was now glad to have us, too. I mean, sure, he still really couldn't hold eye contact with us, but at least he wasn't cowering so much. And sure, he wasn't giving or allowing us to give riotous affection, but his seething, misguided hatred of us had definitely toned down. I could now, for instance, sit at the computer, positioned just above his bunker, and he wouldn't growl at me to get away. Sometimes, when I paused from reading a student's story, I'd feel him watching me, as if he were trying to figure out exactly what my role was in his life, and how long I planned to stick around. "I think you're falling in love with me," I'd say to him, my eyes still on the screen. "I think you're falling in love with your new life. Your forever life. Yes, I think you are." But when I turned to smile at him, he'd quickly look away and pretend to be consumed with something more important—namely, licking his privates.

"Things seem much better," Waylon said one morning outside the building just as I was picking up Rex's poop.

"What?" I looked up at him. He was naked, as usual, except for a pair of overalls with one of the straps undone and a cowboy hat. He gave me an ironic smile and touched the brim of his hat. "Howdy, ma'am."

"Howdy," I said.

"Leroy!" Waylon said, addressing the dog. He had invented a new nickname for our dog, which derived from Le Roi, which is French for Rex. "Leroy! How's my *man?*"

Rex stood there and blinked, no longer afraid.

"He's chilling out. He's acting more like a dog."

"Do you think?" I asked.

"Definitely. He seems much more calm."

"Oh, I'm so glad to hear you say that." I realized I was still standing there with a bag of poop.

And as I climbed the stairs, I realized that what Waylon said was true—Rex was totally *chilling*, man. Soon he would qualify as chill.

This meant we were ready to go to a café, All my life I had wanted a café dog—a handsome, French-looking dog who would laze self-righteously under the table while my lover and I sipped white wine and nibbled each other's earlobes. "Let's do it," I said to Ted on a particularly sunny Sunday. "Let's take Rex to a café!"

"I don't think he's quite ready for that yet," Ted said. "He may not be as aggressive with us, but we still can't be certain about him and other people."

"Oh, come on, please? We're good people. And he knows Stay and Down. And Waylon said he was chill."

Ted gave me that look, one that suggested he knew better than to listen to my cockamamie schemes, but he relented, because I promised to nibble his earlobes and wear a low-cut shirt. So off we went, dog on leash, to a Mexican restaurant with sidewalk tables that faced a relatively quiet street. When our waitress saw Rex she gasped in sweet, childlike wonder and sank down to her knees. "What a beautiful dog!" she said. I started to tell her that Rex had been abused as a pup, that he was afraid of people, that he might bite, but hers was the sort of innocent, pouty-lipped beauty that healed wounds and opened doors, and Rex melted beneath her touch. He spread himself under the table, belly up, and let her scratch away.

"He likes you!" Ted said.

I said, "Could we order some drinks?"

Ted suggested we order our food right away as well. "Rex is being good now, but I don't want to push our luck."

Our drinks came—big, salty margaritas on ice—and as I took a sip I had one of those moments when you realize you are exactly where you want to be. I was at a sidewalk café on a beautiful summer evening with my handsome boyfriend and our handsome dog in the most magnificent city in the world. I lit a cigarette, blew the smoke out of my own pouty lips in a very French way, and announced: "I'm happy." I meant it, and Ted said he was happy too. "You're so pretty," he said, taking my hand. "I wish you wouldn't smoke."

"I bet that waitress smokes," I said. "You can't be that thin and not be addicted to Marlboros."

Just then a homeless man came up to our table and asked for change. Ted said we didn't have any. Which was true—all we had was a fifty. For dinner. But the man continued to beg of us. He enveloped our table with his beggings and his smell. Rex's fur began to rise. Ted told the man he should really move on to another table, because he was beginning to agitate our dog. Rex, as if on cue, began to growl—a low rumble at the back of his throat. Ted said, "Hold on to him!" but before I could, Rex had already sprung into action, tipping the table over as he lunged. Immediately Ted caught Rex by the collar, and the man shuffled off unharmed. But still, the mood had been dampened. Our drinks were smashed on the pavement, and a bottle of hot sauce had rolled off the curb.

"Oh dear," our waitress said, arriving with our order. "Should I wrap this up to go?"

Farther down the sidewalk, I could see the homeless man zigzagging helplessly, as if he had an invisible, unruly shelter dog at the end of a leash.

Ted and I didn't speak on the long walk home. We passed by one of those toys-and-T-shirt stores common in the lower rent neighborhoods of Manhattan, and outside, on the sidewalk, was a bucket full of tiny turtles. All of them scrambled and struggled in the shallow water, trying to climb up the sides. But they all slid back down again. Rex approached and sniffed.

"Don't let him stick his face in there!" Ted said.

"*You* take him then."

We turned the corner and saw the Marching Band Man, walking his children and singing, "How much is that doggie in the window? The one with the waggly tail. . . ."

"There you are!" he cried. "Have you bought the California Natural dog food yet? I'm telling you, it's the best! It's expensive and hard to find, but it will change your liiiives! God bless you for saving that beauuuuutiful dog!"

When we reached our building I told Ted I would check the mail. He took the dog upstairs. In the mailbox were the usual things: invitations to art openings, a flyer for the Manhattan Theatre Club's latest show, my student loan bill, a newsletter from MoMA, a postcard from Ted's mother, and—hey!—a letter from *The New Yorker*. I'd sent them a story months ago, back when I was just another writer without a dog, and their turnaround time is pretty slow. The envelope was thin. It was a rejection letter, of course. But this one had a signature on it, from a real-live editor, who revealed her name, and told me to "please try again." And as I climbed the stairs to my apartment, it seemed to me that there was great wisdom, an essential teaching, in this clipped little note. I knew writers who wallpapered their offices with these letters, to inspire them to keep going. And I always thought that was kind of weird: like, why collect and display these clear signs of failure? Why diminish the inspiration to go on? But now I realized, for the first time, that you were supposed to see this as encouragement, not rejection.

Try again. That's all we could do in this city, in this world. And that is what we would do with Rex.

CHAPTER 6

Love Is in the Air

Then it was August. Love was in the air. Rex, our pugnacious pound pooch, our lean, mean, fighting machine, was finally softening, like the very muscles of a welterweight boxer after a four-hour massage. Only in Rex's case the massage had been going on for about two thousand and sixteen hours, and we hadn't been kneading his tense shoulder muscles (because he hadn't allowed us to touch him) so much as his ego, and his wounded puppy heart. And finally, our months of devotion and effort were starting to pay off!

He now felt confident enough to make eye contact with us. He began to lift his ears when his name was called. He didn't flinch *at all* when we petted him. He started to talk to us—earnest, varied barks that seemed to be an attempt at communication. The best part was Rex started to actually wag his tail! Like a dog! Now, whenever Ted or I walked into a room, we would be greeted with a brisk, musical thump thump thump that matched the beating of our hearts.

"Listen to that!" I'd say, taking Ted's hand. "Isn't that a wonderful sound?"

"It's the best sound in the world," he'd say. We moved toward each other in a Hollywood embrace.

"Who's a waggy?" Ted said to the dog. "Who's a waggy boy?"

I was delirious with pride and excitement. It felt as if I were being reunited with a relative who had spent three months in a coma, or a long-lost friend. And anyone who ran into me on the Lower East Side was sure to hear about this exciting new development. First I'd give the Spiel—the paragraph-long "He was adopted; he was abused" excuse that we used with anyone who wanted to know (or who did not want to know) why this dog was so psycho, and now I could amend that spiel to incorporate this happy progress. "He used to hate us, and all people, and all other dogs," I would tell strangers on the sidewalk. "But now he's actually starting to like us. He wags his tail when I say his name. And yesterday, he gave me my first kiss!" I felt alive in a way that mattered, and I assumed it mattered to all these other people, too.

And then I would describe the kiss: how I was kneeling on the kitchen floor in front of Rex, checking his paws for glass, when I realized he was watching me—watching me the way a man in a bar will stare, mouth half-open, at an attractive girl. So I looked up at him shyly, almost flirtatiously, and said, "What?" and then he leaned in and licked me on the mouth. "It was incredible," I would tell people. "I felt like Barbra Streisand in *The Way We Were*." Non–dog people, at this point, would be looking frantically up the avenue for a fast, empty cab, but dog people totally understood. "What a good boy!" the mother of Molly the mastiff said to Rex when she heard the kiss story. "What a good little kissy-face boy." She used the same frightening baby voice that I now used far too often in public in the presence of dogs, and then she knelt down in front of Rex, trying to score a kiss for herself. But Rex had standards. He loved only me. And Ted.

My friends started to get worried. They seemed to see, with a clarity and an objectivity I no longer had, that I was headed off toward la-la land, toward a house full of needlepoint spaniel pillows and calendars featuring puppies of the month.

"First of all," Tara said, "you let him kiss you on the *mouth*?"

"Well, you kissed S____," I said, naming someone from grad school with enough hair on his back to cloak a wirehaired terrier.

"He was *human*," Tara insisted. "Or barely. But still. I was drunk. You're completely sober—you who never meet me at Moomba anymore. You're telling me you're in love with a dog."

"It's all relative," I said. "Sometimes love walks into your life on two legs; sometimes on four."

They say there's nothing like your first love, and I'd argue that there's nothing like your first dog love. Once Rex decided that he loved us there was no limit to his love. Now, our simply walking into the room was a joyous occasion for the dog; he would leap and wag and spin. Plus, it seemed as if Rex and I were reaching new, unspoken understandings every day. He learned several more words and phrases: Paw (which meant: shake hands), Kiss, and his favorite: Do You Want to Go for a Walk? At this, he'd leap and twist and spin, and jump on us, paw at the door. "Stay still!" Ted would say, happily, trying to get the damn collar on. "Sit!" By now, Rex knew Sit so well that he did it within seconds of the command. And I didn't think I'd ever tire of the thrill of this phenomenon. Every time he planted his little spotted rump down on a street corner in response to the word *Sit* I felt like Anne Sullivan with Helen Keller. It was as if Rex had put his little paw under the faucet and suddenly understood the meaning of *water*. He had grasped the very waterness of water, and I wanted to grab passersby and shake them and exclaim: He understands me! Behold the Rexness of Rex! And if said passerby was another dog person, say, the Marching Band Man, then I *could* grab him, and he would understand my joy. "Look at him sit!" I would say. "Look at that good boy sit! I don't even have to push his rump down."

"Oh. My." The Marching Band Man stopped in midsentence, waved his hand in the air, kind of like a choking mime, and paused to wheeze. "God!" he finally said. "Get *out*! Hallelujah! What an out-*stand*ing dog! Thank the Virgin! Did you thank the Virgin?"

"Not exactly," I said. I couldn't bear to tell him that the only thing I still retained from Catholicism was the mental self-flagellation and the fear of eternal damnation if I sinned. "But we're giving the dog a lot of treats."

"Of course you are," he said. "Of course. It's music to my ears. You're good people, Holy Mother of Mary you are *good* people. Rescuing this poor abused dog. And now look at him. God bless you. Tell that handsome boyfriend of yours I think he's wonderful! Both of you. God!" He seized his heart and staggered off.

At school, I was having breakthroughs, too. Now, instead of spending anxious mornings bemoaning my seeming inadequacies, I would simply flaunt them. Back in graduate school, my favorite writing professor used to announce without flinching that she did not know anything about grammar, or how to spell. I remember being stunned by this pronouncement—it was the first time that I realized one did not have to be perfect at *everything*. That we all had strengths and weaknesses, and weaknesses were nothing to be ashamed of. My professor knew she was a talented writer and a supremely gifted writing instructor—spelling be damned! I had a dog who kissed my face.

So the next time, during a short-story workshop, when my intimidating philosophy student started to wax poetic about Beckett, Goethe, and Kant, I playfully interrupted him and said, "We *can't* talk of Kant." Everyone at the table smiled expectantly at me, because by then they were used to my sarcasm. "At least I can't talk of Kant," I explained. "Because honestly I've never read him. In fact, I hardly know who he is." And then I brought the subject back to something I did know, which was how to make a smooth transition between paragraphs, or how to create a character with a Last Chance to Change.

I'd leave the campus exhilarated, marveling at the beauty of the quad, the augustness of the university's grand library, and the sheer inexplicability that I, me, was actually teaching there. On those days, the campus seemed nothing short of utopia, the land of new beginnings, and I felt somehow connected to that—to all that vast knowledge, and earnestness, and learning. I felt I could make a difference in my students' lives, in New York City, in the world. All because, for the first time in my life, I knew unconditional love.

And then, turning a corner, I'd be on Broadway, in an entirely separate world of noise and city traffic, of Chinese restaurants that smelled of grease, of homeless men selling their wares on the sidewalks—things they'd found in the trash. Even this was beautiful; it was so *New York*—the randomness, the good and bad. It was a city that made you glad to be alive. Especially if you passed a doggie on the sidewalk. With his summer haircut and a wagging tail. "Who's a waggy?" I started to say to these dogs I didn't even know. "Who looks so cute with your little summer bob?"

Half a block later, I'd realize I hadn't even made eye contact with the human. But it didn't matter. Love was in the air. Back at home, Rex would be happy to see me. Wag, wag, wag went the tail. Then, the ecstatic kiss. Then the baby talk, and some writhing around on the floor. On the mornings Ted did the early walk, he too came home with color in his cheeks and a seize-the-day look in his eyes. "We had a good time," he would say, in his happy Rex voice. "Didn't we? Who had a good time?" I loved hearing Ted's happy dog voice.

Other aspects of Ted's life were on an upswing as well. Rex's level of obedience was so advanced we no longer had to meet Greta in the training field. Ted was thrilled. He loved having a dog that stayed down when told to stay down. Who knew not to hop on the bed. It pleased Ted to have that kind of control, to have a least one member of the household doing what he told them to do.

And it pleased me to see Ted pleased. He finally had reclaimed that one missing part of his childhood—a confidant, a faithful companion, someone to gaze at him raptly when he played his guitar. Ted loved having a pal to take walks with. He loved having a competent athlete, one without knee braces, with whom to play fetch. "You're my best friend," he began to say to the dog on a regular basis. He said it while he put Rex's collar on; he said it when he refilled Rex's drinking bowl with fresh Brita water. "Who's my best friend? Who's my little companion?!" His voice, as he said this, cracked in that way I loved. "My father used to tell me I was his best friend all the time when I was little," Ted explained, stroking the dog with a smile. And I could tell, from the way he said it, that this statement had meant a lot to him back then, and still did. And I could tell, from the way Rex raised his face to Ted's, that our dog enjoyed having a best friend, too.

On Sunday mornings, I'd watch them, Ted picking out some Grateful Dead song on his guitar while the dog sat at his feet. Ted couldn't sing very well, but he didn't care. I could sing well but was too shy to do it in front of anyone unless I was drunk. But we began to sing little made-up songs to the dog.

And don't they always say happiness is contagious? On the sidewalks, people smiled at us. Other happy couples gave us a knowing look (happy-couple-dar). Everyone commented on Rex's beauty. So much so that I trusted that soon Rex and I would appear in the Styles section of *The New York Times:* he with his handsome braided leather leash and collar, I with the matching shoes.

"Look at that doggie!" little girls would say. "Mommy, can we get one just like him?"

"Oh, can we please get a dog?" girlfriends would say to their boyfriends. "Let's go to the shelter this weekend. Let's just go look."

Four weeks ago, I would have been walking around with a megaphone and a red flag, shouting to all these girlfriends: "Don't do it! Don't get a dog!" But now I was giving these strangers the name of our shelter. "You'll love it. It's where JFK Junior got his dog!"

It started to happen everywhere we went. Our dog was a chick magnet, a babe magnet, a Crazy Dog Lady magnet. "Where did you get him?" they'd all shout. "He's so cute!"

"Isn't he though?" I'd say. "Doesn't he have the cutest face?"

Every time someone complimented my gorgeous dog, I began to feel a surge of pride move through me, to the surface of my face, bringing a certain glow to my skin. It was the same rush of pride I felt when someone with good taste gushed over my latest thrift-store find. It meant that, in a world full of roughs (and ruffs) I knew the diamonds. It meant, I guess, that I could do things right.

Plus, beauty has a way of radiating outward, and if you happen to be standing next to a beautiful creature, well, that means you're gorgeous too.

Bit by bit, parts of our old life resumed. I finished at NYU and found another temp job—at a public television station where I only had to come in four days a week. On the fifth day I read manuscripts at the literary magazine. And I loved this job. I loved the women who worked there, and I loved the intimacy of the small office space—a loft near Union Square. And I loved spending a day buried in words and stories. Reading those words was quick and easy and efficient, and the editors loved me because I was fast and had a good eye. Five of the stories I pulled from the slush pile got published.

As for Ted, he took odd jobs related to his documentary film production field. He did camera work for some local independent films. He helped an art-gallery friend interview outsider artists who were so outside the establishment they lived in cardboard boxes, and you had to climb down a hidden ladder into a subway tunnel to ask a homeless person named Tweezerman if he had seen a guy named Bokov around. Between such projects, Ted would work on his photography and send out cover letters and résumé tapes, certain the right job would come along. Sometimes, in the afternoons, he'd bring his camera along on his dog walks, wander around the East Village, and take shots of sidewalk graffiti, and wall murals, and those Missing Persons posters that were taped to every bus shelter and telephone pole. He also took snapshots of dogs. Ted's Missing Persons pictures were brilliant and haunting and well composed, but as we sat side by side looking at his contact sheet with a magnifying glass, I only had eyes for the dog photos. "Look at that basset hound! Where did you find him?"

Ted pointed to a black-and-white shot he had taken of Tompkins Square Park in the rain. "Don't you think this one looks like an Alfred Stieglitz?"

"Look at that pug!"

Now that our working lives were returning to a somewhat working order, we came up with a new Rex schedule. A revised schedule worthy of Mrs. Flint. We alternated dog duties depending on who was working when. Every other morning either Ted or I would get up early and take the dog out solo for his Morning Walk, and every Sunday morning we'd sleep late and all go out together (the Late Morning Walk) as a pack. Whoever did the Early Morning Walk was exempt from doing the Late Night Walk (a quick "relief walk" around the block at eleven P.M.) the evening prior and was also allowed to complain about having to get up early on his/her appointed day. We made a point to all go out together for the Mid-evening Walk, just after dinner, as the sun was beginning to set. Ted always pointed out that Rex was happiest when the three of us were together. He'd trot along more perkily, his tail held high, his ears pressed down with a sense of adventure, as if he felt complete and purposeful, and every few yards he'd turn around and smile at us, to make sure we were all still there. "Here we are," Ted said. "Here's your family right here." If Ted ducked into Starbucks for our morning lattes, or into the bank for a quick withdrawal, Rex would stop and wait—perplexed, confused—and he'd strain toward the door through which one of our pack members had disappeared. "Come on," I'd say, tugging him. "Let's go look into that shop window—those new handbags are gorgeous." Rex refused to budge. In the two or three minutes Ted was missing, Rex would whine, pace, and lower his tail. And as soon as the door opened, his body would tense, he'd stop breathing for one second, and then, seeing it was Ted, he would spring into the air with joy. Together at last— hurray! A pack of three, existing as one!

I also had moments of "Hurray!" When I prepared to leave for work in the mornings and kissed my dog and my boyfriend goodbye (in that order), I realized Rex had somehow given us the relationship we'd always wanted. All that worry I had had about losing myself, about losing my sense of identity and all that time to devote to my career, proved to be wasted. I hadn't *lost* anything by giving my time and energy to Rex. In fact, I realized that giving brings you nothing but gain. I had gained a whole lotta love.

But no relationship ever remains on a plateau. The advent of love into one's life, as we all know, always brings with it other, more complicated emotions, such as possessiveness and jealousy and fear. Once Rex decided he loved us, he seemed to realize he couldn't possibly live without us, and he started to act out. He wanted to know where we were going at all times, and wanted to come with us to boot. If I so much as walked downstairs to the mailbox without him, Rex would throw his body against the door and howl. He started to follow me everywhere, click-click-clicking behind me on the hardwood floors. And of course there wasn't really anywhere to *go* in that apartment, but he followed me nevertheless. He followed me if I moved three feet from the stove to the refrigerator. He followed Ted if he walked the two feet from the sofa to the TV. He even followed me into the bathroom, trying to wedge his body in when I sat on the toilet seat. "Will you get out?" I'd shout, and he'd back away, eyes worried, which naturally made me feel bad.

Of course, this can't-live-without-you devotion was the very thing we had pined for at the beginning; but sometimes it drove me nuts. This fifty-five-pound creature was underfoot all the time. And I'm not that coordinated. I started to trip over him in the kitchen. At my writing desk, I'd more often than not roll the Aeron chair right over his tail. Followed by Rex's startled yelp. For Ted, all this following around meant that Rex often got him where it counted, for his snout just reached the level of Ted's crotch. "Ouch!" he'd say, and I didn't even have to look up from the computer to know what had happened in the other room. "Get away!" he'd shout. I had to bite my tongue to keep from laughing.

Ted and I started to get worried. If we ventured farther than the mailbox, he protested even more. *A-woooooooo-waaaaah!* he would yell, so loudly our neighbors would peer out of their doors, eyes wide, and ask if everything was all right. "Oh, he has separation anxiety," I'd tell them nonchalantly, glad that science had given this disorder a name.

One book I consulted (Ted called it *The Hypochondriac's Guide to Overprotective Dog Care*) suggested that we leave behind peanut-butter-stuffed marrow bones and cheese-stuffed Kongs to keep the dog occupied during our searing absences, and we tried this many times. But when we returned we'd find both Rex and the Kongs exactly where we'd left them, the former with his eyes squeezed shut and his head draped mopily between his paws. "I don't get it," I'd say to Ted as we tried to duck out for a quick drink with Chip. "All of a sudden he's acting like my ex-boyfriend, who only wanted me in his life when I didn't want to be in his."

Another book (called *The Paranoid's Guide to Overbearing Dog Care*) suggested that we leave the apartment for five minutes, then ten, then fifteen, as a way to convince the dog that when we left we would always come back again. "And no emotional greetings!" this book said. "You must leave and enter your home with an air of practiced nonchalance. You must have the dog believe that neither your leaving nor your coming home is a big deal." But not even this could assuage Rex, who thought every time we left him we left forever. He would Not Get Fooled Again. He'd emit the primal Roger Daltrey scream.

And of course if you use a term like *separation anxiety* I'm going to get anxious too. Did Rex believe we would abandon him the way his previous owner had? Was he thinking of the day his mother disappeared from the box he was born in, never to be seen again? These questions led me to take the advice of *The Hypochondriac's Guide* a few steps further. I decided to stop going out altogether. Permanently.

Welcome to the beginning of the end of our social life.

It started with our going out less at night for drinks, opting instead for a quick, early dinner. Then we stopped eating out so much. We decided that as responsible parents, with a limited income and a dog to support, we should stay home and cook more, and so we started with the basic things, like spaghetti with vodka sauce, tofu with sautéed greens. But our kitchen, with virtually no counter space and an eighty-year-old stove, was not exactly conducive to such activities as cooking. And then there were all those tedious trips to the grocery store. Why, Rex would be left alone for at least two hours during those trips, and we'd worry about him the entire time. And worry expends energy.

So then we started ordering in: pizzas, and Chinese food, and Mexican and Indian and Tibetan and Senegalese, and Rex would get pizza crusts and pieces of nan, or bits of tofu served to him on chopsticks, or pieces of stir-fried beef that Ted insisted we soak in water first, so as to remove any traces of chili oil. Eventually, Rex came to accept the delivery men as part of his inner circle. So here was another coup—no more freaking out at the doorbell. No more attacking strange visitors who tried to come in. Rex, in fact, began to expect that all visitors came for the specific reason of bringing him something—hopefully containers of hot take-out food.

"Let's meet for a drink after work," Chip might say, calling in the late afternoon, but that would mean at least two hours without the dog. Our film-critic friend might suggest we go to Film Forum for the Eric Rohmer retrospective, but one movie, plus the subway trips to and fro, added up to at least four hours. And one of my books, *The Persecution Theorist's Guide to How to Prevent Your Dog from Getting Killed,* said it was "cruel" to leave a dog home alone for more than five hours.

So we would make excuses that everyone could probably see right through. "Oh, we're tired. We've had a long day." Meanwhile, the dog would be staring up at us expectantly, with a smile on his face and a squeaky toy at his feet.

And which would you choose? Going out again, into the chilly night, wearing heels on a cobblestoned street? Or staying home with a warm fuzzy-wuzzy (and, oh yes, your boyfriend) and pulling on a pair of sweatpants, and playing with a squeak?

Yes, the scale was tipping. And Ted and I were very aware of what was happening. We could sense it in the way the party invitations stopped coming. We could see it in the way eyebrows were raised when we announced that it was time to go home, after having spent only one hour at a friend's poetry reading at Limbo (the café, not the abstract concept). We could hear it when we came home from our dog walks and that electronic voice on the answering machine told us we had "No ... New ... Messages" in such an unsympathetic tone. Sometimes, I would once again pine for my pre-dog life. That life when everything seemed more fluid and free. And yet, even as I had this thought, I realized that I no longer saw Rex as something that limited me, something that held me bound.

Despite all this, a few friends still thought we were normal for some reason, and continued to invite us out.

"Come to New Orleans for the weekend," my writer friend Chowder said. "They're staging a reading of my play at the Tennessee Williams Writers Conference and they're putting me up at the Marriott. You can share my room."

"Come with us to Southampton," our trust-fund friends Matt and Hillary would say. "We're going to have an extra bedroom for an entire week. And this weekend is the final match of the Mercedes Benz Polo Classic."

It was like a veritable Greek chorus: come to the Pete Townshend concert, come kayak around Staten Island, come out to Lloyd Neck and golf; come out, come *out,* wherever you are!

Tara said: "Meet me at Bryant Park Café. We might get a glimpse of Leonardo DiCaprio if we stay out late enough."

"Ugh, *Leo,*" I found myself saying. "I'm so sick of him. He's so overexposed."

"Oh, come anyway," Tara said. "The food is great and I haven't seen you in like seven years."

"Oh, I think we're just going to stay in and hang out. We're tired. You know. We're probably going to just order a pizza and watch a movie."

And as soon as I said this, I gasped. "I have to go," I said quickly, before Tara could get in the final word.

"Did you hear what I just said?" I said to Ted as I hung up the phone, my heart pounding.

"What?" He was busy tossing a tennis ball to the dog and telling Rex he was his best friend.

"Pizza and video! I said we were going to stay in, order a pizza, rent a video."

Ted let the ball bounce to the floor.

"Wow," Ted said.

Sooner than we could ever have believed possible, Ted and I had become what we swore we would never become: a pizza-and-video couple.

But was it so horrible to stay home with your loved ones and order in? With Rex around, this wasn't horrible at all. While we ate, he'd lie on the floor underneath the table, his snout tucked under his back leg like a swan. Now, whenever he could, Rex would press his body against us, leaning with all his weight against our legs. Every night, at eleven o'clock, Ted and I would sit down on our tiny analyst's couch to watch *Seinfeld,* and Rex would decisively climb between us, shimmying his body down until he was comfortable and we were not. Then, at ease in the world, he would let out a little sigh of contentment and rest his head on my knee. "The Rex sandwich," we called it. All we needed was a fireplace, and the picture would be complete.

Then, one night in late August, a friend of Ted's from college who had lived in Japan for the past seven years was in town for the weekend, so we were obliged to go out. This man, whom I'll call Stan, was the only member of Ted's tightly knit group of college friends I had not yet met, and I knew that part of our purpose in going to this dinner was for me to be "presented."

And so, we left Rex at seven with a marrow bone, two Kongs, five CDs of relaxing classical music set to play in random order, and a sincere promise that we would be home by twelve. Then we rushed down the stairs and tried not to listen to the Roger Daltrey howl.

We met up with four other couples, plus Stan, at a Japanese restaurant on the Upper East Side. Each of these couples, all married, incidentally, had already expressed approval of me, and now every time we went out together they—especially the females—observed Ted and me closely, to see if and when we might get engaged. The women listened for talk of ring shopping and wedding dresses; the men wanted to know if and when we had met each other's parents, and if and when we all got along. But the group with which we dined that night in August must have been sorely disappointed, because there was no talk of weddings. All Ted and I wanted to talk about that night was the dog. "He looks like an expensive stuffed animal from FAO Schwarz," Ted was saying from his end of the table. "But when we first got him he tried to bite me when I tried to pull him off the bed."

"He's much better now," I said to the table at large, in case they were worried. We had just been served drinks at this point, and Ted's friends listened to us with wide eyes, nodding with what I assumed was interest.

"Oh, yes," Ted said. "He's much better. He's much less inclined to try to kill strangers now. He's even stopped trying to kill us. At night, when we watch TV, he puts his head on my lap."

"And I got my first kiss!" I shouted.

By the time our meals were served, everyone was looking back and forth from me to Ted as if they were watching a dull tennis match on television. Stan looked like he hoped someone would get up and turn the sound off.

One couple in attendance had just had a baby three months earlier. So all they wanted to talk about was the baby. "I'm already thinking I won't go back to work," Mary said. "I can't imagine leaving my baby with someone else."

Good Lord! I looked at my watch. Most dog books claim that dogs have no sense of time—that five minutes is no different to a dog than five hours. But any dog owner can tell you the greeting you get after a brief absence is different from the one you'll get after a longer absence. Which meant to me that Rex *knew* it was almost midnight. Rex *knew* we had left the apartment at seven P.M. I tried to give Ted the "We need to leave" eye, but he was reminiscing with Chip about their Grateful Dead days.

Mary was now bringing out the photo albums—three full photo albums bound in blue leather and trimmed in lace. Now, I'm as willing to look at photographs of children as the next person, but eighty pages of an inert newborn are not going to raise my pulse. Plus, *my* baby knew how to come and stay and heel and sit. And kiss! As the meal progressed, it seemed that for every charming little anecdote they had about their son, Roland, I had to top it with one about Rex. "He's a really easy baby," Mary said. "He's already sleeping through the night."

"Rex is finally sleeping through the night too," I said. "It's funny, when we first got him, he would pace around the apartment all night long, as if he were trying to figure out the best way to kill us, or plotting his escape. So none of us got much sleep in the first few months. But now Rex trusts us enough to sleep in our presence, and, boy, does he sleep. And he's so cute when he wakes up. His eyes get all puffy—he looks like an old man, right, Ted?" (Had the lighting been better in this restaurant, I would have noticed that Ted was wincing.)

When I stopped gushing, I realized that Mary was looking at me with her mouth kind of hanging open, as if she had just eaten too much wasabi. And Stan from Japan was training a rather incredulous eye on Ted.

"Man, it's been a long time," Stan said.

"Don't compare our dog to other people's babies," Ted said on the cab ride home. "People are going to think we're freaks."

"I know," I said. "I just can't help it though."

"And I can't believe you actually passed Rex's picture around the table after they finally put those baby albums away."

"Terry wanted to know what he looked like," I said.

"But he's not our baby," Ted said. "He's a dog. And why did you have to announce to the table that Rex chronically licks his penis?"

"Karen's brother has a Lab. I thought she might, you know, know something about such behavior."

We passed that sign on FDR Drive that said: FDR CLOSED 1/2 MILE AHEAD—SEEK ALTERNATIVE ROUTE. But the thing was, that sign had been hanging there for about seventeen years.

Finally Ted laughed. "I think that's the last time we'll ever be asked to dinner."

"I'm sorry. I just can't help myself." I bit back an idiot smile.

"That baby was cute," Ted said, moving closer. "But Rex is much cuter."

He spoke with such love and tenderness I got tears in my eyes, thinking what a good dog-father he made.

"Do you think it's okay that we left him alone for five hours?" Ted said.

When we walked into the apartment, we found Rex—not slumped on the floor with his eyes squeezed shut, but stretched out on the analyst's couch, his face all puffy from sleep.

"Who's that good boy?" Ted said as we walked in the door, while I chimed in, "Who's that little sleepyhead?" Rex began to rapidly wag his tail, and his thumps were muffled cutely by foam. Within seconds we were both on our knees in front of the dog.

This analyst's couch had come from Ted's mother's office, back when she had a practice in child psychiatry, and it had become, without any irony on Rex's part, his favorite place to nap. Sometimes, when he slept with his legs vulnerably splayed and his belly exposed, I'd joke that he looked like Manet's *Olympia*—a regal, pampered figure lounging naked on a fainting couch without a care in the world. But tonight, as we sat on our knees and covered the dog with kisses, I realized that if Rex was Olympia, wouldn't that make me the rather harried-looking servant presenting the flowers? Now it occurred to me that Rex had seemed rather, well, relaxed when we came in. And suddenly I saw that analyst's couch as nothing less than an altar, and I wondered if perhaps we were taking our worship of this dog a little too far. Maybe *we* were the ones with separation anxiety. Good grief. I mean, a full sushi plate, some tempura, and a few glasses of sake did not distract *us* long enough to stop thinking about Rex.

Meanwhile, Ted was covering Rex's snout with kisses, even though the Monks said that was a sign of subservience on the kisser's part. "No emotional greetings!" I said. "Who are you to defy the Monks of Steel?"

"I don't care," Ted said. "I love his little snoutie." All the while kissing away.

"Hey! It's my turn."

"Rex," Ted said. "Give your mother a kiss." Rex leapt over Ted and licked my cheek, overjoyed to see me. Ted kissed me on the other cheek at the same time. I thought back to all those nights out drinking, all those parties we attended before the dog. More often than not, it seemed I had only *pretended* to have fun. But there was no pretending here. Our lives felt totally real.

CHAPTER 7

How to Lose Friends
and Alienate People

N ow that our social life seemed to have taken a big leap out the window (I would not allow Ted to say it had "gone to the dogs" because I refused to become one of those dog people who talked in doggie clichés), we faced two choices: make new friends, or keep the old, which meant that until Rex's separation anxiety abated, we would have to invite our current friends into our apartment.

"We really *should* be having people over anyway," Ted said. "We've been here almost a year, and everyone we know has had us over to dinner at least twice. It's rude not to reciprocate."

"I think it's rude to subject anyone to this apartment."

"Everyone understands," Ted said. "No one in New York has a decent apartment."

"It's just so embarrassing, this apartment. I take my environment seriously, you know? I believe a home should be a reflection of one's tastes and interests. This apartment makes it look as if I have no taste at all. As if I grew up in a garage or something with a bunch of shelves and rakes."

"I'm telling you, no one will care. Besides, don't you want to hang out with our friends?"

"Of course I do. But who's to say he won't attack any of them?"

Sure, Rex loved *us*, and was willing to let us kiss and hug him and touch him on the head, but there were still scattered incidents of him, oh, lunging at other people. Mostly men. He had lunged at the meter reader, he had lunged at a nice young banker in the park who merely wanted to pet him, and he had even lunged at his godfather, Chip. Then there was the time, just days before, when we went to Verizon to get a new cell phone and boldly brought Rex. We made him sit while we inspected the different models, and then, without warning, Rex lunged at an elderly white man in a baseball cap who had come up to the counter behind us. Rex shot up at him like a rocket and snapped, and Ted caught the dog in midair and slammed him down, and apologized profusely while the man angrily wiped the paw prints off his pant legs and left. We left too, without a cell phone of course. We had to go to Sprint.

Rex had also snarled and snapped at virtually every male member of my family, except for my handsome brother A.J., who gives off a vibe of peace and tranquility and wears his hair like Jesus Christ. In fact, the only large, heavy-set man Rex hadn't lunged at was Ted's father. "That's because he's a smart dog," Ted said. "He knows my dad's a lawyer who could sue him for personal injury." Rex had, however, played such a fierce tug-of-war with Ted's father he pulled the dear man right out of his chair.

Ted and I had all kinds of instructions on how to socialize the dog, of course. We were supposed to introduce him to people on the sidewalks. We were supposed to tell our guests to ask our dog to sit before they petted him. We were supposed to ask our guests to come armed with treats to reward him when he sat. We were supposed to ask them to cooperate with us while we trained the dog not to jump on people. We were supposed to say, "Would you mind bringing over your small child so we can see if Rex will jump on her or not?"

"Maybe we should start hanging out with more dog people," I said to Ted one lonely evening. "We see them every day at the park. We could ask some of *them* to help us socialize the dog."

"You mean like Charlie?" Ted said, referring to the Vietnam veteran who attached a walkie-talkie to his dog Fergie's collar, and sat at one of the chess tables at Tompkins Square Park and barked orders into the collar if Fergie ran too far away. "Or Marie-Claire?" Ted added, referring to the woman we often ran into on the sidewalks, who always had two or three dogs with her and six or seven bags of poop. She would stand there and talk for forty-five minutes or so, complaining about the way Mayor Giuliani was driving all the starving artists out of town, all the while waving, *wafting* those bags of poop around as she gestured with her hands.

"Okay," I said to Ted. "I get the point. But I *know* we can find normal dog people in Greenwich Village. It's a better demographic over there. Plus, with dog people we can talk about the dog."

"True," Ted said. "And who's the most interesting topic in the world?" he said to Rex, who was lying under the computer table. "Who should be interviewed by Barbara Walters on prime-time TV?"

The dog beamed and thumped his tail.

In our pre-dog life, Ted and I used to stop at the Washington Square Park dog run every time we walked through the Village. We'd stand there for twenty minutes and smile at the camaraderie and play that took place inside its fences. I loved to see the dogs romping and chasing. I loved to see the wrestling matches—the dogs on the bottom thrashing back and forth like fish, trying to kick off their opponents with their back legs; the dogs on top teasing their felled prey with little nips. I loved to hear their little yowls and grunts, and I loved to see the dogs engaged in lip locks and hear the clacking of teeth. And I loved the way the humans laughed. In the summertime, hordes of tourists and locals lined the fences of the dog run, all of them enjoying the spectacle and commenting on how much fun dogs had. And how they'd love to get a dog themselves, but they didn't have the room or the time.

How great it would be for Ted and me, I thought, to finally be in that inner circle.

Our first walk to Washington Square Park with our new dog took twenty minutes. I held the leash while Ted carried his vintage video camera (he wanted to document the dog's first visit to the dog run). We hurried along with excitement, and it seemed our enthusiasm was contagious. All around us, Greenwich Village buzzed with that hopped-up New York energy. Shoppers flowed toward the Soho flea market, and NYU students filled the cafés. On a street corner, a group of kids were playing drums, while nearby, a man standing on an overturned trash can preached about God. Rex dragged us past the sidewalk book vendors, the twenty-four-hour pickup game at the West Fourth Street basketball court, and even past a man in a business suit who was probably in this foreign neighborhood to score a dime bag. Rex dragged us straight into the park. We followed his bobbing tail.

At the dog run, a big red stop sign was posted at the entrance with a list of rules that we were warned were "strictly enforced." No alcohol, no food, no children under five. No more than three dogs per human, no bitches in heat, no aggressive males.

"I guess that rules you out," I said to Ted.

"Yes, yes, very funny," he said. "It also says no bitches in heat."

"I'm not in *heat*," I said. "It's not even that hot today."

Stepping into the dog run was like entering a foreign arena; it didn't feel dangerous, just strange, a place whether neither Ted nor I knew how to act. It was like visiting an ice-skating rink for the first time—all those experts gliding around in sparkly, skimpy costumes while you struggled clumsily just to get your laces tied.

We found ourselves in a dusty circle lined with trees and green park benches. People sat in groups—the smokers at one end, the coffee drinkers near the entrance, the loners off in the corners underneath the trees. And all around them: dogs. Most of the dogs played pig-pile and tug-of-war and keep-away, while the loner dogs stayed off in the corners chasing balls. The gray-muzzled old-timers sunned themselves at the foot of the benches, yawning and stretching out their legs.

Ted and I unsnapped Rex's leash and remained standing, both of us prepared to leap if Rex got into a scuffle. Ted hung the camera around his neck. Rex stood there with his nose twitching. It seemed as if he didn't know how to act in this unfamiliar arena either. He seemed to consider dogs some other species, as foreign to him as cars. It was as if, early on, in his puppy days, Rex had decided (to paraphrase the great nature writer Farley Mowat) that there was no future in being a canine. As if being a dog offered no promise of vast fame and glory. No, even, financial reward. And so Rex, somewhere along the line, seemed to have decided to claim a new identity for himself, a new species, that allied him neither with the canine nation nor the human one. He was simply Rex, Le Roi.

So there was Le Roi surrounded by dogs in a dog run. A king mingling with the teeming masses. When a basenji ran up to him to sniff his haunches, he reared around and snapped. When another dog—a pit bull—came forth and made a play bow, he leapt backward as if threatened, and then growled and chased the dog away. A third dog came forward to introduce himself and swatted playfully at Rex's head with his paws. And this Rex took as a threat on par with Mike Tyson, as if this dog were next going to try to bite off his ear. So he growled and lunged again. "It's okay," we kept telling him. "It's okay." I crouched down next to him and tried to hold him in a protective embrace.

But the dogs kept coming, like a series of villains in a video game. Rex got overwhelmed as he fought them all off—friend and foe. Finally he managed to creep slowly backward, holding his tail between his legs, until he'd backed his vulnerable butt up again the fence.

"First time, eh?" a friendly-looking man with a bichon frise said. He was strikingly handsome, in a Gatsby sort of way. "He's a gorgeous dog," said the man's partner. He turned to us and smiled an equally dazzling smile. You could tell they'd had their teeth whitened. We said yes, it was Rex's first time, and launched into the rescue-dog spiel. The men nodded their heads as they listened and smiled in kind recognition. "You can always tell when they're rescue dogs. But the good news is they all come around."

"Did you hear that, Rex?" Ted said. "It won't always be so terrible. It's like riding a bike. Try it. It's fun."

He nudged the dog toward the arena with his foot. "Here's Rex at his first day of school," Ted narrated into the video camera. "He wants his mommy. He wants to go home."

I smiled at Ted. He really was a good photographer. I'd always considered myself grossly unphotogenic: in photographs I saw a crooked smile, sallow skin, and eyes glowing red like Beelzebub. But Ted somehow managed to capture flattering images of me. And this was one of the reasons I had fallen in love with him. He managed to coax all this beauty out of me that I hadn't known I had.

Rex ran away from the bichon. Just in case you don't know what a bichon frise looks like, picture a tiny little fluffball with an albino afro and a lot of 'tude. The dog chased Rex, yipping in a tough-guy stance.

Meanwhile, Ted was running alongside our frightened dog, holding the camera at dog angle, to get what they called a motion shot.

"It's his first time at the dog run," I explained to all the people who had gathered around to watch Ted. "He's scared." I felt it was important to explain so that we wouldn't get any more wasabi looks.

But lo and behold, everyone at the dog run understood. "I brought my camera here the first time Cannoli came in," a woman with a Spinone Italiano said. "She was just a puppy then. Maybe four months old."

"I *hired* a photographer," another woman with a dachshund said. I immediately snuck a peek at her watch, which, in New York, is how you can tell the wearer's income bracket. But it was just a Timex with an imitation leather band.

"I'm not *rich*," the woman said. "I'm just a shitty photographer. And there's this woman in town—my neighbor in fact—who is one of the top pet photographers in the country. So I said, why the hell not? You only live once, and these babies grow up in no time." She picked her dog up and rocked him like a swaddled child.

At that moment we heard a dog scuffle. Two warning barks, and then a swirl of escalating snarls. It was Rex and the bichon. Everybody rushed toward them shouting Hey! Hey! Ted grabbed Rex by the collar and lifted him into the air. Then the bichon leapt up with an athleticism I hadn't known existed in those little lap dogs. This one was going for Rex's throat.

"Fang, that's *enough*!" one of his owners said. He picked the dog up by the back legs, dangling him like a chicken. "Every time we come in here it's the same thing. You pick on the big boys and then you get mad when they ask you, *politely*, to leave them alone. Bad dog!" He gave the dog one quick spank and said, "Here, take him," to his partner. He handed over the dog, who was still upside down and squirming and growling with all his might. I saw that he was wearing a blue rhinestone collar.

"I am so sorry," the man said to us. "This boy is trouble. His name used to be Fluffernutter, but now we call him White Fang. *Bad* boy, Fang. Bad!"

We apologized too. "Rex should have known better," Ted said. "He's four times your dog's size."

"It's the Napoleon complex with Fang," the men said. "All little dogs have it. Watch out."

"Well, that's strike one," I said to Ted on the way home. Rex was now hurrying home as eagerly as he had left it two hours ago. "You know, they say if your puppy isn't properly socialized within the first six weeks, chances are he'll always be hopeless."

"Don't call our dog hopeless," Ted said. "Imagine being thrown into an arena with about twenty strange dogs. We overwhelmed him."

"But what if it's true that you can't teach a dog new tricks? Not even a trick like playing?"

We bought another book. This one on the body language of dogs. We found that, just as Rex didn't know how to read dog signals, neither did we. We did not know that a growl could sometimes be playful. Or that a tail wag could sometimes be a threat. But this is what we learned: A dog waiting in the sphinx position is offering a sign of friendliness. A dog staring, feet firmly planted, with his tail held high and rigid, is most likely dominant, and prepared to show his dominance over the other dog. We learned that raised hackles could either signal aggression or merely that the dog was alert. An arched back and a tucked tail meant the dog was fearful. And a yawn didn't necessarily mean that a dog was tired or bored—a yawn signaled to another dog that he wasn't a threat. We learned that dogs talked mostly with their eyes, and that a stare was seen as a challenge, and that the lower-status dogs would quickly look away. We learned a lick on the mouth meant a dog was hungry, or subservient. (But I still preferred to see it as a sign of affection.) Ears, too, told a story. Ears pricked up meant curiosity and relaxation. Ears pressed back meant fear—but also peppiness and pride. And tails, of course, sent clear signals. We learned that a tail held straight back meant the dog felt the approaching dog was guilty until proven innocent. A tail curled upward meant confidence and friendliness. A wagging tail: bliss. In fact, tails were like flags on the masts of ships, announcing themselves from a distance as friend or foe.

Next, we learned that there were specific dog terms, such as "mock fighting," "play biting," and "play growls," all of which mimicked the actual thing. Dogs engaged in mock fights would bite, nip, growl, and pin their opponents to the ground like any welterweight wrestler, and then clamp their jaws down on their opponent's neck. This alarmed me. I couldn't quite yet tell the difference between mock fighting and real fighting. Where did you draw the line? Rex played with his teeth bared and his hackles raised. These were signs, I knew, of an aggressive dog, but Ted kept insisting he was playing.

In fact, all of the men at the dog run, I noticed, were more apt to say that an alarmingly intense game of roughhousing was "play." They tolerated the bared teeth and the deep growls. Whereas the women tended to be overprotective and cautious with their dogs. They encouraged their dogs to be gentle, to calm down, to "be nice." They didn't like it when other dogs humped their dogs, whereas the men all laughed and said, "Ah, he's just being a dog. Keep trying, Jake, but it ain't no use. You don't have any balls, remember?"

We learned that a mock fight could turn into a real fight at the drop of a hat. Or the drop of a rope. If two alpha dogs were engaged in a tug-of-war, and each one refused to back down, a fight usually broke out before you even had time to lift the lid off your coffee cup. Then we learned that when a fight between two dogs broke out, all the other dogs would gather round and watch with interest, barking encouragement (as if they had placed bets). The bigger dogs—the gentle giants like the mastiffs and the Great Pyrenees—would bark solicitously with pleas for peace. And all the smaller dogs—the terriers—would egg them on with self-important little yaps. Eventually all the humans had to drop their coffees and their cell phones and leap in to break up the fights.

Then we learned that treats could cause fights, too, and that, no matter how stealthily you reached into your pocket and unzipped the Ziploc on your treat bag, dogs from all over the city would hear it. Suddenly you'd be surrounded by packs of them, all of them wanting a liver snack. "It's the sound heard round the world," Ted said that first time. He seemed amused at his sudden popularity and was prepared to dole them out. But then we learned that there is something called "food aggression" and that the more dominant dogs would fight to the death over one cubic inch of freeze-dried beef.

Rex of course would catapult himself into the center of any Ted-induced treat fight, snapping right and left. That treat was rightly his. But still. We kept having to leave the dog run shortly after these free-for-alls, which Ted would end by alpha-rolling the dog right in the center of the arena and shouting "No!" aggressively right into poor Rex's face. It seemed the other dog people were taking note of this, counting strikes. On our way out, we'd pass by the sign reminding us about aggressive males, like a moral from a fairy tale.

Despite this, Ted and I were diligent about visiting the dog run, convinced that Rex would eventually catch on. And that we would catch on, too. Just as there were Rules of the Run for dogs, there seemed to be some rules for people, too. Unspoken rules. You never asked personal questions of the humans—what they did, where they lived, how much they had paid for their apartment. And you never asked them their names. But you could ask them anything about their dogs.

I cannot repeat some of the things I have heard inside the New York City dog runs. Some of it is just too embarrassing. But I will give you a few examples.

It always starts with a shy hi, a good morning or evening or afternoon, and then you ask, "Which dog is yours?" And then your new acquaintance will point toward a pit bull or a shepherd, or a feisty Jack Russell marking every few meters of the fence, or the Rottie humping the Doberman, or the elderly basset hound hiding under a bench. And then you ask the dog's name, its age, whether he/she is male or female, and then, like that, the conversation takes off, veering in directions you'd never, in a million years, expect.

"Actually, we think our dog is a lesbian," a gay couple with a female pit bull announced. "She pees like a male, she humps all the female dogs, and if we let her loose she'd probably run down to Chelsea and buy a strap-on."

"Ew," I said.

"My dog found a dildo in the park once," another woman chimed in. "In Central Park. In the Ramble. It was one of those flesh-colored ones, made to look anatomically correct. My dog came running toward me with it in her mouth, all happy. She wanted me to play fetch with it."

"Clearly your dog is *not* a lesbian," one of the men said.

Then the conversation would segue smoothly into other taboo subjects: rashes, crotches, castrations, engorged nipples. In fact, at the dog run, you can freely violate the FCC codes with such words as penis, vagina, and anus, as long as you are talking about your dog. First thing in the morning, you can find yourself discussing diarrhea and loose stool, and what your dog ate, and what your dog threw up. You are free to describe the contents of your dog's throw-up, and the subsequent smell of the dog's breath. "I heard about a dog near the East River who almost died of a drug overdose after she ate some homeless person's feces," said the woman with the basenji. "And believe me, it wasn't high-quality shit. The guy was a junkie, clearly."

At first I found these conversations scary and, at best, mundane. Why weren't we talking about what we'd just read in *The New Yorker*? Why weren't we talking about the Whitney Biennial, which was up that year? But soon I found that, despite myself, I was enjoying these conversations. I enjoyed hearing about Pepper's crotch rash and Nymphomania's tarry stool. I enjoyed hearing about the latest doggie chew toys, made of dried bulls' penises, and/or the proper way to "evacuate" your dog's anal sac. Because I realized that these conversations were more pertinent to my life than, say, Chip's talk of his golf scores at Lloyd Neck Country Club. I *learned* from these conversations. I expanded my horizons. And I connected with like-minded individuals—high-functioning, intelligent people who happened to be dotty about their dogs.

And isn't it true that you can only find true contentment in life when you find your inner calling? When you find a way to live and express your True Self? I'd always thought that calling for me was writing. And buying vintage clothes. But maybe it wasn't. Maybe my calling was dogs.

Ted's calling seemed to be to disagree with almost everything I said. *Par example*, at the dog run everyone wanted to know what kind of dog Rex was. We still didn't know a thing about his history, and I had all but given up on finding out anything from the shelter. You may recall that we were told he "might be" a setter mix. (But note, gentle readers, that this is the same shelter that routinely posts pictures of, say, a Bernese mountain dog on Petfinder.org and lists him as a Jack Russell terrier.) So as more and more people asked us to define Rex, the more determined I became once again to figure out Rex's breed. Back we went to the dog encyclopedias at Barnes & Noble, back we went to the Internet and compared notes. But we could never agree. Ted wanted to believe our dog was an English setter— maybe a purebred, a Llewellyn or a Laverack. "Look at the shape of his head," Ted would say, pointing out the telltale setter bump on the top of Rex's noggin. "Look at the fringe on his legs, and his markings, and his tail. He's a setter all right." Rex, uncertain about all this scrutiny, tried to hide his head under his back right leg.

I was open to Rex being an English setter. You often see setters in paintings in the apartments of the rich and famous, and once, when I took Rex into the intimidating Ralph Lauren flagship store, one of the floor men shouted, "That's a Lauren dog!"

But then I ran into a woman at the Washington Square Park dog run whose father had bred English setters (she didn't reveal this fact until after I had announced that Rex was a Lauren setter) and had looked Rex up and down and said, rather haughtily, "Are you sure? My father had six setters and kept them at the hunt club."

"She's a bitch," Ted said when I repeated our conversation. "I thought they didn't allow bitches in here."

"Shhh," I said.

Next, I became certain that he was an English springer spaniel, or possibly Welsh. He had all the telltale markings of a springer: the sparkly white coat, the liver spots, the *woo-woo-woo*. He weighed seventy pounds by then, however, whereas the biggest springer typically weighs fifty. So then Rex became a field setter, because some woman on Lafayette Street shouted at me from her passing taxi, "Is that a field setter?" And I had shouted back, in the spirit of the moment, "Yes!" both of us joyous at the discovery that a field setter could be found on fieldless Lafayette.

But then a self-possessed German man with a pair of perfectly behaved German short-hair pointers at the dog run insisted that Rex was definitely a German wire-haired pointer. Then some Irish guy at McSorley's said he was without a doubt an Irish red and white setter. After we left McSorley's, Ted and I looked up the red and whites on the Internet and saw the spitting image of Rex. I was excited. I'd love to have an Irish dog. It was like finding a pot of gold. I began to plan what kind of costume I'd make Rex wear on St. Patrick's Day. Ted brought out an old green turtleneck and said that Rex could wear that. But when I told a woman at the dog run that Rex was an Irish red and white setter, she looked me up and down and said, "My family bred red and whites. Are you sure?"

It was always one step up and two steps back, in terms of Rex's identity.

Sometimes I still looked for Rex's mother on Petfinder.org. I looked for his long-lost littermates in the faces of other New York City dogs. Perhaps he would socialize well with *them,* his own kith and kin. At the dog run, I sprinted toward any other dog that was white or brown or spotted or had fringe. "Where'd you get your dog?" I'd ask the humans, and I got the usual variety of Lower East Side answers: from the Center for Animal Care and Control, from the street, from a junkyard, from Nassau County Pet Rescue.

"What?" I said to this last answer. "When?"

"Oh, almost two months ago," the human said. Her dog, named Igor, had many Rex-like qualities. He was mostly white, with black spaniel-ish markings and a great plumed tail. He stood a good four inches taller than Rex, but he had one black ear and one white ear and a Phantom of the Opera face. Igor was always trying to run away from Rex, or vice versa.

"I wonder if they're related," I said. I told this woman how we had adopted our dog two months earlier as well, and that his history was a mystery. I told her how my boyfriend was now pretty fixated on the idea that Rex was an English setter, but that I was not convinced. I told her that each time I concluded that Rex was an English setter, every breeder and her father came out of the woodwork to tell me I was wrong. "But now Ted has seven books on English setters and he's certain all those other people are wrong." In fact, I told her, the only time Ted didn't insist Rex was an English setter was when I concurred. "He hates to agree with me," I said.

"Uh-huh," she said. "Igor, get down! Excuse me, I have to—" She motioned toward Igor, who was humping a Dalmatian.

And I was left standing alone.

From there on out, whenever that woman saw me coming into the dog run, she would quickly leash up Igor and leave.

For a while, I was hurt and perplexed. I still didn't get dog people. I thought all they wanted to talk about was dogs. Maybe they only wanted to talk about *their* dogs.

Then, the excellent magazine *Whole Dog Journal* ran an article about flower essence therapy or some such thing, and in this article was a picture of a dog that looked absolutely, unequivocally, Just Like Rex. Immediately I called the editor on the phone (you can do that sort of thing in the dog world). "That's a French spaniel," the editor told me. "I can give you the breeder's number if you'd like." Le jackpot!

And what is a French spaniel anyway? According to the *chien de chasse* websites, an *épagneul français* is a rare breed in the United States, more common in Canada and France, used to hunt quail and grouse. They say the French spaniel has been around since the Middle Ages, and that the breed came about from a union between an English setter and a French pointing spaniel. The French spaniel is loyal, loving, stubborn, and smart. A Rex by any other name.

It made perfect sense. I'd always felt that Rex came from pure bloodlines that went all the way back to the spaniels of the duc de Duhart. I pictured his noble ancestors sitting at the feet of kings at breakfast, hunting all day in the vast fields and valleys of the estate, and sleeping at night inside the château with the servants, whose job it was to keep the dogs warm rather than the other way around. These were the ancestors who whispered to Rex when he passed a mere pigeon on the city sidewalks: *"Ne les regardez pas. Allons. C'est rien, cet oiseau. Il n'est pas un vrai oiseau! Allons vite!"*

"He's a French spaniel!" I shouted to Ted when he came home from the photo lab. I showed him the photograph from the magazine. "Oh my gosh," Ted said. "That looks just like him." He knelt down to hug the dog. "Who's a French spaniel?" he said in his happy voice. "Who's an *épagneul Français?*" Rex beamed and thumped his tail.

We began to speak to the dog in French. We began to remark that his diet was a little, how you say, proletarian. We began to sense that it was an outrage that his collar didn't quite match his coat. And of course Rex got a new nickname. "Who's a Spinach Boy?" Ted would say when he came home from work. "Who's my little *épinard*?"

I should at least attempt to explain this nickname. *Épinard* is one of my favorite words in French, and it means spinach, which explains why Ted called Rex "Spinach Boy." I always thought that nickname was adorable, but as I write this I realize you never really expect anyone else to understand or appreciate your doggie's nicknames. It's too much to ask.

Anyway, Rex didn't *always* remain a Spinach Boy in Ted's eyes. I began to notice that whenever we had some mundane disagreement—over, say, whose turn it was to clean the toilet or why Ted never wanted to visit my family—suddenly Rex was an English setter again. And I would insist he was a French spaniel. And on and on it went, never resolved.

Inside the dog run, our English setter/French spaniel continued to get in a little squabble every third or fourth time we visited, then every fifth or sixth, but he was getting better. And I swear he never *started* the fights, but neither did he ever back down. Some obnoxious little Jack Russell terrier would nip at his heels and egg him on, and then Rex would say enough was enough and lunge angrily at the dog. Then a small scuffle would ensue, and Ted would grab Rex and the snippy woman would grab her snippy dog, and then I'd apologize and that would be that. Except that Ted didn't think we should have to be the ones apologizing.

"That little shit started it," he would say of the Jack Russell.

"I know he did," I'd say as we dragged Rex out of the run. "But still, I don't want to be ostracized."

"We're not going to be ostracized. He was playing, and that terrier started it."

That's when I recognized another unspoken pattern at the dog run. You liked people who liked your dog. You tended not to like the people who didn't like your dog. And you didn't like the dogs who didn't like your dog.

Sometimes I sensed that not many people in the dog run liked Rex, in those early days. They certainly took an interest in him at first, because he was so unique-looking, and so handsome, and everyone loves to hear the story of an abused dog given a second chance; but once they witnessed one of his little squabbles, well, the interest in him kind of waned. It seemed to me that people started to keep their distance from us. Ted thought otherwise, but I saw the averted gazes, the tightened grips on leashes when Rex came near. We were unpopular. I felt like a kid on a school playground.

After several weeks spent visiting the dog run and trying to make friends there, it still felt as if we were in some sort of social limbo. In many ways we'd migrated beyond our Lower East Side friends. But we didn't want to be certified dog people either. I pictured a long life sitting in front of the television with just Rex and Ted.

But the good news is, Rex's separation anxiety—like most of his other behavioral problems—abated as more time passed. It was safe, once again, to venture back out into the world. We decided that it was important for us to do two work-related events per week—one for me and one for Ted, which we would both attend—and two social events per week (typically dinner or drinks). Work-related for Ted meant a film or a lecture or a photography exhibit; for me, a book party or a reading. We remembered how much we enjoyed dressing up in city clothing and seeing and being seen. And we remembered what it was like to schmooze, for that is the true reason New Yorkers go out all the time. Everyone is always trying to get something from someone else.

Chip had a new girlfriend, and she was a gracious person with refined social skills. Twice a week, we dined with them, and by our second meeting Kristen had already surmised that I liked to talk about dogs, and she used this knowledge as a tactic to draw me out. We might be talking about Orson Welles or Goethe, and Kristen would lean over the table and touch my hand and say, "How's the little froufrou?" She had a delicate gold chain around her neck that quivered as she spoke.

I'd glance over at Ted, to see if he was listening. I knew it was important not to get any more wasabi looks. I knew I was supposed to curb myself, to rein the subject in, to talk of *books* for God's sake (and not dog books!), but still, inevitably, stories of Rex would slip out. Ask, and it is given.

I'd sit up in my seat and lean toward Kristen, my face animated, my eyes bright, and find myself telling her that yesterday I had met a woman with a dog named Otis, and that this was what a previous, horrendous boyfriend of mine had called his penis, and that now I was going to have to avoid this woman whenever I saw her and her dog Otis approaching us on the street. "Because," I said, "who wants to be reminded of an ex's Otis?" Or I might tell her how I had started to cook for the dog, because the quality of commercial dry dog food was so inferior, even dangerous. "I read that most brands are actually carcinogenic!" I whispered conspiratorially, as if the president of Iams might be at the next table. "I read that at least ten of the major brands were found to contain traces of euthanized animals! And elephant carcasses and baseball gloves."

"How horrible," Kristen whispered. "No wonder you make his food. I would too."

"And it's funny because in the mornings, I'll stand there with an apron, sautéing ground turkey and cubed potatoes, and Ted will say, 'Will you make me an English muffin?' and I'll tell him, 'Help yourself.'"

We laughed loudly. Ted had a certain look that I called the Crow. And when he gave me that look from across the table, I knew I had crossed some line. He gave it now.

And yet, it was becoming harder and harder for me not to talk about the dog in public. Every conversation, in my mind, could lead to Rex. Talk of the Yankees segued into talk of Rex's morning romp around the baseball field. Talk of the Clinton administration segued naturally into talk of Bill's dog Buddy, and how the country needed more generous off-leash laws. Talk of the food we ate, or the wine we drank, or the countries we had visited—all roads, whether in Cambodia or Romania or Madrid, led back to our little Rex.

But no one is interested, an inner voice kept telling me. The voice sounded like Obi-Wan Kenobi. *Use the Force, girlfriend. Talk of other things, talk of your writing, stop talking about the dog.*

It got so I literally had to bite my tongue to keep from doing this. It was like having Tourette's. I grew oddly silent during our social engagements. Biting my tongue made me sit with an odd smile on my face, a slightly pinched smile, like that of a recovering alcoholic in the presence of five bottles of gin. Ted never stopped talking, no matter what the situation, and he'd look at me from across the table or the banquette, and smile, and say, "What's wrong?"

"Nothing," I'd say, with the pinched look, and I began to wonder if his friends saw me as reticent, or boring, or a snob. Perhaps they thought Ted and I were fighting and on the verge of breaking up. Little did they know I was trying to spare them the pain of another cute dog story. Little did they know I was becoming someone else.

Late one Saturday evening, while the rest of the world was seeing the final performance of *Rent* on East Fourth Street before it moved up to Broadway, Ted and Rex and I went again to the dog run. Ted brought one of his vintage cameras with black-and-white film. I sat down on a bench while Ted followed the dog around like some kind of tracking device. Next to me was a nice bland girl with undyed hair and terrific legs. She was wearing Tevas and not necessarily flattering shorts. But she seemed not to care. She told me she lived in Inwood, two hundred blocks north, and told me that she drove to this dog run every day. This stunned me and I stared at her. "I just like to hang out with my dogs," she said. "On weekends we go hiking and climbing, and on weekdays we come here."

I could tell she lived a simple life. Hers were two of the friendliest dogs in the arena: two plump chocolate Labs who trotted side by side with a plastic water bottle in their mouths, playing a benign tug-of-war. "Which dog is yours?" she asked me. I pointed toward a solitary Rex, who paced along the north fence as if looking for an escape route.

I mused: "Sometimes I wonder if dogs represent the worst of us, or the best of us? Or both?"

"What kind of dog is he?" she asked. Her voice was kind and uncomplicated. I could tell she didn't get all worked up because she couldn't afford Prada sandals. I could tell she didn't get depressed because her name had not yet appeared on Page Six. No, she just *was* and it showed in her face. I decided to say Rex was an English setter.

"Aren't they great dogs? I grew up with setters. Yours is so handsome."

Her dogs ran up to Rex with their tails wagging. The one with the bottle put it down and nudged it toward Rex with his snout. Rex sniffed it hesitantly, then took the bottle into his mouth and ran. He bounded and dodged and sailed over benches as the other dogs chased him. With his lips stretched over the bottle, he looked as if he was smiling. And why not? He had finally grasped that being chased in the dog run was *fun*. I clapped my hands and shouted, "Ted, look at Rex go!"

We recognized the signs of dog happiness: his tail held high, his ears flattened back in what looked like pride at his own talent and cleverness. "Look at that happy boy!" Ted shouted.

I always felt that if you have known great sorrow, you can appreciate joy that much more, because you have experienced its opposite. And I've always felt that dogs do have memories, even though some of our dog books claimed this wasn't true. But why else would a dog flinch around a baseball bat if he didn't remember the pain it had caused? Why else would a dog run to the door every time you put on your coat? It's not just conditioning. So as I watched Rex run around with his tail held high, I wondered if he was finally going to forget his troubled past. Or at least let it go.

Rex cut away from the Labs like a linebacker and paused, play-bowed, and darted off again. Maybe dogs simply had good days and bad days, just like humans, I thought. And maybe Rex would always be a little bit unpredictable. But why not accept that? No relationship is ever 100 percent normal and stable after all—not even a relationship between dogs. So why not just savor those moments when everyone gets along?

Behind us, the sun was setting, which made the triumphal arch at the northern border of the park glow orange. It wasn't a giant Arc de Triomphe, like its Parisian counterpart, but in the orange light it looked grand and impressive.

"Come here, Rex," I called. "Come here, happy boy!" He came and jumped onto the bench and kissed me. I laughed with delight. And at that moment Ted snapped my picture. I heard the click, and I could tell it was going to be a perfect picture—one that he'd carry around in his wallet for years to come.

As we walked home that night, I decided not to tell Ted that someone had confirmed Rex was an English setter. I decided that he could have his truth and I could have mine. That way we'd all be happy.

CHAPTER 8

Domestic Animals

I n summer in New York City, all your hopes and dreams boil down to one thing: air-conditioning. But Ted and I didn't have an air conditioner yet. All we had was one of those tiny table fans that barely managed to whisper, like an old man on his deathbed. And you don't think about the implications of these things until a heat wave comes, but there it was: a dying fan. I tried not to read too much into this, but aren't large appliances the sort of purchase *married* couples make?

That summer was to be the hottest summer on record in New York City. Like, in the history of mankind. Everywhere, throughout the city, tempers began to boil. At city hall, Mayor Giuliani lashed out at reporters during a testy press conference on quality-of-life violations, while, out in Queens, five policemen were accused of shoving a plunger up Abner Louima's ass. So now you have some context. If you were foolish enough to walk outside in daylight, it seemed, you put yourself at risk.

Meanwhile, the temperature rose. The Department of Health issued a warning to stay indoors because of poor air quality, so I could only take Rex on the briefest of walks. Here was a dog who had just gotten used to a maniacal routine of a one-and-a-half-hour walk in the morning, two or three half-hour walks throughout the day, and another hour-long trip to the park at night. And now that routine had evaporated like steam. I could only take him out for short relief walks, and we'd stagger around the block like geriatrics, panting, one labored step at a time. Everyone walked like this: the people, the dogs (especially the northern breeds like huskies and Samoyeds)—all of them staggering forward, like those slaves forced to build the pyramids, laboring in the baking sun with their feet chained. There was the heat to contend with, plus the humidity, plus the fact that, in our neighborhood, the sidewalks absorbed the heat like sauna stones and the windows on all the buildings beamed the sun right back at you, singeing your eyeballs with demonic force. It was like being in a tanning booth all the time. Without the benefit of even getting tan. It got so hot the gum on the sidewalks—those ubiquitous black patches that had been pockmarking the streets for centuries—had turned molten and pink and was starting to ooze like a special effect from a DreamWorks film.

I began to worry that the same thing would happen to Rex's feet. And sure enough, when we paused at intersections he'd stare at the ground and pant and pant, lifting his feet one at a time like a tap dancer, as if trying to find a way to avoid the heat of the pavement. Watching him, my heart would ache, and I'd hear the old mantra, "In the city?" and I'd wonder once again if New York really was a terrible place for a dog. So we stayed inside as much as we could.

But inside was only slightly better. After our walks, Rex would lie on the floor of the kitchen and pant and pant. This was a noisy, rhythmic, endless pant—the stuff of prank phone calls. His whole body heaved, and his tongue lolled out of the side of his mouth at twice its normal length. *The Hypochondriac's Guide* spoke of the possibilities of heat stroke and heart attacks, and advised me to keep cold washcloths on Rex's belly and give him baths. But don't make the bathwater too cold, the book cautioned, or you might send the dog into shock. Another book warned that most dogs hated baths and that dogs saw forced bathing as a sign of dominance, but Rex seemed to enjoy having expensive organic shampoo massaged into his neck and shoulders. And who doesn't like a massage? As I knelt next to my dog and rubbed in the lavender oatmeal conditioning rinse, he'd get a little gleam of appreciation in his eye, and I knew that despite the heat he was happy, that he liked his new life. And I knew he knew I was trying my best.

But then the temperature climbed to 800 degrees. Anyone who was sane or who could afford it, of course, left. Ted and I watched from our window as millions of people threaded their way out to the Hamptons, or the Hudson Valley, or even as far as Cape Cod, leaving behind them big heaping clouds of car exhaust, most of which had settled on the Williamsburg Bridge, under which Ted and I lived. The smell of exhaust hung over East River Park like a blimp. The smell from our neighborhood wasn't something I even want to describe. Great vats of human urine, rotten milk, spoiled meat—you name it— stewed in puddles and alleys and at the bottom of metal garbage cans, and filled the air with a noxious haze that turned the entire city brown. It seemed to be worse in our own courtyard, where our neighbors dumped used diapers, chicken carcasses, and empty bottles of Colt 45. The stench rose up from this courtyard and went straight into our living room window. And the only thing I could do about this, other than slit my wrists, was keep all the windows closed. It was like I could either die of heat stroke or die of chemical warfare, so I chose the former. Besides, I reasoned, my apartment could be like a sauna. The heat would steam open my pores.

But I worried about Rex. The smell from the courtyard made him sneeze and pace with the hunched-up, trapped look of a zoo animal. The heat from the closed windows made him lie on the kitchen floor and pant. At least such behavior gave me a glimpse into the future, to a time beyond those ten years the vet was talking about, when Rex would finally be calm.

But still I felt bad, so I did what I could to help him. I served him ice cubes made of chicken bouillon. I froze a dozen washcloths to keep his belly cool. I even showed him pictures of Belgian cart dogs, all tethered and muzzled and forced to work in the heat. "These are your ancestors," I told him. "Dogs used to be forced into labor, and worked literally to the bone, until they *died*. See this picture? See that poor shepherd carting around those giant steel canisters of milk? Look at the look on that poor dog's face! Does he look happy? See how lucky you are to be living in New York City?" I'd look over at Rex to gauge his reaction, but he wasn't impressed. "Get me a Beef Consommé snow cone," his look seemed to say. "And then maybe we'll talk."

Sometimes I thought Ted and Rex and I should move someplace healthier, like Marin County or upstate. But it was too hot to move. It was too hot to think.

Ted, however, had grown up down South. And as a Southerner, he always managed to maintain both his spirits and his social life during heat waves, and so, on the hottest night of the summer, he went out to dinner with some friends. I hadn't joined them because I was lazy, and because leaving the dog in the apartment would have been like confining him in a hot car with the windows rolled up, and you can get arrested for something like that. So Rex and I made do with cold washcloths on our bellies. Who cared if Ted was out discussing politics and Egon Schiele while I was having a conversation with a spaniel? ("Who took a bathie? Who's so clean?") Who cared that I drew pictures of Rex and sang him little songs? We would have been fine just lying on our backs, watching movies, sharing popcorn, and eating packaged cookies (the only, I mean the *only*, good thing about New York City humidity is all your rock-hard packaged cookies will magically become fresh-out-of-the-oven soft) had not Ted called from his cell phone and said he and his friends were on their way over for an after-dinner drink.

"Good God," I said. "Are you sure?" My ankles itched suddenly and I hoped it wasn't fleas.

"Yes, I'm sure. Jeff wants to see the place. And he wants to meet Rex."

"What if he lunges at Jeff?"

"He's not going to lunge at Jeff."

"Why don't we just go out for a drink?" I said. "Did Giuliani give us permission to go outside?"

"Jeff wants to see the apartment," Ted said. "Plus, we're already here." I could hear his voice coming from both the phone and the lobby. Then I heard three pairs of shoes coming up the stairs.

"Don't kill anybody," I said to Rex. "Okay?" But he didn't move from his panting position on the floor.

I rushed into the bedroom for a last-minute look at myself in a full-length mirror. And there I beheld the scariest sight since I discovered my first gray hair at age twenty-six. I beheld a Dog Lady. Not quite a Crazy Dog Lady—that was Stage V. But a Dog Lady nevertheless: I was wearing boxer shorts, an old Robert Plant T-shirt, and some flip-flops I had bought at Rite Aid for $3.99. All of the above were covered with dog hair and stained with drool. At least it wasn't my own drool, but still. I looked like I hadn't showered since that Robert Plant concert in 1983.

And then the lock was turning! And then the second lock, and the third. I had no choice. I threw on a Yankees cap and decided to act nonchalant. I would pretend that they had caught me off guard; that normally I'd be wearing a slip dress and some feathered shoes. "So Rex, tonight I am a normal person and you are a normal dog, okay?"

Ted and his entourage entered, and I warmly greeted Jeff (a broker from Morgan Stanley who used to work in D.C.) and his female friend. She, Liesl, was one of those fragile blond beauties with pale eyelashes and collarbones as delicate as spun glass. She wore a gossamer slip dress of butterfly yellow, and a pair of Jimmy Choo shoes. Jeff explained that they had gone to business school together, and that she was just in town for the night. He had a hungry look on his face when he said all this, which suggested he was hoping to have sex.

I invited them to sit while Ted went into the kitchen to make the drinks. Meanwhile, Rex pushed himself into a standing position and did a Downward-Facing Dog. I watched with a certain amount of trepidation as he lumbered toward Jeff, but he simply veered away when Jeff put out his hand. Next Rex went up to inspect Liesl, panted, and slobbered all over her four-hundred-dollar dress. Then, apparently having approved of her, he backed up and sat on her Jimmy Choos.

Liesl smiled in a tight, crinkly-eyed way that suggested she wasn't pleased.

"I'm so sorry," I said, pulling Rex away. "That means he likes you!" I was about to go into my "He's a rescue dog" spiel, but then I saw that her forearm was slick with drool.

"Oh goodness, I'm sorry."

"It's okay," Liesl said flatly. "I love dogs."

But I could tell she didn't. In grad school I used to dog-sit for an English professor who would dismiss anyone he disapproved of— grouches, fundamentalists, Republicans—by saying: "They're not dog people." When he said this he and his wife would shake their heads, and then start talking baby talk to their dogs. And at the time, I didn't get it; I did not see how someone so intelligent and politically savvy and informed could divide the world between those who loved the canine nation and those who did not. But suddenly, there in my own steam room, I understood. And it felt good in a way. To have found Liesl's flaw.

"Do we have any wine?" Ted called to me from the kitchen.

"I don't think so."

"Any beer? Vodka? Cooking sherry? Jeez, there's nothing in the freezer but washcloths! And something scary in the ice cube trays that looks like urine." Ted stuck his head into the living room. "What have you done with our real refrigerator, sweetheart? The one that had food in it and was clean?"

"We just, um, haven't had a chance to go to the store," I said, laughing nervously. "We've been so busy training this dog."

"Sorry," Ted said to our guests, "but it looks like we're totally dry."

"We have frozen chicken bouillon," I added, trying to be funny. But my guests weren't dog people, so they didn't get it.

For the next few minutes, we sat and stared at one another. I had spent so little time in the company of humans that I seemed to have forgotten how to have a conversation. And what was of interest these days, besides Gentle Leader collars and the pre-union oppression of Belgian cart dogs? Normally you'd talk about the heat, but I didn't want to call any attention to that, because then Ted might want to open the window.

"So what have you been up to?" Jeff said.

"Oh, the usual. Writing, teaching, editing, drinking, searching for the meaning of life. This dog keeps me busier than anything. You know how it is."

They didn't. Silence. Having all these people in a hermetically sealed room was making it hard to breathe.

Jeff nodded toward my hat. "Are you a Yankees fan?"

"No, I'm a Yankees-cap fan."

Liesl gave me a blank look. Was she stupid, I wondered, or did she have no sense of humor?

"And what do you do?" Liesl asked. I told her that I was a writer, and taught part-time at a city university, and read stories for a literary magazine. Ted called out from the kitchen, "She's a Renaissance woman!" and I had one of those moments when I thought we sounded really cool.

None of this got a reaction from Liesl, however. Her face remained so stiff I started to wonder if she had been Botoxed.

"And you?" I asked.

She said she managed funds. She stiffened in her seat when the dog came toward her again. He took four panting steps—one for each leg—and then slumped onto the floor.

"He's totally mellow!" Jeff said. "Chip told me he was a wild man."

Ted came out with a baguette and olive paste and some old powdered lemonade. It was too late to tell Ted that I'd dropped that baguette on the floor, and that Rex and I had played tug-of-war with it. "Yeah, we've been trying to domesticate him. We didn't want to tell you this, but you guys are our first human guinea pigs. So far so good."

As Ted set the tray down, Jeff checked out the apartment. He himself lived on the Upper East Side, in a cookie-cutter high-rise, and had always admired us from afar for our bohemian tendencies. But tonight he could not disguise the, um, dismay on his face as he took in the blood-orange walls, the blue velveteen sofa cover I had scored at a drag queen's stoop sale, and our "outsider" artwork, some of which we had admittedly found on the side of the road.

Liesl was staring at the gold thong bikini I had hung on the wall like a sconce. Ted had given this bikini to me as a birthday present back when we first started dating, and while I was flattered that he found me sexy enough to envision me in such a getup, it really was the kind of thing only a woman with breast implants could wear. Thus, a wall hanging.

"That's interesting," Jeff said, nodding toward the thong. Rex panted and panted in a way that made Jeff's statement sound lewd. Then Jeff started to sweat profusely, a great burst of perspiration that I hoped wasn't induced by the thong.

I didn't want Jeff to notice I'd noticed his glistening forehead, so I picked up a piece of bread. It had teeth marks on it.

"Jesus Christ," Ted said. "Let's open a window!"

"I don't think that's a good idea." I tried to give him a look that said *trust me on this one,* but Ted persisted.

"It's absolutely stifling in here," he said.

"Well, why don't we just go out for a drink?" I said brightly. But when I said the word *out*, Rex leapt up and spun around and started to bark in a manic, psycho way that people who don't like dogs might find alarming. Rex, we were learning, had different types of barks for different things, and this was a hap-hap-happy bark. But Liesl pressed her chin into her clavicle and leaned back, as if prepared to limbo right out the door.

"Stop it," Ted said. "Stop it! Shut up!" Rex's tail knocked the baguette back onto the floor.

"I'm just going to open this window," Ted said. When he did, the stench rose up from our courtyard like one of those nuclear clouds they always showed you in the seventies in science class. The apartment filled with a stunned, solemn silence.

Jeff brought a handkerchief to his forehead. "I should probably, uh, get Liesl back to her hotel," he said. His voice was choked from trying not to breathe and he had giant wet spots under his armpits. I knew we had ruined his chances of getting laid.

As they rose to leave, I felt myself filling with a mild, inexplicable panic. It seemed that when they closed that door, any further possibility of freedom or youth or glamour would vanish. "Well, thanks for coming you guys," Ted said. "I apologize again for our lack of hospitality." Then he added casually that we had been invited to a rave that night by some architect friend. "He's really cool—he designs hair salons if you can believe it, but he does them in a very modern style, and uses a lot of brushed steel. I think I might go."

"You *should* go," I said to Ted. "You should absolutely go to that rave." There was urgency in my voice and Ted looked at me questioningly. It just felt as if there was more at stake than his immediate pleasure—I felt that if he stayed in, he would be setting the tone and the terms for the rest of our lives. We'd be the Dog Guy and the Crazy Dog Lady! It was like we were on a sinking ship and I was telling him to save himself.

"What will you do if I go?" Ted said.

"Oh, I was going to watch a video."

"What movie did you get?" Jeff asked. He'd had his hand on the doorknob for the last few minutes, which was unfortunate because you could really see his armpit sweat. But I appreciated him offering me this one last chance to prove myself, my Last Chance to Change.

And I could have said, *À la Recherche du Temps Perdu*, in perfectly accented French, but why bother? It was too hot. And eventually all truths are discovered. "Um, it's called *Training Your Gun Dog*," I mumbled. I looked at Liesl and shrugged. "It is."

She gave me another Botox look—one that contained neither smile nor frown.

"Oh, I heard that's a *classic*," Ted said. "Excellent cinematography. And Antoine Coppola did the sound."

Jeff shook his head and laughed and said, "You two! You're hilarious. Well, have a good night."

Liesl reached out her slender hand and thanked me. She had a sublime French manicure. My stubby nails were rimmed with dirt. And in that moment, I saw her life and she saw mine. I saw that, at the end of the day, she would go home and wash off the dog drool, whereas I would live in it. And drink of it. And the funny thing was, I didn't even really mind. A few months earlier I had been a woman who worked to buy clothes to wear to work. And what's the point of that? Maybe life wasn't about having a rotating wardrobe. Maybe it wasn't even about having a working air conditioner. Maybe life was all about making others get a gleam in their eyes—all creatures great and small.

"I guess I'll stay in with the two of you," Ted said as our guests slipped away into the night. "I'll stay in and stay warm with my little family."

We had become domesticated animals, I realized. All three of us.

Rex came over and pressed his warm self against our legs.

CHAPTER 9

The Hypochondriac's Guide to Overprotective Dog Care

I n September, tragedy struck the neighborhood. One of the Marching Band Man's dog-children had died. I heard the news one night as Rex and I were walking home from a big night out at Krispy Kreme. The Marching Band Man ran toward me with tears streaming down his cheeks. "My third child, Ginger, died two days ago, from choking on a tennis ball. She was playing one minute and then she was choking, *choking*, and there was nothing I could do. I tried to get the ball out with my own hands, but it was stuck. Plus I didn't want to scratch her throat with my nails. Then I hailed a taxi and told him to get me to the Animal Medical Center, but we didn't get there in time. She died in my arms, precious Ginger. Died right in my arms."

How could I not cry? "I'm so sorry," I said, touching his sleeve. I realized I didn't even know his name. "I guess that's the best place to die, though, isn't it? I mean, if she had to die. With you, in your arms."

"Oh, bless you, yes! Yes!" He blew his nose into a worn pink handkerchief. "For that I am thankful. But listen, honey, you go home right now and get rid of all your tennis balls. Do it for my sake, for Ginger's, for your only child! They're dangerous! Dangerous!"

Ted was not home when I returned to the apartment. I was so distraught over the death of Ginger I didn't know what to do with myself, so I decided to watch the movie version of Milan Kundera's *The*

Unbearable Lightness of Being. This brilliant book tells the story of two doomed lovers who have to flee Communist Prague. Their relationship is rocky from the start—he cheats all the time—and eventually they get a dog to seal their tenuous bond.

Immediately, I fast-forwarded to the part in the movie where they have to put their dog Karenin to sleep. I'd seen this movie twice already, but that was in my pre-Rex days, before I had understood the vast purity of a dog's love. Now I wept as I witnessed the death of Karenin. I wept at the death of Tomas and Tereza's love. I wept over the fact that Rex would someday die. That he would be snatched away, and that I wouldn't get to say goodbye to him. All this love, all this perfect love, would be taken away. I wrapped my arms around Rex's neck and clung to him, hugging him too tightly, my face buried in his fur. He seemed confused by my outburst, but still, he stayed. He seemed to recognize that his job was to absorb my pain, so he licked and licked my face. I sobbed until I was depleted, and silent, and then I heard Rex's heartbeat, just on the other side of my cheek. It was a solid heartbeat, and it seemed to tell me: *Don't be sad. I am here with you now. We are together.*

When Ted came home at midnight, he found me lying on the living room floor next to Rex, still crying and clutching him tightly. "Honey, what happened?" Ted said, kneeling next to me on the rug. Rex took the opportunity to scurry away, having been released from the headlock that had finally begun to cramp his style.

"Ginger died," I cried. "She choked on a tennis ball. He tried to save her but he couldn't. I don't want Rex to die."

"He's not going to die," Ted said. "He's not even two years old. Most setters live until they're twelve. He's going to live to be a tired old man."

"But so many things could happen to him," I said, sitting on Ted's lap. My voice was that of a twelve-year-old. "It's not safe out there."

"I know," he said. "But I'll take care of you. I'll take care of you both."

I sat up and told him about the scene in *Unbearable Lightness.* "After Karenin dies, Tereza confesses to Tomas that she loved the dog more. Then she corrects herself and says that she loved the dog *better.*" I stroked Rex's soft, soothing fur. "I just thought that was so sad."

Ted nodded. He understood. He probably loved the dog better, too.

I slept fitfully that night, and in my dreams kept hearing, over and over again, a piercing, mournful yowl. It turned out that one of the Cat Ladies in the neighborhood had launched a campaign to trap all the feral kittens and find them new homes. But the mothers were still out there, crestfallen, heartbroken, confused. Every night they called out for their babies, and every night their cries echoed off the sides of our building and into our room. "I can't stand to hear that," I said, hugging Ted, in tears. "That poor cat. She thinks she lost her babies. She *did* lose her babies."

"Those kittens all have homes now," Ted said. "They're much better off."

The mother cat wailed.

"It just seems so cruel."

"I know, honey," Ted said. "But let's try to get some sleep."

But I couldn't sleep. I was too worried about losing Rex.

Welcome to the next phase of our life with a dog: hypochondria.

Until I brought a dog into my life, I never considered myself a hypochondriac. And I swear I'm not—not when it comes to myself, that is. If I were, say, bleeding from the palms and the eyeballs, that wouldn't necessarily stop me from being first in line at the semi-annual Barney's sample sale (although whether they would let me into the dressing rooms, or allow me to manhandle the Prada bowling totes, is another matter). And don't get me wrong—I don't mind going to the doctor. I like being in the presence of someone who will listen to my problems and pretend he actually cares. But the thing is, in New York City, the doctors don't listen to you. They schedule a new patient every twelve minutes, make you wait two hours in their plush reception area for your appointment, and spend a total of ten minutes in your actual presence, during which they shine a light into your ears, tap you on the knees, and call you by the wrong name. (Once the tech with the clipboard came out into the waiting room and asked for "Mr." Harrington.) For this you will be charged six hundred dollars, and sent away with a two-week trial sample of Viagra (even though you came in to talk about the inexplicable stigmata on your ribs). At least when I was little I got to choose between a lollipop and a jeweled plastic ring. So, needless to say, I didn't go to the doctor much.

But then Ted and I adopted the dog. We did not know this dog would open up our lives, and teach us how to nurture, and to love nature, and to better love ourselves. Nor could we have predicted that falling in love with a dog would bring out new, seamier emotions that attach themselves to love like demodectic parasites: worry, overprotectiveness, and hypochondria.

All my friends who had birthed human children swore they'd *never* be worrywarts like their mothers. But I witnessed their slow transformations into paranoid schizos who lay in bed at night obsessing over Sudden Infant Death Syndrome, child molestation, and whether the trees surrounding the house should be cut down, for fear that their branches would shatter the nursery windows during a freak New England storm. And I understood this to be a phase they went through, a rite of passage that every parent undergoes with their firstborn child. But I never imagined that I would undergo the same rite with my dog.

You might say it all started with the hundred-and-one books Ted and I had purchased eight weeks earlier. You might say it was the Internet, which provides thousands of websites containing veterinary information, and millions of reasons why you should worry incessantly about the fate and health of your dog. And that's just the websites written in English. (Some say the World Wide Web exists solely to prey on the paranoia of people like me.) Or, more likely, you might say it was something innate within me that was just looking for an excuse to come out.

From the books and the Internet, I learned practical stuff: for instance, that the bump on top of Rex's head was called an occipital protuberance. I learned that dogs have something called anal sacs and that anal-sac glands produce a "sour to rancid-smelling watery brownish secretion that may serve to mark your dog's stool like an identification tag." These anal sacs are often "emptied" explosively in stressful or frightening situations. Eww. Even sneezing, I learned, could mean something disgusting: the presence of a foreign body, nasal mites, nasal worms. "Nasal worms?" I said to Ted. "Can you imagine?"

"It sounds like something they'd do on *Jackass*." This was a show on MTV in which guys vomited, catapulted themselves into bins full of packing peanuts, and pulled other asinine college-boy stunts. (For the record: Ted liked this program.)

I read of puppies choking to death when their collars got caught on crate latches; I read of dogs dying when their stomachs got punctured by chicken bones. And finally, I learned that simply walking down the sidewalks of New York City, or interacting with dogs at the dog run, or chasing a squirrel, could lead to a number of dangerous ailments: canine distemper, infectious canine hepatitis, leptospirosis, parvovirus, peritonitis, allergic dermatitis, giardiasis, intestinal parasites, and worms. To confound it all, I learned that all the symptoms of all the above were essentially the same: scratching, sneezing, panting, straining.

At my temp job, I began to spend six of my eight working hours visiting veterinary websites and recoiling at the graphic images of cocker spaniels with eyes bulging out of their sockets, of unidentified rectal prolapses and hyperestrinism (you don't want to know), of dogs who had been hit by cars. I'd call Ted in tears, telling him to log on to such-and-such a website for proof as to why Rex should not be allowed out of doors.

"You're just upsetting yourself," Ted would say. "And you're upsetting me. Aren't you supposed to be doing some kind of *work*?"

"I sent my daily fax already."

"Well, can't you look at male porn or something? Something that won't make you paranoid? Can't you find something more constructive to do with your time?"

No, I could not.

But Ted, too, worried about how to best care for our dog. He called me as many times a day as I called him. "His poop smells funny," he said. "I noticed on the Late Afternoon Walk."

"Doesn't poop always smell funny when it comes down to it?"

"This is different. It is unlike any smell I have smelled before."

"Well, should we take him to the vet?"

"Maybe," Ted said. His voice sounded grave and paternal. "What do you think?"

That's when I heard the dog sneezing in the background. "He sneezes all the time! We should take him to the vet. He might have something stuck up his nose. Some bizarro substance that's making his poop smell."

That's when Ted changed his tune. He always changed his tune whenever we came close to agreeing on something. "There's nothing wrong with him. We don't need to take him to the vet. You probably just fed him something he wasn't supposed to eat yesterday. Am I right? Some of that midnight Dulce de Leche, for instance? That carton you polished off while I was asleep?"

So we'd had some ice cream, the dog and I, but I remained silent. So did Ted. He was on to me, I could tell. Then Rex sneezed.

"See? He sneezes all the time!"

"Go work on your book!" Ted said, laughing. "You're driving us both nuts."

By "us" he meant himself and the dog. Many women gauge the progress of their relationships by the first time the man says "we." Ted now said "we"—about Rex.

The minute we hung up I looked up " 'EXCESSIVE SNEEZING' AND DOG" on all the various search engines on the Internet. Needless to say, I wasn't getting much writing done on those afternoons, but the *Merck Veterinary Manual* could boast to their advertisers about that month's additional eight hundred hits.

How could we not worry? Our friends with human children could at least comfort themselves with the fact that someday their infants would be able to speak to them and communicate their wants and needs. Our friends with human children passed through the worry-wart phase smoothly, and were able to tell their second children, who might be bleeding from the eyeballs, to "get over it" and "leave us alone." But Ted and I, with our dog-child, would never have that advantage. Rex would never be able to voice his ailments, his hopes and dreams, his pains.

"At least he's not going to tell you he hates your guts when he turns fifteen," my friend Jaylin said. (She and I had recently reconnected, because she had three children and I needed some advice.) "At least he's not going to tell you, as you're getting ready to go out to dinner with your husband, whom you *never have time to see,* that you're a disgrace to the human race."

"Gosh," I said. "I guess I'm lucky to have a dog."

But the bottom line was, our dog could not speak. Sure, he was smarter than the average canine, and knew, to date, twenty words in the English language, but none of those words were, "I have giardia, you know, caused by drinking from a fetid puddle when you weren't looking, out near the old bathhouses in East River Park. Giardia is a parasitical infection and it's contagious! I require an antibiotic and a new bed. Helllllp!"

Perhaps now is the time to confess that I had always been kind of paranoid about the dog's health, from the get-go. In the first, oh, month, we took him to the vet for panting, yawning, flatulence, and the weird black discolorations on the bottom of his paws.

"Those are spots," the nice, patient vet told us of the weird discolorations. "You have a spotted dog."

"Oh," I said. "I thought maybe it was tar. We crossed a street the other night that had some freshly filled potholes and I thought—"

"They're spots," the vet said. We were charged another seventy-five dollars.

(Which was a bargain if you think about it; plus, the vet was cute.)

These early episodes did not dissuade me from continuing to imagine the worst-case scenarios. In June, I worried about heartworm and ringworm; in July, it was fractures and fleas. In August, my biggest paranoia, the thing that kept me up most at nights, became foxtails and burrs. Foxtails and other barbed seed-heads, I read, could easily penetrate the skin and travel down the ear canals or up the genital tract, causing "irritation, abscesses, serious tissue damage, and/or infection." In extreme cases, I read, foxtails have been known to puncture the organs, including the brain. This was not an image I could easily forget, and it didn't help that the warning signs—excessive sneezing, scratching at the ears, pawing at the nose, shaking the head—were gestures that Rex, or any dog for that matter, made with a regularity that could drive someone like me insane.

Which brings us up to the present. "He's sneezing all the time!" I began to say on a daily basis. My voice got screechier each time.

"We live in New York City," Ted said. "In a ground-floor apartment. We like to keep our windows open, under the guise of getting some fresh air. Our apartment is full of dust and car exhaust. Of course he sneezes."

"We need to take him to the vet *now*! He could have a foxtail embedded in his nostrils."

"Are you sure a foxtail hasn't punctured *your* brain?" Ted said.

His biggest paranoia was the rising cost of veterinary treatments, and after the seventh or eighth office visit it was clear we had divided into two camps. There was sense and then there was nonsense, and in Ted's opinion I was full of the latter.

Then Rex began to lick himself. Well, okay, he was always licking himself. (We have all heard the joke that starts with the question "Why does a dog lick his balls?" and ends with the punch line "Because he can!") But Rex's behavior seemed unusual to me. Like, kind of obsessive/compulsive. Plus, Rex didn't have balls. He was licking something far more, um, pointed.

I rushed to my *Hypochondriac's Guide to Overprotective Dog Care*.

"If your dog begins to lick himself excessively," I read, "and has a purulent, foul-smelling discharge coming from the prepuce, he may be suffering from balanoposthitis." My eyes widened and I looked over at Rex, who sure enough was licking himself again. I read the sentence a few more times, trying to figure out exactly what amount of licking constituted "excessive." It didn't say. So then there was the matter of the discharge. I hadn't noticed any per se; but then again I hadn't looked.

Ted walked in the door as I was conducting my prepucal inspection.

"What are you doing?" he shouted. His voice was screechy.

I was positioned much like an auto mechanic under a car. Rex was busy with the task of cleaning out the inside of a Häagen-Dazs carton that I had given him to keep him occupied during the physical exam.

"I'm smelling his pee-pee," I said. "For a purulent, foul-smelling discharge. Come here, do you think it smells funny?"

"Stop it! You're acting crazy."

I sat up. "I think something's wrong with him. He won't stop licking himself."

"Nothing's wrong with him."

"What does *purulent* mean, anyway, do you know?"

"I have no idea," Ted said. He sat cautiously on the analyst's couch. "Rex, come over here. Stay away from your mother."

I stood and walked over to the bookshelves.

"What are you doing?" Ted asked, hugging the dog protectively.

"I'm going to find out what *purulent* means."

"Would you stop it?"

I faced Ted with my hands on my hips. "Why don't you two go for a *walk?*" I said the latter word loudly, so that Rex would react. The word *walk* sent Rex into a tizzy of barking and spinning, and Ted had no choice but to take him out. End of discussion.

Over the next few days, Rex kept up with his licking. And I kept up with my research. I discovered that "a small amount of cloudy, yellowish discharge is not unusual in mature males," but that "an excessive purulent discharge is associated with overt infection."

"Well, there's the word *excessive* again," I said to Ted that night. "And *purulent.* What constitutes a normal amount of discharge?"

Rex settled onto the sofa and began to lick, lick, lick himself again.

"Don't look at me," Ted said.

Then I read: " 'If the puslike discharge is dripping directly from the penis opening, the condition is probably more serious. You should look for foreign material, such as foxtails, inside the prepuce of affected dogs.' " I put the book down. "Foxtails!"

Ted grimaced at the thought. History books are rife with references to Achilles' heel, but they never discuss a man's real vulnerable hot-spot: the Achilles' urethra. "He does not have a foxtail stuck up there," Ted said. "It's impossible."

"How do you know?"

"Because we haven't been anywhere near foxtails. A foxtail couldn't survive in East River Park. I think they grow only in the Pacific Northwest."

"Well, it could be something else."

"But nothing is dripping. You're overreacting here."

At this moment, I swear, something green dripped from Rex's privates.

"Look!" I shouted to Ted, pointing. "Did you see that?"

Rex ceased his licking for a moment and stared at me, a somewhat guilty look on his face. Then he looked over at Ted, rolled his eyes, and lapped up the evidence. He buried his snout in his crotch and resumed with the licking, making a lewd snuffling sound.

"Something is wrong," I said. "I know it." I produced a diagram entitled HOW TO EXPOSE THE PENIS, which illustrated how you were supposed to seize your dog's privates with both hands and push one part forward (the penis) and pull another part back (the prepuce). Having been raised Catholic, I had a hard time even reading those words.

"Here," I said to Ted, pushing the book toward him. "You do it."

"But nothing's wrong with him. He's licking himself. He's a dog."

"But he has a discharge! And when the discharge is excessive, perhaps greenish or odorous, and the dog licks at his prepuce excessively, these are signs of balanoposthitis." I was now waving the book in the air like a preacher with his Bible. "So someone is going to have to extract that prepuce and it's not going to be me!" Rex stood, belched, and then lumbered off to the other room.

🐾 🐾

Because I had to show up at my temp job, it was Ted who had to take Rex to the vet the next day. This is what transpired, secondhand:

DR. MARTER: So, what seems to be the problem today?

TED: Well, my dog is licking himself a lot. On his penis?

DR. MARTER: *(raising his bifocals to look at chart)* He's a male dog, right?

TED: Yes.

DR. MARTER: Well, that's what male dogs do.

TED: Yes, but my girlfriend said she saw—

DR. MARTER: Girlfriends *(pauses to regard Ted over bifocals)* know nothing of licking.

Pan to close-up of Ted's face, burning with embarrassment

It took several years for me to live down this story, and for Ted to get over the humiliation of having brought the dog in in the first place. And of having to pay two hundred dollars for the privilege. He vowed never to listen to me again.

I soon noticed that they seemed to have the same opinion of me at the veterinary clinic. From that point on, every time I brought Rex in for an appointment we got the New Vet, the one who had graduated from Cornell like the week before. And this is not to say Rex got inferior treatment; it's just that I started to wonder: Was I not being taken seriously? Did they see me as a Crazy Dog Lady? How could this be possible when I was only twenty-nine?

Very early on in his career in "The English Setter Patient" (another cutesy nickname Ted had come up with after the thirteenth or fourteenth visit to the vet), Rex had received a written warning of sorts. Ted and I weren't even aware of this, until we discovered in July that someone at the vet's office had written CAUTION in black magic marker at the top of Rex's chart. We're pretty sure we know why he had received the CAUTION warning (it's a long story involving a muzzle and a bordetella shot that I don't have the room to describe here). But I began to wonder if that CAUTION referred to me.

Not even Rex took me seriously. If I, say, admonished him for eating his food too quickly, he'd eat even faster, attempting to finish off his breakfast before I had even placed the dish squarely on the floor. Like many dogs, Rex gulped down his food as if at any moment, six adolescent wolves were going to burst forth from the kitchen cabinets and try to steal it away. (Thus the verb *to wolf.*) But this, I had read, was not healthy. "Hey! Don't eat so quickly," I'd say. "You might get volvulus." He ignored me and continued to wolf. Clearly, *volvulus* was not one of Rex's twenty-three words.

"If you eat too quickly," I continued, "your stomach could bloat, and then distend, and then twist on its axis, and that's life threatening, and we'd have to rush you to the vet. Do you want to have to go to the vet?"

In two more swift gulps he finished his food off, lapped up some water, and then delivered a solid belch. He knew the word *vet* but pretended that he didn't. The belch I took as an insult. And a secret signal that he sided with Ted.

Without the cooperation of either my boyfriend or my dog, I had no outlet for my hypochondria and therefore started to get discouraged. I had pretty much given up on the idea that I would ever be able to properly care for Rex. Or anyone.

And it's usually when you are feeling discouraged and disheartened, when you are convinced that you haven't emotionally progressed beyond the age of sixteen, that a member of your family calls and asks you to visit.

That August, my sister and her husband were taking their first vacation in over seven years. She asked if I would come look after her two young daughters and their perfect yellow Lab. I was overjoyed. First of all, I was flattered that my sister would entrust her two children to me, and secondly I looked forward to spending a week on the Cape. There would be bike rides to the beach in the morning, blueberry picking at dusk, ice cream and fried clams in the early evenings, and then leisurely walks around the cranberry bog with the dogs.

And it was a lovely week, despite the fact that I felt inadequate as a substitute parent. I had always thought that children loved chaos, loved to defy order, and loved to eat candy for lunch, but not my nieces. They, bless their hearts, found true stability in the routines my sister had set up for them. So instead of taking delight in the fact that I was not a rule enforcer, that I was the Cool Aunt, the Fun Aunt, they took it upon themselves to enforce the rules. When I told them the first morning that they could get their own breakfasts (which would have been a thrill to me as a child, as I was not allowed to eat anything other than what my father dictated, which was usually unsweetened wheat squares), they just looked at me with perplexity. "Mom always makes us fruit salad for breakfast," they said. "Mom always makes us banana bran muffins from scratch."

"Mom always gives us lunch at twelve," they would say at three o'clock, with their stomachs rumbling. "Mom always brings sunscreen to the beach," they would say at high noon, as the sun's harmful UV rays beat down upon our fair, white skin.

"It's a good thing I don't have children of my own," I said to my friend Jaylin that night on the telephone. "Can you believe I forgot to feed them dinner? My poor nieces. My sister would have been better off leaving them with a chimpanzee."

"It's understandable," Jaylin said.

"But how do people do it?" I said. "How do people have children? How do you keep track of all these things you're supposed to do and know? How many child-rearing manuals did *you* have to read before your first son was born?"

"None," she said. "I didn't have time. Mothering is just a wisdom we all have within us. You'll see. It's there."

But I didn't believe her. Take my wisdom with Rex for instance:

On the first day of our visit, he basically tried to run my sister's dog Bailey out of town. Bailey was one of those irresistible dogs who uses her whole body to wag her tail. She was pure, honey-colored happiness, and she had enough love to spare for everybody, great and small. So Rex could not have been presented with a more benign dog in a more welcoming setting, and yet he acted, well, beastly. When they first met, Bailey came out of the house all happy and excited and ready to play. "Look, Bay-Bay," my nieces said in singsong voices. "There's your cousin Rex. Go meet your cousin Rex!" Bailey wagged her tail and her body and approached Rex welcomingly, without caution or guile. Yet Rex remained tense, with his tail raised, his forelegs and shoulders rigid. I assumed he would know a cream puff when he saw one. But he didn't. When Bailey came up and licked his lips he growled at her, and when she jumped back, startled, he snapped, and continued snapping as he chased the confused Bailey toward the woods. She hid under the porch for the remainder of our stay.

There were other violations. By the second day of our visit, Rex had burst through a screen door, stolen all Bailey's rawhide chews, and shredded two of my nieces' favorite towels. He played tug-of-war with those towels with a savagery that caused me great alarm. He played as if his life depended on it, as if losing meant he would be thrown to the lions, as if winning meant he could eat his opponent for dessert. I began to wonder if he had seen too many episodes of *Gladiator* with Ted.

"Do you think he'll grow up to be one of those Columbine kids?" I asked Jaylin on the phone that night. "Those Columbine dogs?"

"Just don't let him listen to Goth."

"This afternoon I was reading yet another dog-training manual, and I read that dog aggression is a result of"—and here I adopted an authoritative dog-trainer voice—"*mismanagement by humans.* That some humans don't have the personality to handle a dominant dog."

"Your personality is perfect. Don't upset yourself. He's just a dog," Jaylin said.

Would that Rex were just a dog. He seemed like so much more. He was all my secret fears and failures personified. As Rex got down on his belly and tried to snake his way under the porch to get at poor Bailey, I thought of something I had read in a puppy-training book: If you can't get your dog to come to you when you call, this book questioned, how can you expect your husband to come home from a bar at night? If you can't get your dog to come back to you, how will you get your kids off to the school bus on time in the mornings? If you can't house-train a puppy, how will you potty-train a child? Or control a teenager? It dawned on me that if I ever did have children, the potential was there for my children to walk all over me. In fact, when my children reached their teenage years, they would probably hold me up at gunpoint and force me out of the house. And I, not wanting to hurt their feelings, would let them keep the keys.

"He's just acting out because I'm not there," Ted said over the phone later that night. "He needs his alpha around to maintain control."

I didn't respond. I detected a note of nya-nya in his voice.

"You need to alpha-roll him when he's aggressive with your sister's dog."

"I would if I could catch him. He runs too fast."

"Wait, you've been letting him off-leash?" Ted said.

"Yes," I said. "My sister lives on a dirt road, near a little horse farm. Her nearest neighbors live in one of those earth-bermed houses that's underground."

"I know, but you still shouldn't let him off-leash. What if something frightens him and he takes off? What if he gets hit by a car?"

"He's not going to get hit by a car."

"Don't argue with me. Why can't you just do what I say? Don't let him off-leash."

I decided to let Ted have his way. It made sense, after all. But the thing was, Rex hated to be tethered. At the beach, when I tied him to a stake in the sand, he threw what can only be called a tantrum: barking and muttering and digging a huge hole of frustration in the sand. He kicked sand all over my *New Yorkers*. And a family sitting next to us moved their towels.

Then, back at my sister's house, I confined him to the porch so that I could take my nieces out for some fried clams and ice cream. This was taken as an outrage, and as we drove off, he let out the classic Roger Daltrey yowl and hopped along on his hind legs while paddling his forelegs along the porch rail. "He's playing the piano!" my younger niece said.

I loved how my nieces managed to turn all of Rex's antics into something fun and funny. But his behavior made me feel out of control. I decided to start letting Rex off-leash again and simply not tell Ted about it. It was easier to let the dog do what he wanted than to try to control him, I reasoned. Just as it was easier for some parents to let their wilder children govern themselves.

Rex seemed to appreciate the freedom. He *loved* the Cape. There were so many new smells for him to discover: salt water, lobster rolls, fried clams. There were so many new sounds, too: the peepers in the cranberry bogs, thick layers of cicadas purring in the trees. I loved to watch the way he'd lift his ears and jerk his head around, surprised by all the strange things that surrounded him. His senses had awakened. So much so that on Wednesday morning, when he saw his first butterfly, he tried to catch it, prancing and leaping across the lawn. He looked just like a happy little puppy, a dog seizing the day. I immediately called Ted to tell him about it.

"Was he on a leash?" he said.

"No." Then I added quickly: "But he was on the deck."

My nieces enjoyed Rex's freedom, too. They were happy, loving, sunny children who loved to hug and skip and play. Their skin always smelled faintly of strawberry bath soap and their bathing suits were always slightly damp. If I ever had children, I told myself, I hoped they'd be just like them. They took such delight in my dog's antics! They giggled when he chased Bailey. They cooed his name as he barked at them. They ran around the yard in gleeful mania when he shredded their towels. They loved his white ear/brown ear combo and the big fluffy spot on his rump, which they called his scratch patch. They gave him all sorts of nicknames based on the different flavors of ice cream his brown and white markings represented: Chocolate Chip, Vanilla Fudge Swirl, Rocky Road. Miraculously, Rex tolerated them and let them scratch him on his scratch patch, and he allowed them to praise his cuteness and his dashing good looks. He even stood still long enough to allow my older niece to draw a picture of him (which was very good) and my younger niece to count his toes. But then, on the third day, while I was sitting on the sofa reading an old *New Yorker,* and the dog and the kids were just a few feet from me on the rug, my younger niece suddenly said, "Ow, he bit me!"

"He bit you?" I said. I rushed over and scooped her up. She was a sweet, soulful eight-year-old with a velvety voice.

"He didn't *bite* her," my older niece said. She was an irresistible imp who, as the older sibling, thought she ran the show. "He snapped in her *general* direction. Dogs do that, my mom says, when they want to be left alone. He missed."

"It didn't hurt," my younger niece said. I hugged her and stuck my face into her hair. Her hair smelled faintly of the Atlantic Ocean—a scent so vast and eternal I wanted to cry. I wasn't the Cool Aunt at all, I realized; I was the Lame Aunt. The Dangerous Aunt. "Let's get an ice cream," I said.

"You can't let him go around biting children," Ted said that night.

"Duh!"

"Did you alpha-roll him?"

"Yes, I alpha-rolled him." I left out the part about Rex trying to gnaw me on the wrists as I flipped him over. Plus, it didn't hurt. All I could do was pray to make it through Saturday before anyone got killed.

Friday morning, I was lying on the lawn, reading a manuscript and occasionally marveling (as city people will) at the smell and feel and the color of the grass. Most city people, you may have noticed, will often lie facedown in country grass, drinking it in, getting drunk on its very aliveness. Nearby, my nieces played on the waterslide, while Rex and Bailey were down by the cranberry bog, traipsing around with a giant wolfhound puppy who lived down the road. This pup's goofy presence, or perhaps his size, had sedated Rex somehow, and he no longer lunged at Bailey. Perhaps my dog, too, was drunk on grass. So, it felt, for a moment, that all was well. I began to think maybe I could have children. Why, birthing a child might be a zillion times easier than birthing a book. I kept putting my manuscript down to smile at my nieces and check up on the dogs. The air had a lazy, end-of-day quality to it, soft and supple, and in the distance lawn mowers hummed and the birds had started their evening song. My nieces giggled, a musical, uplifting sound that evoked a lost childhood of purity and innocence. Intermittently, the dogs barked.

But then, my younger niece suddenly ran up to me and said, "Aunt Lee, Rex is limping." And sure enough, there was Rex, hobbling toward me on three legs from the bottom of the hill. The wolfhound pup (named Sasquatch) ran worriedly alongside him like some buck-toothed neighbor, with an "I didn't do it" look on his face. Rex came right over to me—to me!—and presented me with his paw. Suddenly I was surrounded by two children and three dogs, all of them panting from the swift climb up the hill, all of them expecting me to somehow know what to do. Never had I felt so inadequate. Never had I been so aware that I was an adult, at least in theory. In the distance, a pair of seagulls called to each other, and it sounded mocking. The salt air suddenly felt harsh and abrasive. I took Rex's paw in my hand to inspect it, thinking that I had to at least go through the motions of a competent person, and Rex, at least on the surface, seemed willing to go along with the charade. He licked the hand that held his paw. But when I turned Rex's foot over I saw right away that he simply had a thorn in one of his pads. A rosebush thorn stuck right smack in the center. And so I pulled it out.

"There you go," I said to Rex. "You're fine now." Rex gave me one wet kiss and then tore off down the hill again with his pals, to menace the seagulls who had dared laugh.

"You did it!" my younger niece said. "You fixed him."

I smiled. "I did!"

I looked down at the thorn in my hand, feeling extravagantly proud and competent. My pride was disproportionate, of course, but still I let it move through my veins and settle somewhere inside me. I put the thorn in my pocket so that no one would ever step on it again.

I pulled my niece onto my lap and stroked her sun-warmed hair. Together we watched Rex and his pals frolic. Rex was a broken dog, fixed.

CHAPTER 10

The Curse of the
Three-Headed Dog

There is a fable which tells the story of a slave named Androcles, who escaped his master and sought refuge in the forest. There, he encountered a ferocious lion, which, much to Androcles' surprise came toward the man whimpering and holding up his paw. Androcles inspected the raw and swollen paw and found a thorn embedded. From there on in the lion was his friend. Eventually, however, Androcles was captured by his master and, as punishment, thrown into the arena with the lions. There he met again his friend, who forbade the other lions to kill him, and thus Androcles' life was spared, and he was set free. Sometimes I wonder if that lion ever had regrets about agreeing to trust Androcles. I wonder if Androcles ever forced his large virile lion to wear a silly hat.

It was time to play dress-up with my dog. Poor thing—there was no end to the ways I wanted to poke him and prod him and play with his ears. I spent hours staring at this gorgeous specimen of a canine. I was *besotted* with him. I loved the little yin-yang marking on his forehead. I loved his tiny white whiskers, his brown nose, his mismatched ears. I loved the fact that his patches of brown fur were inexplicably softer than his white fur, as if they came from a separate source. And I loved his floppy lips. These lips were pink and speckled with little spots of brown. Mr. Leeps, I began to call him. (We had hundreds of nicknames for him by then—a new one every week.)

"Who has pink leeps?" I'd say to Rex in my special dog voice. "Who has pink spotted leeps?"

"Leave him alone," Ted would say. "He doesn't like it when you poke at his face like that."

"At least I'm not dyeing him pink," I said. (That was the latest trend I had spotted at Bryant Park.)

I loved to stroke the complicated folds of skin and fur under his muzzle. I loved to touch his toenails—some white, some brown. I loved, especially, to wrap his shaggy ears up around his head, like a pillbox hat, and call him Aunt Mabel. Or Jackie O. "Who's so chic?" I'd say, kissing his snoutie. "Who's so Jackie O in his little pillbox hat?" Poor Rex had to restrain himself from snapping like in the good old days. Sometimes he'd groan a little; sometimes he'd try to swat me away with his paws, but mostly he just lay there, sighing with resignation and looking miserable. I had become something he had to endure.

"Would you stop?" Ted said. "He hates it."

"He loves it! So terrible," I'd say to the dog. "So terrible to get so much attention. So terrible to be the most handsome dog in the world."

There was a tiny whorl at the center of Rex's chest, a vortex of fur at which all of the hair of his body—and all of his life—seemed to originate. It was this part of Rex I loved best. In Chinese tradition, there is a center of creation in each person that is called the Dan Tian, and I liked to think of this little whorl as Rex's Dan Tian. At night, I would tickle him there, to stimulate his life force, to ensure a long and healthy life.

"For the love of God," Ted would call from the bedroom. "It's midnight! You've been poking at him for two hours! Can you leave him alone? I'm calling the humane society and turning you in."

"All right, all right. I'll come poke at you for a while."

Into the bedroom went I, to pay attention to my boyfriend. But not before kissing the dog about eighty more times.

Yes, we had tamed the lion. I could rub my dry nose against his wet one. I could stick my fingers in his mouth. I could get him to show me his bottom teeth, which I called "teefs" because they were so babylike and nonthreatening and cute. "Let me see those little teefs" became the Rex phrase of the week, followed by Ted's refrain: "Could you stop sticking your hands in his mouth?"

No, I could not. I taught him the command "Show us your teefs." Then I taught him to roll over and "show us the belly." This was a posture of submission, you may recall, he had not been willing to assume unless it was by force (or St. George). We taught him next to shake hands with other people, which he did grudgingly, like a businessman being forced to make a deal. So in other words, Rex was becoming a circus act. This was a clear sign that I had advanced to Stage IV of becoming a Crazy Dog Lady. But so what? Poking at my dog was my favorite thing in the world to do.

Then, in mid-October, I saw a sign for a Halloween costume contest for dogs! Halloween is by far my favorite holiday, and there's nothing like Halloween in New York City. After all, New York is home to some of the most artistic and creative people on the planet, most of whom will jump at any opportunity to put on a show. Consider the city's eight hundred thousand drag queens, who, just to take a trip to the deli, will put on seven-inch platforms, a sequined butterfly jacket, and a two-foot wig. Now try to imagine such people at Halloween.

In the weeks before this most hallowed holiday, the whole city— not just the queens in Queens—starts to pulsate with a randy, edgy excitement. Shop windows are crammed with bondage gear, feather boas, brocaded undies, and big-hair wigs, the likes of which you haven't seen since the eighties, when heavy metal was all the rage. Disco can be heard thumping through the walls of even the remotest apartments, and even the men of Wall Street break out their DayGlo ties. All those flamboyant colors, sequins, feathers, and rubber masks can bring out anyone's inner drag queen.

And it isn't any different for the dog people. There are more than thirty dog runs in the city, and therefore more than thirty annual doggie costume parades. Each run in the city has its own flavor, and our neighborhood run, called First Run because it was the first dog run established in New York City, was known for 1) the youth of its doggie parents (most were East Village kids in their twenties); 2) the number of pit bull mixes (most of the young doggie parents adopted pits from the Center for Animal Care and Control or found them on the streets); 3) the number of dog brawls that occurred daily; and 4) its legendary First Run Annual Halloween Costume Contest, which drew the likes of Iggy Pop and Lou Reed.

When I first saw the sign for this contest, I stopped dead in my tracks. In that moment, I felt my entire universe expand. Dogs in costume! What fun! What joy! I told Ted in no uncertain terms that we had to go.

"You're not thinking of dressing Rex in a costume."

"Of course I am."

"He'll hate it."

"No he won't. He'll think it's fun. Oh, we have to go!" I said. "We'll be hip!"

I managed to convince Ted to let me create a costume by promising that I would do all the morning walks for one straight week. We—or rather I—had decided to dress him up like a little hiker. I think it all started with this brown wool hippie hat that Ted had worn in his stoner days. The hat had been hand-knit in Peru, and was slightly pointy on top, and had two strings that you could tie under your chin. I suggested we put it on Rex, just for kicks.

"He looks so cute," I shouted. "Oh my God. Get the camera before he shakes the hat off."

"The poor boy," Ted said. "How humiliating for him." But still Ted got the camera.

The rest of Rex's Halloween costume quickly fell into place. Rex already had his own little backpack, for camping trips, and Ted agreed to donate a pair of ratty old hiking shorts he'd been meaning to throw away. He started to have regrets about the whole thing, however, when I spent thirty dollars on a little wool sweater and cut strategic holes in his shorts to accommodate Rex's tail and privates. (Men just don't like scissors going near crotches, I guess.) But by then it was too late. The contest was one day away.

"You're going overboard," he said the next morning as I gussied up Rex. "Everyone else will probably show up with their dogs in cat ears and witch hats."

"So what?" I said. "We'll win." For a final touch, I put a Catskills trail guide in the pocket of Rex's backpack, so that there would be no doubt that he was a hiker.

That Saturday itself was one of those perfect fall days you read about: crisp, cool, clear, with the scent of autumn leaves and hot cider doughnuts lingering in the air. I insisted on dressing up Rex at the apartment and couldn't contain my excitement at the cuteness of it all. I started to have visions of Rex being in the movies, of his starring in dog-food commercials, of his face gracing millions of cutesy-dog greeting cards. A photographer from the *Times* would definitely be at the contest—one came every year. So maybe finally I'd get my picture in that paper. With my award-winning dog. "Oh my God, he's so cute!" I said for the millionth time. "Will you take a picture of him before we leave? It's his first party, in his first party suit."

"Let's not prolong the torture," Ted said. "The poor boy." Admittedly, Rex looked downtrodden, as if he wished he had nothing to do with the human world. He kept lifting his eyelids, and twisting his head left to right, trying to figure out what was on top of his head. He also tried to pull off the backpack with his mouth, but he couldn't quite reach.

"Let's just go!" Ted said.

I enjoyed all the attention we got on our twenty-minute walk to the dog run, but Ted clearly did not. "Look at that dog!" people on the sidewalks exclaimed. "That's so funny!" All around us, people laughed and pointed and smiled. I basked in their praise; I enjoyed being in the spotlight, even indirectly. But Ted seemed pained.

"He's such a dignified dog," he kept saying as we walked through the East Village. "This isn't right. You're humiliating him. He's going to grow up to be a pansy. He's going to be like Hemingway, who was all screwed up because his grandmother dressed him in girlie clothes."

"No he's not," I said, undaunted. I stopped to talk to strangers and told everyone endearing little anecdotes about Rex. "He used to be a shelter dog," I would begin. "And he used to hate us. And he would never let us touch his head. And now look at him with his little hat. . . ."

"Rex, come," Ted would say, pulling on the leash.

"Rex was enjoying himself," I said to Ted when I caught up to him.

"That's because that woman petting him had a doughnut in her hand."

"No it's not. It's because she told him he was cute."

On and on this went, all the way to the park. It wasn't until a horde of pretty girls in go-go boots ran up to Ted to ask what kind of dog Rex was that the tight, slightly pained look left Ted's face.

When we reached the grassy area of Tompkins Square Park, Rex immediately went into hunting mode. His steps slowed, his torso sank lower to the ground, and his nose twitched with the precision of a sonograph as he picked up subtle scents. You could tell he had forgotten he had a little ski cap on, and a backpack, and a toddler's sweater, and silly shorts. "Look at him stalking those squirrels!" the girls in the go-go boots called out.

"Poor Rex," Ted muttered. "The poor emasculated boy." But this hadn't stopped him from bringing along his video camera. He followed Rex along, zooming in for close-ups, as Rex crept slowly toward a squirrel.

When we finally reached the dog run, I was astounded at what I saw. You're always going to find, at every canine Halloween contest across the country, a Lab in Christmas antlers, and one or two Dog-zillas, and a golden retriever in a store-bought Yankees cap. But try to picture a Harlequin Great Dane dressed up as a giant sunflower. Or a matted gray Shih Tzu dressed as a mop and accompanied by a short gay man dressed as a frumpy housewife. The costumes were spectacular. There was a shepherd mix in a curly black wig and Gene Simmons makeup, wearing a tiny leather jacket embossed with the logo KISS. There was a couple dressed up like farmers, carrying baskets of produce, and tucked among the vegetables was a tiny Chihuahua in a pea-pod costume, shivering nervously the way Chihuahuas do. There were pit bulls sporting cow udders, and six dachshunds spray-painted yellow to look like a bunch of bananas, accompanied by a giant man in a gorilla suit. "Wow," Ted said. "I'm impressed."

"I'm *depressed*," I said. One of the great, but also one of the rotten, things about New York City is that no matter how creative you are, no matter how talented or clever or smart, there's always going to be someone out there who's smarter and more talented and more creative than you. Every second of every day.

"Uh-oh," Ted said, teasingly. He pointed toward a malamute in a little brown uniform who approached us, hauling a miniature brown truck that said UPS. "It's a UPS truck. Hold on to the dog!"

Rex threw himself onto his back and tried to rub the backpack off in the dirt. He twisted and shimmied, legs flailing like a break-dancer's.

"Hey, cut it out!" I said. "That sweater cost money."

"Look at *that* costume!" Ted said. And there I beheld my nemesis. Across the run, wearing expensive Gucci sunglasses and surrounded by adoring fans, was a man with a golden retriever, whom he had fashioned into a Three-Headed Dog. From a distance, the two extra heads looked realistic, and they continued to look lifelike even as we got close. "How did you do that?" someone asked. "With Styrofoam," he explained. The crowd surrounding him was now three deep. "I do special effects for Miramax." And he went on to describe how he had begun constructing the heads back in August, how he had required his dog, Butterscotch, to pose for an hour each evening as he painted her likeness on the busts, and how it had taken him three weeks to find the best "suspension mechanisms" to attach the heads to Butterscotch's collar. Then of course he had to go out and find the perfect cape to conceal the suspension mechanisms. And the cape had come from Shanghai Tang (a high-end Asian-themed boutique on Madison).

"That shawl had to have cost six hundred dollars," I said to Ted as we slunk away. "And did you see that the eyes on the Styrofoam heads actually blinked?"

"It's amazing," Ted said. "It's a technological marvel."

"I don't even have socks from Shanghai Tang," I said resentfully.

"Aw," Ted teased. "You're jealous."

"If I had known people were going to spend *six months* on their costumes, I would have put more effort into Rex's."

"There's always next year," he said.

When we got to the registration desk, we found out we had to have a name for Rex's costume. I hadn't thought of a *name*. To me, Rex looked like a little hippie kid, a Trustafarian going off on a hike. "How about Happy Camper?" I said to Ted.

And don't they always say First Thought, Best Thought? Because then, for some reason, I decided that I needed to have a more literary name. Something more clever and tongue-in-cheek. I thought then of Jon Krakauer, the author of *Into the Wild*. "What does Jon Krakauer have to do with a dog in a wool cap?" Ted said. "No one is going to know what you're talking about." But I reasoned that we were in the East Village, a neighborhood full of artists and writers and tortured souls. Any of the above would certainly have heard of Jon Krakauer, because *Into the Wild* was the book of the moment, and Mr. Krakauer was the current "it" writer, an outdoorsman who would soon spawn millions of imitators, all of them writing about the dangers and perils of the great outdoors.

So we—or rather I—registered Rex as "Jon Krakauer." Ted gave me that look I call "The Crow." We took our place in line to wait for the parade to begin.

The contest began with everyone parading their dogs around the perimeter of the run in a group, after which the contestants circled the perimeter one by one. The whole dog run was lined with giddy onlookers who hooted and clapped and cheered as each contestant was called forth. The sound of so much applause was uplifting, and suddenly I was having a good time again, but then Rex's name (and the name of his costume) was called. The MC said: "And here's Rex the English setter mix, posing as, um, Jon Kra . . . Jon Cracker I guess?" The crowd, who had just been cheering madly for the mastiff-as-ballerina before us, fell silent. In this void, I told Rex to heel and we promenaded along. I smiled nervously and fakely, like a beauty-pageant contestant who has just found out she was eliminated after the first round. The applause was polite at best. I tried to make eye contact with Ted, who was out there somewhere with the onlookers, but I couldn't find him in the crowd. Rex, miraculously, held his Heel.

Then our moment was over. Rex and I returned to our place in line, and some other dog's name was called. "Those were our fifteen minutes of fame," I said to Rex. "And it was only about sixty seconds long."

The Three-Headed Dog won, of course, and soon his costume designer was surrounded by photographers from the *Post* and the *Times*. I took off Rex's shorts and backpack so he could go hump the ballerina and bite other dogs' necks.

"I should have just called him the Happy Camper," I said to Ted, folding the shorts and the hat into my bag. "At least people would have had a clue."

A crowd surrounded the Three-Headed Dog man, and people were congratulating him over and over again. He seemed a bit too proud of his achievement, a bit too smug. He had not once taken off his Gucci sunglasses.

Ted thought the whole thing was hilarious. "Jon Krakauer," he said over and over again. "*Into the Wild!*" He trained the video camera on me and said: "This is Lee after Rex just lost the Halloween contest. This is a stage mother, crushed."

"Turn that thing off!" I said.

As we were leaving the park, a nice young woman came up to me and touched my shoulder. "I thought yours was the best costume," she said.

"Really?" I turned to her and smiled. She had a great short haircut and a pair of those funky black eyeglasses that are the staple of all New York editorial assistants.

"*He* should have won first place," she said.

"Thanks."

"See?" I said to Ted as we passed through the park gates. "Some people got it." I was happy all over again. It felt like she had asked for my autograph.

"Yes," Ted said. "One in twelve hundred people gets you." He put his arm around me. "Make that two."

Rex, as if he understood us, turned around at that moment and looked at us with what we called his treat face.

"Make that three," Ted said.

We went, then, to an expensive French bistro on Avenue A, and sat outside at a café table with our tired, humiliated dog. The service was excellent, and in French, and the food was exceptional. Ted had steak frites. I had a poached sole. Rex got pieces of buttered baguette and a few fries. I wasn't really dressed for the occasion—I was in my dog-run clothes—but who cared? We had a bottle of wine on the table—a pretty good cabernet—and a bouquet of roses.

Such restaurants always put Ted in a good mood—well-prepared food helped reaffirm his cherished belief that the world was a properly functioning place. And soon he was saying he was glad he had come out today. "Look at you staying under the table like a Parisian dog," Ted said to Rex, giving him the last bite of his steak. "Who's sitting under the table like a good boy? Who's a café dog?"

"Let's make today Rex's birthday!" I suddenly said. "Why not? We don't really know when he was born—he's probably one year old by now. And it would be so fun to have his birthday on Halloween."

"I'm fine with that," Ted said. "Halloween is a good day for a birthday."

"But wait. Maybe we should make it next week, so that we can plan the party ahead of time. We could get little hats and balloons and one of those liver-flavored cakes."

"Please," Ted said. "Let's just get him some special food for the way home. Liver and bacon or something."

"Let's order another steak frites!"

"Good idea."

And so, arm in arm, we headed home, with a genuine doggie bag in Ted's free hand. Rex trotted alongside that hand, making little leaps, because he was so excited at the special birthday meal that lay ahead. The window boxes along First Avenue overflowed with chrysanthemums and pumpkins and decorative squash, all in their final bursts of color before the decay of the winter set in. We passed one of those makeshift churches, a high-spirited Baptist church in a storefront that had once been occupied by a florist. The music was so loud and energetic we could hear it through the closed doors. They sang, "Hallelujah! Glory be!" Rex leapt up and grabbed his leash and began to trot more quickly, as if to hurry us home. "Leash biting should not be tolerated!" Ted said, quoting our old acquaintances the Monks of Steel. But he was laughing. I laughed too.

So we hadn't won any prizes. But Rex had a dog-smile on his face.

"Who's having a birthday party?" Ted said. "Who doesn't have to wear a hat ever again?"

I didn't tell Ted that I was already plotting next year's costume—a lime green gown, a dusting of bronzer on his fur, a blond wig, à la Dogatella Versace. But we had plenty of time for that.

CHAPTER 11

We Are Not Responsible

When I was in college, my best male friends had a sign in their group house that said: WE ARE NOT RESPONSIBLE. The rest of it—which probably said something to the effect of FOR ITEMS LEFT BEYOND 30 DAYS—had been torn, or burned, or perhaps even chewed off. That was the kind of crowd I hung around with, and in those four years of our tight, intense friendships, *We Are Not Responsible* had been a sort of motto for us—a saying we found simultaneously hilarious and profound. But now I was almost thirty. I had a live-in boyfriend and I had a dog. So I had to finally ask myself: Wasn't it time to, like, move on?

We Are Not Responsible. I saw it in all my major life choices to date; I saw it in the fact that I didn't have health insurance or one of those—what are they called?—IRAs. I saw it in the way I neglected my horrifically mounting student loan bills, and how I justified that irresponsible neglect by telling myself I would be able to pay it off in one big chunk, once I sold my book and struck it rich. My financial situation, I always told myself, was *temporary*. In fact, any New Yorker will tell you that the reason they stay so long is that they believe their miserable career/relationship/living situations are temporary. You have to believe that the Big Change is right around the corner.

Ted always told me that I was a dreamer. That I didn't have a practical bone in my body. And I could never disagree. I didn't even see this as a flaw. I was an Aquarius, after all; he was a Sagittarius. Even before we met, our roles had been carved in stone. He would be the responsible one. I could float around with my head in the clouds. We complemented each other in that way. And we also had the potential to drive each other crazy for the rest of our lives.

That November I was assigned a new temp job. This time around it was at some banking-type place, for an executive who already had an executive assistant—Penelope—who in turn had harangued him into hiring an assistant for *her*. I was to report directly to the executive, however, which was fine with me. My job was to transcribe Mr. Bobkins's morning memos (from an actual Dictaphone), edit them for grammar, and then deliver them to his desk promptly at ten. Then I was done for the day. I spent three hours writing, one hour at lunch, and the remaining three hours talking to Ted on the phone about the dog. Mr. Bobkins was fine with all this. He liked me because I was pretty and had been honest with him about my desire to write. He also had a dog. "I like to see you young people realize your dreams," he said kindly. "Just don't let Penelope see you writing, or she'll have both our heads."

In the olden days—five months prior—I would have gotten a secret thrill out of having another opportunity to get away with something and to "beat the system." In the olden days, I would have enjoyed the scenario of Penelope appearing suddenly at my desk, and me, within seconds, minimizing my novel on the screen and revealing, underneath, a maximized memo. I would have enjoyed ignoring Penelope, and staring at this memo intently, as if the difference between using a comma or a semi-colon was going to cost thousands of jobs. But now, at that office, away from my doggie-dog, I began to realize that a potentially real life was getting away from me.

We Are Not Responsible. I saw it in the fact that I had been making my living as a temp for the past *three years*. Since graduate school, basically. All that time I had been telling myself that it was the writing aspect that made temping so attractive. (Believe me, there are thousands of writers in New York City who are forced to work at tiny desks underneath their loft beds, hunched over their keyboards like primates, without even enough room to stand up and stretch.) But now it was becoming more apparent that it was the noncommittal aspect of being a temp that most appealed to me. I did not have to get involved in office gossip or politics. I didn't even have to clarify the pronunciation or spelling of my name. Most people knew me as "the temp," and as the temp I could be anonymous, unaccountable, and paper-thin. I was beholden to no one, and no one was beholden to me. But without a true connection to anyone or anything, wouldn't I eventually disappear or melt away? Or, worse still, would I die alone, dogless, on the Bowery, without an IRA?

I pondered this for days. After I'd typed up Mr. Bobkins's morning memos, I'd stand at the window of this tall office building and gaze south toward the Lower East Side, feeling like Rapunzel trapped in a tower. Down there was my real life and my real dog. Up here I was surrounded by a bunch of men with cufflinks, who hovered too close to my desk and used terms like *due diligence* and said things to me like: "I sure could use some coffee. Wouldn't you like some coffee? I think the pot is low."

I'd always put my hand over the receiver and tell them all, "I'm on the phone." Then I'd go back to my conversation, not even trying to hide the fact that I was talking to Ted about the dog. "So how was your walkie?" I'd say, straightening out the photo on my desk—the one of Rex and me at Coney Island.

"Oh, it was great. On the way back from the park we stopped into that new dry cleaner's and they had a gerbil in there, in a little cage. It was spinning on that wheel, and the dog was mesmerized. He pressed his little nose against the cage and the stupid gerbil just kept on running along on his little wheel. And then Rex knocked the cage over, of course. You're going to have to pick up my dry cleaning from now on."

"What is he doing now?" I said, using my special Rex voice.

"He just had his dinner." Ted's Rex voice was musical and matter-of-fact.

"What did he have?"

"Food."

"Did he make a belchie?"

"Of course. It was a very good belchie. He's very talented."

We had a whole language, Ted and I. We knew how to discuss

Heidegger or the systematic annihilation of Tibet by the Chinese. But there was never any talk of worldly matters anymore. Instead:

"Did he make a poop-a? Was it stink-a?"

It was better than arguing, of course. It was better than *work*.

Clearly, I felt most alive during those eight-hour workdays when I was talking about the dog on the phone with Ted. I felt positively sizzling with life in the dog's actual presence. I was a true morning person now. I actually *liked* waking up. For the minute I opened my eyes, there would be the dog's face: smiling, alert, ready. Lord knows how long he'd been standing there, resting his chin on my pillow, waiting, waiting, waiting for me to get up, but I could tell by the slight motion of his head and the pillow that, behind him, he was wag-wag-wagging his tail. The morning swish, we called it. He waited there, panting with excitement, and his breath was warm and sour and completely tolerable. (Not like someone else's morning breath who shall not be named.) "How is it he knows when we've opened our eyelids?" Ted always said. "Is it possible he can hear it? Or does he just sense it in the way dogs do?"

Who cared how he knew? What mattered was that he did know. I loved being attended to like that. I loved having a being in my life who was interested in my every movement. This sentinel to my dreams.

You might say that waking up to that dog-face was the highlight of my day. Then, the second highlight: the morning walk. When you have a dog, especially when you have a dog in New York City, you are constantly re-astounded at what a pleasure a morning walk can be. All your stresses, all your worries, all the nagging tasks you have to accomplish that day . . . all this disappears when you are walking to the park with your dog. There's that dog-rump, first of all, bobbing along ahead of you. My dog's gait was chipper and purposeful, and he held his ears flattened back with pride. He didn't stop to sniff much on the way to the park. He didn't bother to say hello to other dogs. He just did his business and then hurried along, determined, focused, eyes straight ahead, like any New Yorker on his way to work. I never tired of seeing this dog's enthusiasm. Or of being part of it. Especially on work-a-day mornings, when most of the people we passed on the sidewalks looked miserable or pissed off or even murderous. Everyone walked with their jaws set, shoulders hunched, elbows close to their sides, in case they needed to hip-check anyone out of their way. Rex and I would cut through these hordes easily. He sat now at every intersection without my having to tell him, and once the traffic light turned green, and the entire seething mob on the sidewalk moved forward en masse, he always tried his damnedest to snake his way through, and to get to the front, which he seemed to think was his rightful place. The veritable leader—forgive the cliché—of the pack.

And I *loved* that Rex knew what was ahead of him. That he couldn't wait to get there. I loved that he now *expected* joy. He expected walks, he expected meals, he expected cuddles on the couch. And we delivered. We had given him a future, I realized. A future in which he knew all his needs would be met. And in exchange, he brought me into the present.

It's hard not to be in the moment when you are with a dog. If Rex stopped suddenly along the East River promenade and tensed his body, and lifted his head slightly toward the west and sniffed at the air, I would turn west, too. And I might see something I might not have seen had the dog not alerted me: the great white glare of sunlight on the World Trade Center towers, a bouquet of red balloons floating off toward New Jersey, a woman wearing the latest Tuleh dress. When he snuffled through the overgrown brush of the abandoned soccer fields, I caught glimpses of ferns and clover and morning dew. And just to see dew in New York City brings you down to earth. It reminds you that every day is a new day.

On those mornings, I'd return to the apartment with my senses heightened and my mind clear. I'd feel that life was simple and uncomplicated, that any obstacle I met that day and any day could be easily and swiftly overcome. Rex rejoiced at every turd or leaf he found, following any old course, not caring if he wasn't following any particular plan, and I tagged happily along. I realized the only thing that had stood in my way, all through my life, had been me. So what if I had never been the type of person who seized the day? So what if I had always been too shy, too fearful, too uncertain, too noncommittal, too doubtful to believe and expect that my needs would be met? I now seized the leash of a being that seized the day, which meant I was going somewhere. I could learn from this dog. He would take me along for the ride.

I started to show up at my temp job later and later. I started spending two hours at lunch, shopping at Century 21, not even bothering to hide the shopping bags even though I'd told them I had a dentist appointment. Most of the afternoons were spent on the Internet, reading about congenital diseases in spaniels and ordering expensive squeaky toys. When Penelope snuck up behind me to peek at my computer I wouldn't even bother to minimize my novel on the screen. I felt somehow beyond her now. I felt no need to pretend.

Was this irresponsible? Or was such behavior the first necessary step toward maturity?

"When was the first time you realized you were an adult?" I asked Tara.

"The first time someone called me ma'am."

Jaylin: "When I began to understand the cartoons in *The New Yorker*."

Ted: "When my parents got divorced and I realized I was on my own."

Me? I'd always assumed I'd be an adult when I had real furniture. But Rex had turned my attention outward somehow. I didn't quite believe that furniture was going to do the trick after all. Or clothing. Or cars. And that, I realized, is when you become an adult. Pre-adult years are those you spend in self-absorption, dedicating most of your waking hours to trying to figure out why you and the entire world are so fucked up. Pre-adult years are spent writing bad, mopey poetry, blaming your parents for your incurable mopiness, loneliness, and yearning, listening to Death Rock, and throwing your beer bottles out the window so that the police don't find them in your car. And then, suddenly, you realize you are done with all that. It is time. You realize it is your duty, as a human being on Planet Earth, to help make the world a better place. For yourself. For your community. For your dog.

And because they say the solution to all the world's problems begins in your own neighborhood, I began to see our neighborhood with new eyes. I suppose I had noticed before Rex came into our lives that used diapers lay splayed out on the sidewalks, that people would toss full garbage bags from their windows right onto the street, and that these bags would often hideously explode just as you were walking by. But I guess I thought that the garbage was something we could choose to ignore, the same way we ignored the men who gathered on our street corner late at night and furtively exchanged money and plastic bags. In a certain light, these conditions could be seen as backdrop, as something that gave an edgy glamour to our lives. Why, it was just like the musical *Rent,* and we could tell our friends on the privileged, pristine Upper East Side that no Tony Award–winning musicals were being made about *their* neighborhood.

After Rex, however, the grittier elements of our lifestyle were exposed for what they really were: hazardous, ugly, polluted, depressing, and dangerous for the dog. He could get attacked by a pit bull! Stolen! Pierced with a heroin needle! Infected with AIDS! He could cut his poor little pink paws on the glass! "Why don't the police do anything about the junkies?" I would say to Ted in the mornings as we steered the dog around the used needles. "Or those tents?" The homeless people—mostly trust-fund kids from the Pacific Northwest—were so brazen they set up campsites, complete with laundry hanging off tree branches and morning fires.

"The police are all busy on the Upper East Side," he would answer. "No, wait. Giuliani has them all at Rockefeller Center, making sure people don't cross against the lights."

"Why can't they arrest that drug dealer on our street? Every morning the schoolchildren pass by him and he just stands there, staring them down."

"They already did arrest him once. He even spent time in jail. Now he's back, only on a different corner."

"How did you know that?"

"Waylon told me. He told me he's connected to the Sanchez brothers gang."

"Well, there's no reason why he has to do his business on our street."

Rex looked up at me with his ears pricked up. Why were we asking him to do his business, he seemed to wonder, if he had already gone twice?

"I meant the drug dealer," I told the dog in my Rex voice. "You're a good boy." Then I assumed my new responsible-adult voice. "It just pisses me off that the city neglects this neighborhood so much. Who is our district councilman?"

"Who knows? Probably one of the Sanchez brothers. Listen, nothing you do is going to change the way things are."

We walked past a car that had recently been set on fire. A traffic officer was writing out a parking ticket for it.

"Maybe we should just move," I said. "No mayor yet has managed to make this neighborhood a better place, so who am I to think I could?"

"But we can't move," Ted said. "We can't afford it. Not until we both get real jobs."

"Oh, right."

In November I got a surprise phone call at work from some headhunter who knew who I was and where I was working and wanted to know if I was interested in a permanent position.

"Why would I want to do that?" I said. I told him to take my name off his headhunter list, and to never, ever call me again.

"You tell him," Tara said later. "The perv. How did he even get your name?"

"I don't know. He probably talked to my father. They always ask you at the agency whether you want Temp or Temp-to-Perm. But I *never* choose Perm."

"*Perm,*" Tara said later. "Perms are so eighties."

After Tara and I hung up, my heart was pounding. I felt violated in a way I can't even explain. It felt as if that man had seen into the window of my soul, and had tapped into my deepest fear, which was that I would never publish my novel, that I would never be anything beyond an office assistant. That the thirty thousand dollars I spent for a creative-writing degree was a bust. That health insurance is actually a really good thing.

I mean, writing is a challenging profession in the sense that you don't necessarily see immediate rewards. Some would argue that you never see *any* rewards. You just write in this void, day in and day out, and allow yourself to dream that someday, someone might actually read your words. Someone besides your mother. And sure, I had earned a handful of publications and some actual money. Still, it wasn't like every day editors were swooping into my kitchen and dancing around and telling me that the one measly paragraph I'd written that day was the best, best, best thing they'd ever seen, and thank you, thank you, thank you for writing this! But if I gave the dog one biscuit, one taste of my lobster bisque, he'd bark and spin and *a-woo-woo-woo* with all the zest and celebration of a marching band.

I probably don't need to restate at this point that the dog's limitless enthusiasm made me very happy. But I'll restate it anyway. Because it's just plain fantastic when your efforts pan out, when something you attempt actually works, when your dog does not send you an unsigned, form rejection letter saying, "While we read your story with interest, it does not suit our needs at this time."

"'Suit our needs,'" I said to Ted when I got another rejection letter, this time from *Harper's*, where I knew the editor for God's sake. "This makes me wonder if what I need is suits. Suits to wear to my dull unfulfilling office job that pays actual money."

"Don't get discouraged, honey," Ted said. "*Confederacy of Dunces* was rejected countless times before it got accepted."

"But the author committed suicide!" I said.

"Still, it got published," Ted said, laughing. "Would it make you feel better if I told you you suit *my* needs?"

"You're so sweet," I said. I hugged him.

"Plus, I keep telling you, all your book needs is more sex. That's all any book needs. Sex. Then it will sell millions."

"My book is fine as it is," I said. "You don't need gratuitous sex."

Ted raised his eyebrows.

I couldn't help but wonder: Had I reached some turning point? Was I going to give up writing for my dog? If I really thought about it, that seemed preposterous. But it felt like *something* had to change. With Ted, with me, with *us*.

"Can I tell you a secret?" I asked Tara. "Sometimes I think of moving to the suburbs and just getting some *job*. I've been thinking about that ever since we went to the Cape. My sister has such a charmed, stable life. She has a yard."

"One word," Tara said. "No, two: Mini. Van."

"She has a minivan, true. At least the minivan would be bigger than our apartment."

I looked out the window. Some man was shouting obscenities and kicking at the tires of a double-parked car. I thought about how it would be so much easier to raise the dog in the suburbs. In the city, you have to gear up with leashes, poop bags, keys, pepper spray, cell phone, pager, your BlackBerry, and a copy of your five-hundred-page manuscript in case you happen to run into some famous editor on the street—just to walk out to the curb. In the city, you have to brush your teeth and comb your hair. Because you never know just when the ex-boyfriend is going to turn the corner, or when Hugh Grant is going to be shooting a scene from his latest movie right on your block.

"Well," I said to Tara, "it'll probably never happen anyway, this move. We're too indecisive. We're still all talk, no action when it really comes down to it."

After we hung up, I tried to remember what had made me happy on the Cape (other than the fact that I hadn't inadvertently killed my nieces). I remembered the flowers and the grass. So if I couldn't change the grittiness of our neighborhood, at least I could beautify our own immediate environment, right away. The next Saturday Ted and I took Rex to the Union Square Greenmarket to pick out some plants. Neither of us had done much gardening before, nor had we been so inspired. But here we were, walking to Union Square, Rex trotting alongside us looking pleased with himself.

The market was full of nature's bounty—flowers bursting with color, summer fruits piled high—and the air had that early-morning, pre-traffic-jam freshness. We wandered through the stalls: Ted and the dog moved instinctively toward the Amish market, where they sold fresh cheeses and homemade pies. I gravitated toward the flower section with its rows and rows of potted plants. Soon I had gathered up several pots of geraniums and Gerber daisies, petunias and kalan-choes, and an exotic-looking plant with purple flowers. In my arms they smelled fecund and earthy; in my arms they smelled of bounty and evolution itself, and I swear I felt something ancient and fertile within me stir. "Let's get herbs, too," I said when Ted arrived. I was already picturing myself in an apron and a kerchief, making lemon basil omelettes and rosemary tea. "Let's get one of those tomato plants."

"You can't grow tomatoes on a fire escape," Ted said.

"Eli Zabar has an entire organic garden on his."

"That's on his rooftop, from what I hear. And it's an entire block long."

"Well, we're not going to feed the entire Upper West Side. I'm talking about two tomato plants."

"Who wants a tomato that tastes like car exhaust?" Ted said. "Besides, our fire escape doesn't have the right kind of light."

But to me there was light and no light. Like many city people, I had little concept of flora and fauna. Seasons were not measured by when the lilacs bloomed, or when the crocuses pushed their way above the thawing ground, but by what the legendary socialite Nan Kempner wore to the Metropolitan Opera Gala each year. So I piled Ted's arms with pots of verbena and rosemary, and spearmint and thyme, and had no doubt that they would grow.

"We're going to have to carry all this stuff home, remember," Ted, always the voice of reason, said.

"We'll take a cab."

"Who's going to pick us up with the dog?"

"A cabdriver who likes dogs."

Ted didn't believe that this was possible, but when I threw my arm up on Fourteenth Street, a dog-loving driver came right along. I felt like a part of it: New York, New York.

Back at home, I was absolutely transfixed by my new herbs and flowers. I arranged them on the fire escape with feelings of awe and reverence, pleased that I had turned such an ugly, rusted place into an oasis of life. And as the days wore on, I found that I enjoyed watering the plants and talking to them. I loved saying the word *verbena* and touching my nose to its fragrant leaves. And at certain moments—on those late summer evenings when the air was soft, the plants had been watered, and the dog had been walked—I began to feel that I truly was connected to the universe; that I was part of the great ecosystem. I was helping these plants and animals to live, and they were helping me. It all made sense—the pursuit of life, love, happiness.

Ted seemed more connected to the universe, too. It used to be that when he ventured out into the city, something would always happen to piss him off. He'd return to the apartment from Film Forum or the photo lab, and greet me with: "Some motherfucker almost killed me on the way home. Stupid asshole drivers shouldn't be driving fucking cabs. People are such *idiots.*"

But now, on Sunday mornings, he'd take the dog out, for some "quality time with his son," and come home two hours later, refreshed and exhilarated and in the best of moods.

"I thought you were just going on a shortie," I said. "I was worried about you two."

"Oh, it was such a nice day out we decided to go up to Ess-a-Bagel and get some breakfast." He held up a paper bag, which contained lox, bagels, capers, two containers of French butter, and Hero fourberry jam.

"A real New York breakfast!" I said. "Here, let me get some plates."

"Three different people stopped me this morning to ask me what kind of dog he was, and to tell me how handsome he is," Ted said as he took the dog's collar off.

"Isn't he though?" I smoothed back Rex's ears. "Who's a handsome boy?"

Rex lifted his face to mine so that I could scratch him under the chin. The look on his face was that of a sunbather raising his face to receive the sun. "Who's the handsomest dog in the world?"

"Rex is," Ted said.

"And who's the handsomest man?"

"Waylon?"

"You!"

While Ted put out plates for our bagels, I fed the dog and then mixed up some frozen pink lemonade. I felt very Martha Stewart at that moment—my life contained beauty and order and a Mexican glass water pitcher with a set of four matching blue highball glasses— so, on a whim, I threw a few fresh mint leaves into the pitcher.

"Mint lemonade," I announced proudly. "With herbs fresh from the fire escape." I couldn't have been prouder than if I had just spent eight hours stewing a bouillabaisse.

"You made me lemonade!" Ted said. "What a good girlfriend you are." To Ted, food was love. To me, food was work. But this was a start.

We ate breakfast in that leisurely Sunday way, and flipped through a few sections of the Sunday paper. Time slowed down. Rex lay at our feet on his side, slowly blinking his eyelids shut in unbeatable fatigue. Finally, he heaved one last sigh and began to snore. It was 2:08 P.M., which meant the sun would shine through our window for approximately four minutes. Sure enough, a shining ray poured through the window, lighting up Ted and the sleeping dog. I felt so grateful for my life at that moment. We had planted roots. We belonged to civilization. We were part of the Great Cycle of Life.

But once you tap into the Great Cycle of Life, and recognize that each and every one of us is connected to the ecosystem, chances are you'll begin to feel self-righteous. As in, anyone who isn't plugged in to the Great Cycle of Life doesn't belong. Anyone who doesn't have as his mission to make the world a better place *has* no place—not in my backyard. That drug dealer, for instance, on the corner of Suffolk and Stanton. It bothered me to see him in the same landscape as verbena, a blue sky, a successful morning session with Rex. It bothered me to see him up before I was, staring us all down with his bird-of-prey eyes. So I began to do what generations of self-righteous city women have done before me: I gave the man dirty looks. Heart-stopping, soul-snatching, dirty looks. Or so I thought. The man completely ignored me. Me! A rising Martha Stewart!

So one morning, when it was my turn to walk Rex, I marched right up to him and said, "Can't you go someplace else?"

He looked at his watch and took out a pack of cigarettes. He didn't even raise his eyes once in my direction.

"Look, we don't want you here," I said, in the same tone I would use to scold the dog. "Can't you just leave?"

He lit a cigarette and threw the match at my feet. Indignant, I looked to Rex for a reaction. He who used to lunge maniacally at a little old lady's outstretched hand was now as calm as could be in the presence of the drug dealer. Perhaps the man smelled of pot.

"Jerk," I said.

"You said what?" Ted screamed when the dog and I got home. "Do you realize how dangerous that was? That guy is evil. He could kill us if he wanted, and he wouldn't even care."

"He's not going to kill us," I said, pouring the dog his kibble. It rained musically into the stainless-steel bowl. "I don't even think he's coherent enough."

"That's my point. He's barely human! Jesus Christ!" Ted grabbed his forehead. "Don't you remember that three people—including a toddler—were gunned down on Clinton Street in a 'drug-related incident'? Don't you know that a landlord on Clinton hired a hit man to kill two of his tenants so that he could replace them and raise the rent?" He lifted his eyes as if to solicit the wisdom of the heavens, but was met with a burned-out light bulb and a cork-board ceiling stained from forty years of use. "This is not good," he said, starting to pace. "This is just not good. We're going to have to move."

"No we're not," I said, tying a little frilly apron (from Catherine Malandrino, no less) around my waist. My voice was suspiciously Stepford. "We have nothing to worry about at all."

What Ted didn't understand was, I had become a *nurturer*. And you can never underestimate the breadth, depth, and power of an Earth Goddess. *Par example:* Rex and I were waiting at a light to cross Houston, and when the light turned green, a giant pedestrian mob and I surged forth. But a cabdriver, determined to turn right come hell or dead people, cut us off. People shouted "Jesus!" and "Asshole!" but my attention was caught by a woman at the head of the mob, who pushed a stroller. She had a baguette in her hand, and she raised it like a sword with all the fury of Joan of Arc and brought it down on the cabdriver's hood. "How dare you!" she shouted. "I am a mother!" This was how I felt when I called that man a jerk. Rex and my plants needed me to protect them, and protect them I would.

For the next few days Ted insisted on escorting me to and from the subway station, even though it was only half a block away. He even climbed onto the roof of our apartment building to take some pictures of the drug dealer, in case he had to pick someone out from a lineup. He was convinced that I would be offed in such a gruesome way the *New York Post* would write about it on page two. "But not Page Six?" I'd say. "All my life I've wanted to be a boldface name on Page Six."

"Stop joking. This is a serious situation you've gotten us into. That psychopath knows where we live!" Ted would continue. "How could you have been so irresponsible?"

"I was actually being *responsible*. They say the catalyst for great change begins at home."

"Why did you bring the dog with you? He's the only dog of his kind in the city. What if something happens to Rex?"

I wish he hadn't said that. But he did.

For days I couldn't stop worrying. I worried about the dog, I worried about the plants, I worried about Mother Earth and the orbiting of the planets. A few nights after I'd called the drug dealer a jerk, a storm blew into town, pummeling my flora with bullet-sized drops of acid rain. I sat up in bed, worried that they would lose their petals, or suffer bruises, or drown. "Go back to sleep," Ted said, and he reminded me that modern houseplants and their antecedents had been growing without my aid for centuries, and that, every season, despite me, flowers bloomed. But still, I felt responsible. I was the one who had taken those flowers home from the Greenmarket. So I climbed over Ted and spread newspapers on the floor and opened the window to the fire escape and brought the plants in, one by one. They seemed to whisper, *thank you, thank you, Earth Mother*—but then I realized the plant with the purple flowers had become the launching pad for a dozen helicopter-sized flies. Suddenly they were all over the apartment, buzzing steadily like the little beepers they give you at restaurants to let you know your table is ready. Rex opened one eye and raised an eyebrow, but Ted continued to snooze. We didn't own a flyswatter because, frankly, not many insects can survive in New York City, and we didn't have the space. But we did have plenty of old *New Yorkers* lying around, unread because we spent all our spare time with the dog, and it was those I used to kill those flies. One by one. Rex lifted an eyebrow for every thwack of the magazine, but Ted, being that sort of guy, slept right through it. It wasn't until I went after the final fly—an elusive, plump, General Patton type who perched haughtily on a blade of the ceiling fan—that Ted woke up. To be precise, he woke up when I fell on top of him, because I had placed a kitchen stool at the foot of the mattress, and had tried to reach the fly by climbing on top of that. When the stool fell, which was inevitable, I bounced off Ted and onto the floor. Rex jumped up, startled, and began to vigorously lick my face.

I thought of college for some reason and started to cry.

All this responsibility went hand in hand with worry, it seemed, and was it worth it? Was becoming a mature adult an opportunity for growth? Or was adulthood just a burden that ultimately made you feel worse? "I can't save anything," I said. "I can't even save plants."

Rex leaned into me, pressing his rib cage against mine. I felt his heart beating, and stroked his soft fur, and he placed his head on my lap, and thumped his tail, and then looked up at me imploringly with kind, understanding eyes, and he seemed to be trying to tell me: "Don't worry. I am here. I will take care of you."

"But I'm supposed to take care of *you*!" I said. Ted thought I was talking about him.

"We'll all take care of each other," Ted said, kneeling down on the rug to embrace us both. Rex thumped his tail even faster. "Look at him. Look how much he loves you. Look at how much he loves his mother."

I looked at Ted with tears in my eyes.

"You're his mother now."

"I am?"

"You're his Mrs. Flint. You have been all along."

"You're right. I guess I haven't allowed myself to believe that, even though there have been moments when I thought it was true."

"Remember the days when you thought you would never be able to handle this dog, to care for him, to provide for him, to meet his needs?"

I nodded.

"Well, how can you forget that? We *did* all that."

These are some of the reasons why I always felt I could never have children: Didn't have the stamina. The patience. The nurturing gene. Could never be responsible enough. Didn't have the faith in myself or the world. But when Ted said, "You're his mother now," I saw that I could believe in a doable future. One without fangs. We had given Rex a future. And he had given *us* a future, too.

At my temp job, I asked Mr. Bobkins about the option of going Perm. "Just to have the insurance," I added quickly. "I'd still write." He nodded and said he would look into it. And twenty minutes later he came back to my desk with a report: "Penelope wants someone more committed to the firm," he said. I nodded in understanding. "In fact, she wants to fire you. She's noticed that you've been coming in late. Leaving early. Not getting coffee for her men."

I nodded again, like a twelve-year-old caught stealing.

"Maybe this is for the best," he said. "Maybe now you'll really finish that book."

"Thank you," I said. I had to go into Penelope's office to get her to sign off on my paperwork. She wasn't there, and I glanced at her desk to see if she had any photographs of a husband or boyfriend. Instead, I saw a rejection letter. From a poetry journal. With a handwritten comment that said "Please try again."

"Maybe it *is* for the best," Ted said at home. The dog was splayed out between us on his back, waiting for his belly to be scratched. "You've been saying for a year that you just need to focus on your book full-time in order to polish it up. I'll tell you what. Why don't you stay home and write for the next month and finish your book. I can continue to support us with the money from my grandmother, plus the money I've saved. Then, in December, we'll both start looking for full-time jobs."

"You'd really do that for me?"

"I want to support your writing. I admire how hard you work, and I know this is something you really want."

I leaned over the dog and hugged Ted as hard as I could, so that our hearts would press together. I concentrated on our heartbeats, mine thumping into his, and tried to will that something essential pass between us, that we be eternally linked. Rex squirmed between us, trying to set himself upright, to get in on this hugging action, and we moved apart to let him in.

CHAPTER 12

Unleashed

Thus I became a stay-at-home mom. Ted, ever the responsible, practical one, took a job as an assistant cameraman for a local shoot. It was a Hollywood blockbuster wannabe about a giant space-ship that had positioned itself above New York and remained suspended there for weeks, threatening to annihilate the whole city. Oh, the irony. My eternally unfinished novel had been hanging over my head like that for the past five years. But this month I would finish. I would finish for me, and for Rex, and for Ted.

I found that I loved writing at home full-time. I loved the luxury of it, and the ease of managing my own schedule. I loved being able to sit around all day in the same yoga pants I had slept in, and never showering, and being able to pretend, whenever I ventured out in public, that I was just on my way home from the gym. I loved the fact that I didn't have to *talk* to anybody (not counting the high-pitched baby talk with the dog). And I *loved* the fact that there was a dog under my desk. He was just so soft and furry and calm—the perfect writing companion, the perfect place to rest my feet. All morning long he remained there, lightly snoozing. And as I typed away, I had the sense that he was guarding my words, my stories, my successes and my failures. (The very dog that used to cower under this very desk!) He lay there on the good writing days—those days when I felt brilliant and creative and everything flowed. He lay there on the horrid days, too—days in which my mind wouldn't work, and four hours would pass, and I still hadn't ironed out one simple transitional sentence of the same damn paragraph.

All the while, his unwavering presence and his uncomplicated canine vibes somehow wafted up to me, like the radiant warmth from a space heater in the wintertime. He lay there without judging, resting his head on my feet, sighing with contentment and bliss. And when I pressed the Save button, and shut the computer down, he would leap out from under the desk with excitement. It didn't matter whether I ended the session feeling pleased with myself or knotted with frustration. He danced, he leapt, he a-wooed, reminding me it was *this* that mattered. This very moment. Happiness awaits! Come, come away!

Then, in rolled a cold front. It was a chilly November that year. Now, every dog person out there knows that their beloveds get friskier when the cold fronts roll in. They know dogs get more animated and need more exercise and less sleep. Every dog person knew this except me and Ted. And then, suddenly, we found out. The dog we thought we'd tamed just one month earlier was suddenly panting again, pacing, spinning in circles inside the apartment, jumping on the windowsills and demanding to be taken out *Now! Now! Now!* This was a different kind of hyperactivity than when we'd first adopted Rex—it wasn't threatening or fear based, but rather frisky and peppy and, in Rex's mind, fun. But hyper was hyper, whether you were dealing with a Dr. Jekyll or a Mr. Hyde.

Which meant that the apartment started to feel claustrophobic. Both Ted and I were home together during the day now. The windows were closed. The heat kicked in from the radiators in shocking clanks, as if some ghouls in the basement were pounding on the pipes with baseball bats. We jumped every time the radiator clanked or the dog barked. On colder days I could barely get any work done. I felt that giant spaceship pressing down on me again. I began to nudge Rex away with my foot when he tried to crawl under the desk.

"Don't kick him!" Ted would say.

"It wasn't a kick, it was a nudge."

"What kind of mother are you?"

"Mommy dearest," I said. "He's just bugging me. All he does is pace and pant. He never gets tired."

"Well, take him out then."

"It's *your* turn."

"I'm doing research right now." "Research" for Ted was watching television. "You're not even working. I haven't heard any tapping of keys. You're just sitting there kicking the dog."

"I did the Morning Walk. Which means that *you* do the Late Morning Walk. Rules are rules. Get out of here!" I said to the dog as he tried to pounce on me.

"Don't yell at him!" Ted said.

"Don't yell at me!"

Good Lord! We were arguing in the same way we had argued when we first got the dog. Only back then we could blame the dog. And I suppose we could blame the dog now, too. But let's be honest. Ted and I always got along best when there were a few state lines between us. We had dated long distance for the first year of our relationship, and we always joked that those were our glory days. And every New York City couple knows the reason for this: Distance gives a couple the room to recognize each other's positive qualities. I was able to appreciate Ted's generosity and intelligence; his sense of responsibility and his capacity to plan. Ted liked my sense of playfulness, my romantic vision, my commitment to my art.

But anyone who lives in a three-hundred-square-foot studio apartment can tell you that the thing you love most about your partner can also be the thing you hate most in the end.

"Do you think you could find a new song to play?" I'd say, hands on hips.

Ted was ten feet away from me, trying to figure out the chords to "Uncle John's Band."

"Do you think *you* could go to Starbucks and write your Great American Novel?"

When we bickered, Rex would spin around and jump on us, and bark, bark, bark.

"I just wish we could let him off-leash in the park," I said. "He gets so tired after he runs around."

"He can't go off-leash. Do you want him to run onto FDR Drive and get killed? Do you want him to run off and attack another dog?"

We went back to the books, to the chapters on "Diet and Exercise," in case there was something we had missed the first eighty times around. But even *The Hypochondriac's Guide* claimed that a twenty-minute walk in the morning was considered "sufficient daily exercise" for a house pet.

"Maybe for a gerbil," Ted said. "But not a hunting dog."

"If he really is a French spaniel—"

"English setter."

"Whatever. Let's say he's half English setter and half French spaniel. Well, that would be on par, energywise, with a cross between a Michael Jordan and a Flo-Jo."

"That's funny," Ted said. "You should go write that down. I'll pay you to write that down."

"But it's my turn to walk the dog," I said. Rex, this whole time, had been jumping on the windowsills, clawing at the door, demanding to be taken out *Now! Now! Now!*

"We'll both take him," Ted said.

But these walks were still just that—*walks*. What he needed were gallops, a fox hunt, a weekend in the northernmost region of Minnesota, flushing out grouse. Nothing short of four hours running at top speed, over the river and through the woods, was going to tire out this dog. But there are no woods on the Lower East Side of New York City. And to cross the river we had to take the subway, on which dogs were not allowed.

Every morning, as we headed into the park, he would pull us past the vandalized bathhouse and the hoopless basketball courts, and he would not stop pulling until we had reached a dilapidated fountain, surrounded by benches and trees. There were three or four ratty gray squirrels in those trees, and Rex would spend the next hour trying to get at them. First he would poise himself tensely at the base of the tree and spring straight up, twisting his body in the air like an acrobat. Then he would try to crawl up the tree trunk, taking longer and longer running starts, but he couldn't get very far because we always had him on the leash. He'd spring into the air, as if trying to launch himself into orbit, and then look disapprovingly at us, for we were clearly cramping his style. Next, frustrated, he would sit and stare up at the squirrels and bark, and bark and bark and bark, and still the squirrels would not come down and present themselves to him, bellies up. So then he'd rear back and *bite* the tree savagely, as if he were trying to pull the thing down. Ted and I would look around nervously to see if anyone was watching (you can get a two-thousand-dollar ticket for molesting trees), and there would be those aliens from Planet Future with their Starbucks and their stroller and their perfect yellow Lab walking by. And then Rex, knowing that we weren't looking, would lunge at the tree again. "No!" Ted said, yanking the dog back by the collar. "Stop!"

"That wasn't exercise," Ted said on the way home. "It was an exercise in frustration."

"He was much better on the Cape," I said. My new mantra. The Cape, the Cape, everything was better on the Cape. "Since then, he really hasn't been willing to accept city life so much."

This was true. He had been to Cape Cod. He had seen seagulls, he had seen rabbits, he had seen, at the shores of the Atlantic, the expansive horizon, and hints of the great beyond. And once you have encountered such expansiveness, and the glory of a sunrise, how is it possible to accept a view of an air shaft? Our apartment was starting to feel like a men's locker room before a football game. With all that pent-up energy and hot panting breath, all that tension and testosterone, and the closed windows, a sweaty film was starting to form along the ceilings and walls.

"When were you inside a men's locker room?" Ted said.

"What you have is a teenager," the Marching Band Man said. "A teenage dog. So you better get yourselves a large bottle of Stoli, because it's going to be a looooong winter. He'll test you, he will."

He was right! We had a teen. By then, a distinct personality had arisen in Rex—a personality that was part canine, part human being. Ted and I assumed, of course, that this was his true personality, his *original* personality, the one that had existed before his alleged abuser slapped it out of him. And we were glad to see his Original Self emerge.

"Well, you know," I said. "They say that you don't really start to show your true colors until you've been dating someone for four months."

"Interesting," Ted said. He was looking at me as if trying to remember *our* first four months.

Rex's canine qualities included his love of stick chasing, of *always* tugging at his leash when we walked him, of writhing ecstatically in the grass, mumbling and wooing with pleasure. His human qualities included a distinct sense of humor and arrogance about his heritage and his looks. He was intelligent, manipulative, and stubborn. Passive and aggressive. Smart and creative. Sometimes a cream puff, sometimes unpredictable and temperamental. In other words, a combination of me and Ted.

Because of these personality changes, Ted and I of course began to anthropomorphize the dog's behavior and channel all of our secret wants and desires onto him.

"He's depressed," I'd say to Ted. "You didn't walk him enough today. He feels cheated. He's not getting enough attention from you. He thinks you work too much."

"He's tired," Ted would respond without lifting his eyes from the television set. "He's had a long day. Leave him alone. Can't you see he just wants to sleep?"

No, I could not. In fact, I now believed that Rex had a complex range of emotions that swung as widely as mine did in the throes of PMS. "He's angry. He feels like he missed out on a true childhood. He misses his mother."

"He just wants to have some *space*," Ted would say. At this point he'd pull a pillow over his head to blot me out.

Soon I figured out that the best way to get what I wanted was to tell Ted that something was for the dog. "I think he needs to get away for the weekend," I'd say. "I think he'd like to stay at a nice B and B."

Ted would say, "He thinks that would cost too much money. Money that would be better spent on a winter coat. For him." Ted picked up the remote and patted the spot on the sofa next to him. "Come here, Rex, hop up."

The dog hopped up, spun two circles, and settled himself next to Ted with a grunt.

"See?" Ted said. "He just wants to hang around this weekend and watch *Seinfeld* with me."

But the funny thing was, sometimes when Ted said this, Rex would give him a kind of disdainful look, jump off the sofa, and walk to the door, where he would again turn around a few times before slumping to the floor with a grunt. Our behavior seemed to embarrass him, like any true teen.

The teen had outgrown his puppy toys. We'd bought him "educational" toys from the Suckers R Us pet catalog and the excellent Petco—toys that were supposed to "stimulate the mind"—but he would take one look at them, get a whiff of their plastic commercialism, give us a look that said, "Oh please. Don't insult me with such childish games," and then walk away. He walked away from the talking ball; he walked away from the Smarty Bone. He walked away from the Buster Cube, a hollow plastic cube designed by a Danish behaviorist to "alleviate boredom and stimulate the brain" by releasing treats if you rolled it just right. *Why would I work for my kibble when I can call room service any time of day?* his look seemed to say.

The only toys he liked were things that he could play tug-of-war with, or toys that he could kill.

Yes, we had a teenage boy.

"This is why parents who can afford it ship their teenagers off to boarding school," Ted said. "And with the amount of money we spend on him, we could do it, too."

"We could let him off-leash," I said, a bit more petulantly than I'd intended.

"No!" Ted said.

I decided to poll my fellow New York City dog lovers, to see where *they* stood on the off-leash issue, and how they exercised their teenage dogs. I posted a notice on Manhattan Dog Chat, an online forum for city dog owners where even your silliest, most asinine question was treated with concern and respect. You could ask what flavor of canine toothpaste to buy, how best to evacuate your poodle's anal sac, and whether that hangdog look on your new basset hound's face was a sign of depression, or if that was just how bassets looked. And you'd get dozens of answers, all of them helpful and sincere. These Manhattan Dog Chatters would even offer their home phone numbers, and suggest you meet them for coffee, or even that you come to their apartments, to talk in further depth about the anal sac. And it was safer than any online date.

About sixty Chatters responded to my first posting within half an hour. Drugs, was the main suggestion. Prozac. Ritalin. Send him to obedience class, said another. Send him to boarding school. Move to the Cape. I decided to meet some of them in person. Dog owners can get chummy very easily—we may be crazy, but we are sincere. First there was John and John, a gay couple who lived on the Upper East Side with their spoiled Pomeranian, Petunia. "Our apartment is big enough that Petunia can exhaust herself just running from the kitchen to the library," John said. Petunia sat self-righteously on his lap.

"You have a *library*?" I said. "We have to keep our books on the floor in the bathroom."

"Would you believe she prefers the library?" said the other John. "Most dogs you'd think would be hanging out in the kitchen, but Petunia is very refined. She likes Balzac."

"No, she doesn't," John said. "She likes Rudyard Kipling. He wrote lots of stories about dogs."

"What do you do if she has to go to the bathroom?" I asked.

The Johns looked at each other. "We hired someone who carries her out three times a day and lets her do her business."

"I'm not sure I understand what you're saying," I said, even though I did.

"We don't want her little paws touching that filthy pavement—"

"Let alone the fur on her belly," the other John interjected.

"As I was *say*ing," the first John said testily. He began stroking Petunia, breathed deeply, and seemed to regain himself. "So when she has to go pee-pee we hold her, you know, so that she's kind of hovering over but not quite touching the ground."

"Our little Hovercraft, we call her." The two Johns smiled and joined hands.

Next I met a cinematographer who had a special rubberized surface installed on the roof garden of his Tribeca loft apartment, so that his vizslas could pee up there. "And it never smells," he said. "Not even in the summertime when it's hot as Hades up here." He was on his hands and knees, sniffing the rubber surface in a way that smacked of S and M. "C'mere," he said. "Smell."

"What do you do for exercise?" I said, backing away. "For the dogs."

"Oh," he said. "We have a country house."

Our friend's friend Tony got a bulldog specifically because that breed doesn't need that much exercise. "Look at her!" he said proudly as we stood inside the Tompkins Square Park dog run. "She can't even breathe! I have to drag her here—literally drag her! And then once we get here she just sits around." Poor Flora had shimmied her wide body under a bench. A cocker spaniel puppy came up to sniff her, but she just wheezed. "Come on! Go play!" Tony nudged Flora with his foot. "Ah, it ain't gonna happen. But you gotta love her. Come on, baby, let's go home."

"I think we're talking to the wrong people," I finally said to Ted one weekend. "What we're trying to find out about is exercise. We need to find someone with an English setter or something. Someone who doesn't have a country house." And that's when I realized: no one else on the Lower East Side had an English setter. I thought of that website again: *It is cruel to keep this type of exuberant hunting dog in a city apartment.*

We happened to be sitting that night in Chumley's, an old speak-easy in the West Village, where two overweight yellow Labs were lying on the floor. At least they used to be yellow Labs. Now they were more like sea lions, all fat and passive and breathing in smoke. They were so catatonic and lazy that if you held out a French fry they wouldn't even get up to take it from you. "You have to bring it to 'em," the bartender shouted. "They're spoiled. They've been here too long."

"How old are they?" we asked.

"Oh, about six."

"Do they ever get, um, exercise?" I asked. The male had to be three hundred pounds.

"I took them to Coney Island once to see if they would, like, swim, and they spent the whole day lying next to the concession stand, waiting for fries. They're city dogs! Give 'em a couple burgers and *The New York Times* and they're fine!"

"I think it's time to get my bike out of storage," Ted said.

In one of our dog catalogs, we had seen a contraption that attached like an arm to the body of the bike, to which a leash could be fastened, but the dog they showed in the picture was a tiny wheaten terrier who was happily trotting along, hair flowing back like Farrah Fawcett's. Somehow we knew that our experience would differ greatly from that portrayed in the catalog. So Ted opted to hold Rex's leash and ride alongside him as they braved the paved paths of East River Park. At first, it simply seemed that Rex enjoyed the opportunity to trot more quickly than he was used to, but the faster Ted pedaled, the faster Rex galloped. Soon you could see them barreling down the footpaths like horses in a Western while Ted shouted: "Rex, slow down! Rex, go straight. Not that way, Rex. No! No!"

Within days, Rex seemed noticeably calmer after these bike rides, but Ted's voice was growing hoarse, and he had begun to grind his teeth. So I offered to take a turn at what we now called "running the dog with the bike."

"The trick is you have to keep talking to him," Ted said. "If he senses you're not in control for one second he'll take off." He handed me a helmet and for a moment I felt like a storm trooper, off to risk my life. First of all, to ride a bike in a park in Manhattan, you always have to be on the lookout for Rollerbladers, joggers, families of eight who walk side by side, indignant mothers with strollers, and, finally (and perhaps worst of all), other, better cyclists, who wear snazzy outfits and speak French and have no patience for the likes of you: the casual weekend cyclist. Especially not those with a dog in tow. Or rather, those being towed by a dog. "On your *right!*" these cyclists would shout disdainfully, muttering something about the dog. So there was this to deal with, and the fact that Rex kept trying to pull me toward Squirrel Town. I didn't have the strength or the stubbornness to keep him on the paths the way Ted did, and continually found myself veering off toward shrubs and trees. It was like a giant, never-ending game of Chicken—one I was convinced I would lose. And, sure enough, Rex saw a feral cat, of all things, and I knew I was a goner. "Rex, sit!" I shouted as he brought his pace to a full gallop. "Sit! Sit! Sit!" It was the one word I knew he knew, the one command he would always eventually succumb to, and I shouted it until I was hoarse. But Rex didn't hear me. The only thing on his mind was Cat, and Cat was scrambling up an oak tree on the other side of some benches, and Bike would soon be over Bench and up that tree as well. So I let go of the leash.

And letting go of that leash seemed to change Rex's world. He sprinted after the cat at full force, like a rocket released from a launching pad. The cat scurried under a bench and Rex flew over it—majestically, without effort—and ran circles around the tree. When the cat clawed its way up to a branch and hissed with its back arched, Rex barked and leapt into the air, twisted his body around, and somehow landed facing forward again. He tossed his head and barked—the heraldic bark of a foxhunt trumpet. The cat climbed higher up. Then Rex spotted a squirrel in a nearby tree. He charged, the squirrel scampered up, and Rex barked at it from the base of the tree. Then he saw another squirrel. And another, and another. Rex sent all of them scampering. I would later learn that there was a verb for this: to tree. But for now, I set my bike down and watched with fascination as a transformation took place in my dog. After treeing the fourth squirrel, his demeanor changed. His style. His face. All at once Rex looked proud and serious, almost presidential. His eyes were narrowed, lips closed, ears flat. He looked around slowly for more squirrels. It was as if some ancient instinct had finally been awakened in Rex. He had tapped into the Universal Canine Force. Those first four squirrels were his warm-ups. This was the real deal. I realized my dog was a killer.

An unsuspecting squirrel scampered across the grass a few yards away, searching for nuts. I saw him first. Rex's nose twitched, and he turned his head, a Patriot missile homing in on its target of destruction. He crouched. He lowered his body into a point—that position I had seen in dog encyclopedias, and in hunting prints, but never in my own dog. Every fiber of his being was focused on his prey. Slowly and fluidly, he crept toward his victim, paw by paw. His nose twitched. When he paused, his muscles remained primed and tense. The squirrel sat up quickly, acorn between its paws. Rex froze, his front right leg held in midair, his plumed tail pointing straight back. Only his nose moved—a subtle twitch. Then he unfurled in one great leap. I realized just at this moment I should try to step on his leash, to save the poor squirrel's life, but Rex was yards away already. The squirrel had been treed. But Rex did not seem to mind that he had lost another victim. He was ecstatic. To him, this was not about the end but the means, the glorious thrill of the chase. He tracked and treed another dozen squirrels, who all managed to scramble up the trees at the last minute. The squirrels started to chatter to one another, a series of clucks and cheeps to warn all the squirrels in all five boroughs that a new dog was in town. Rex had found his Inner Bird Dog.

When I shared this observation with Ted back at home, he said, "Don't let him off-leash."

"But you should have seen him! He's so cute running around. His ears flop back and his face stretches into that smile. And he gets so much exercise chasing all those squirrels."

"Don't let him off-leash."

"Okay," I said.

And of course I respected Ted's point of view—he was the responsible one, after all. But I guess I respected the dog's needs even more. Here was a dog that was bred to hunt and chase and flush and point. And by not letting him off-leash, we weren't allowing him to realize himself. We weren't giving him mental exercise. It was like me with my writing—if I did not or could not write for a few weeks, I began to feel all out of sorts and grouchy and unsettled. No wonder Rex had been hyper all the time! He was not yet a Realized Being. And now, with him unleashed, and myself unfettered by a desk, and Ted out filming boldly in the streets, we were all realized again.

So every other day, when it was my turn to run the dog on the bike, I let the leash go. We seemed to have an unspoken agreement that if I gave him his freedom, he would not stray. I trusted, unequivocally, that he would come back. And he always did.

I liked keeping this little secret from Ted. It made the dog feel more "mine."

For the next few weeks we had a calmer dog, and a calmer relationship. Rex and I would return to the apartment with secret little smiles on our faces. Ted smiled at our smiles. But then Ted's bike got stolen. We'd been leaving it locked to the stairs inside the building, just as we had seen many other tenants do. But one day it was simply gone.

"It's that drug dealer," Ted said. "I know it. He knows where we live. Why did you have to call him a jerk?"

Rex walked in between us and sat on my foot. He faced Ted like a chess piece.

"I don't think drug dealers bother with petty theft," I said.

"This city!" Ted said. "You never get a break! We live in this shit-hole apartment, and even a shitty ten-year-old bike gets stolen."

"How can you be so certain it was the drug dealer?" I asked.

"Who else could it be? All the criminals in this neighborhood are related. We're going to have to move," Ted said.

"We say that all the time."

"Well, now we have no choice. Come on," he said, grabbing his keys and the dog's leash. "Let's go get the Sunday *Times*."

On our way to the deli, we saw a couple walking home arm in arm, at dusk, carrying a pint of Dulce de Leche and the Sunday *Times*. I knew they were going home to read the real estate section and start making calls *right away*. Everyone was always one step ahead of you in New York.

And have you ever tried to find an apartment in New York City? Have you ever had your toenails extracted? Two thousand a month will get you a basement unit with a bulkhead entrance. For an extra $600 they'll throw in a hot plate and maybe a sink. But you have to fork over at least $3K if you want to have a bathroom. $3,200 for a bathtub and a kitchen. And they don't tell you ahead of time that in that price range the bathtub is *in* the kitchen.

"Are you serious?" Ted would say every time the Realtor swept out her arm to present the apartment, like some hostess on *Jeopardy!*

"This is a very desirable neighborhood," the Realtor said. She had an alarming habit of licking her lips. Like a serpent. "And you better decide soon, because there are already seven applications down on this, and two couples are able to pay a full year's rent in cash."

"If they have that kind of money," Ted said to me, "why would they be living in that place?"

"Because it takes another kind of money to get a place you'd actually like."

We started to lie about the fact that we had a dog, to increase our chances, but nothing really materialized. I hated the apartments Ted liked and he hated the ones I liked (probably because I only liked the ones I saw at the back of *The New York Times Magazine*, and they cost twelve million dollars). Ted would accuse me of being unrealistic, and say that I was disagreeing for the sake of disagreeing.

"But that last apartment we saw was ugly. It was depressing. And I don't think it's too much to ask that the kitchen *not* be in the living room."

"You're just going to have to lower your standards," Ted said. "You need to get a grip on reality. We can't afford anything better than what we have now."

And that, to me, was the most depressing thing about living in New York. Unless you Made It Big, moving was never a step up, a step forward. It was more like a sidestep. If you were lucky. And got your application in first.

But we never got our application in first, because we always waffled. And you cannot waffle in the world of New York real estate. If you do, you'll be burnt toast.

So we had no bike, no apartment, and, in Ted's mind, no further way to exercise the dog. That's when I made my confession about letting the dog off-leash. "Come, I'll show you. Let's go to the park."

I think Ted was mad at me for not being honest, but he maintained his silence on the way to the park. Once we got inside the ball field, I unsnapped the leash and Rex took off for the squirrels.

"What if he doesn't come back?" Ted said.

"He'll come back," I said. "It's like that saying from the seventies: 'If you love something set it free. If it comes back to you, it's yours; if it doesn't, it never was.'"

There's something about witnessing freedom in action that makes your heart soar. That's why it's so fun to watch an off-leash dog. In the distance, we could see that Rex had chased a squirrel up the fence that lined one of the baseball fields, and was now following the squirrel around the entire perimeter. His joy was boundless, and the love I felt for him filled me like helium. In the farther distance, downriver, we could see the Statue of Liberty, welcoming the free and the brave. If you didn't know she was holding a torch, you might think she was toasting Staten Island with a bottle of beer. It was a fine image, a cheerful one, which made me feel as if I had a great perspective on life. Perhaps all my negative karma had been purified.

By then Rex was out of sight, and Ted began to shout his name and to call for him to come back. But I held fast—to my conviction, and to Ted's hand. Rex wasn't just mine. He was ours. Our dog came galloping toward us from the opposite end of the baseball field.

"What a good boy!" Ted shouted. "Look at how he's coming back. What recall!"

As he neared us, he slowed down. He had a funny, sideways way of trotting that made him look like a figure skater following a steady diagonal line. (Ted, by the way, was convinced this was an early warning sign of hip displasia, and was already saving for the surgeon's bills.) Yet when he galloped, that misalignment vanished. That's when I realized: When you take tentative steps, you don't necessarily plow forward. But if you surge ahead at full force, without fear or hesitation, you can follow a smooth, straight course. I realized that Ted, at that moment, was my life's biggest ally. And I accepted that maybe Rex would never get tired in this lifetime. But neither would we ever get tired of him.

A few days later, Ted spotted his bike on Delancey Street, being pushed along by a ten-year-old boy. The front tire was bent, and the boy said he was taking it to be repaired.

"That's my bike," Ted said.

"No, it ain't, my brother just bought it from a guy down the street."

"What guy?" Ted said.

It turned out to be one of our neighbors. An old man who kept one of those old junk shops that everyone knew was a front. An old, one-eyed cat guarded that shop at night and Rex would often throw his body against the glass trying to get at it. I'd always had a bad feeling about that man. In any case, Ted convinced the boy and the big brother to give his bike back. But we never bothered to run the dog on the bike anymore.

Now we were the people to whom Rex came back.

Having a dog off-leash opened up new worlds for us. Gone were the near brawls of the dog run, gone were the endless hours of being dragged across town. "What a health benefit," I said. "No more dislocated shoulders and misaligned spines." Out in the park, Ted and I could hold hands again or even tango, right in the middle of the ball field, which we tried a few times. I wasn't a very good dancer, though. I was too self-conscious to dance, even out there in the park, even though we were mostly surrounded by dogs.

Having a dog off-leash can also open up a world of danger, however: your dog is at risk of being attacked by another dog. It happened on a Wednesday, on a day so ordinary I never once looked at my watch or questioned my existence. There I was, walking Rex, and thinking how much fun it would be to be a dog walker. I mean, who could resist walking behind a pack of rumps as we trotted along Delancey Street? Imagine multiplying Rex's happiness times three. Look how excited Rex was to go to the park! He knew good things lay ahead at the East River, and he pulled me, trying to gain momentum as he trotted, his muscles alert and strained. Traffic was at a standstill on Delancey Street, so for seven blocks we were assaulted by the sounds of "Fuck you!" and honking horns. I watched the way his ears flopped slightly and the fringe on the backs of his legs fluttered as he moved. He was not affected by the traffic. He did not notice the cacophony of the construction on the Williamsburg Bridge. He wasn't bothered by the fact that the bridge had been under construction for years and showed no signs of being finished. He didn't view the unfinished bridge, in his moments of doubt, as a metaphor for me and Ted. No, he just bobbed along, always happy, always looking forward, never back.

Once we reached the green safety of the baseball fields, I let him off his leash. He sprinted away immediately, heading for Squirrel Town, and I watched with pride as he crept stealthily a few yards ahead of me, circling a tree. It was that hour of day when the sun was setting and evening was about to cast its spell on the city. Although in parts of the city this could be a sinister spell, if you happened to be walking past drug dealers who lurked under bridges and streetlights that didn't work. From this emerging darkness came a large white boxer, who charged straight toward Rex. But Rex was in the Zone, the hunting mode: nose down, eyes focused, his whole body aligned into a muscular point. He ignored the boxer. The boxer ran circles around Rex, and barked at him, and Rex gave him a look that said, *Do you mind?* and then returned his attention to the squirrel in front of him. He lifted one paw at a time and placed each noiselessly a few inches forward on the earth. All at once, the boxer attacked Rex. He snapped once, twice, with escalating growls. I shouted hey! And then I was in the midst of murderous violence. Rex reared back fiercely and lunged.

The boxer met him in midair and tried to take him down by the neck. He caught Rex's shoulder instead. Rex yelped, fell onto his back, then twisted away. I felt terror for a second—*he's going to die! He's going to die.* And then I went into my own Zone. A mother's zone. A no-one-is-going-to-fuck-with-my-dog zone. I ran between the dogs, and shouted and swore. I kicked the boxer. He dodged. Both dogs circled away from me, each trying to latch his jaws on the other's throat. Rex caught the boxer's lip, and tugged. It stretched hideously. It gave. I tried to grab the boxer's collar. He leapt past my hand and finally caught Rex by the throat. Rex's eyes widened. He went down. Thrashed. Breathed in heaves. Kicked at the boxer with his back legs. "Let go!" I shouted. The boxer growled and tugged, trying to rip open Rex's throat. The skin around Rex's neck stretched, showed blood. I dove in, like the legendary mother who lifted a Volkswagen off her trapped toddler. I somehow got my hands inside the boxer's mouth and pried his jaws open. Released, Rex fell back and then rolled away. I shouted for him to sit, but Rex wasn't finished. He just dove right back in. He circled us—I say *us* because somehow I had the boxer's collar and kept him restrained. All I had to do, I thought in those swift illogical moments, was keep my body between my dog and this one. Then a woman appeared, a jogger, and asked me if I needed help, and I said yes and asked her to grab my dog, but Rex resisted capture, dodging skillfully away from her outstretched hands. "Grab his back legs," I shouted, which she did, which was good, because this enabled her to haul my dog off, like a wheelbarrow. Funny the images you think of in the middle of violent episodes.

A man appeared on a bicycle—a handsome but harsh-looking man with olive skin and heavy-lidded eyes. "Let go of my dog," he said.

"Oh, good, he's yours?" I said. "Can you take him? He's got something against my dog."

"Get your hands off my dog," he said. His face was blank and unsmiling, and I started to get alarmed.

"I'm holding him because he attacked my dog," I said. "If you could just take him and put him on a leash, I'll get my dog on leash and then we can separate them."

"Let go of my dog," he said.

The female jogger stepped forward. "Just take your dog out of here," she said to the man. "Why can't you just take your dog and get out of here?"

The man stepped off his bike and came toward me. He had his chest thrust forward in a way that suggested confidence and skills in the martial arts. I was crouched down, to keep my hand on his dog's collar, and then he crouched too and reached for his dog, smiling at me in a disingenuous way. "Thanks," I said, and let go of the boxer and so did he. The boxer charged off after Rex again. The female jogger screamed.

"You asshole!" I shouted. "What the fuck?" Somehow I managed to seize the boxer again.

"Get your filthy hands off my dog."

"He's crazy!" the jogger shouted. "Let's just get out of here!"

"Look." I glared at the man. "Just take your dog and get *out* of here. Don't be such a prick!"

That's when he hit me. A solid punch right on the forehead. Automatically, without thinking, I tried to hit him back. I was *not* going to be trodden upon, by him or anyone. He caught my feeble fist, as it were, in his own hand and twisted my arm behind my back. "Oh, my God!" the jogger was shouting in the background. "I'm calling the police!" And she ran off across the field, toward FDR Drive.

"Let go of me," I was saying to this guy, who was trying to twist me to the ground, and I noticed that evening had completely descended, and that we were being watched by two Puerto Rican fishermen who sat on a bench, impassive and motionless, and that the streetlight nearest us hadn't gone on yet, and that my dog was nowhere in sight, and that I was spiraling to my knees, and the grass was dank. "Help!" I finally shouted. "Help!" At that, the Boxer Man let go of me, and spat on me, and then hopped on his bike. "If I see you or your dog again," he said, "you're dead," and then he whistled and his dog followed him off.

My head hurt. I could literally hear the blood pounding inside my skull. And where was Rex? I only had to turn toward the stand of trees to find him, circling a poplar, as oblivious to me as he ever was. I started crying then—childish whimpery sobs that didn't quite feel real.

The jogger returned, sprinting across the field in an impressive fifty-yard dash. "I found a policeman," she said, catching her breath with her hands on her knees. "He's on his way."

"Thank you," I said. "I'm so fortunate that you came."

"That's the weirdest fucking thing I ever witnessed," she said, shaking her head. "I'm so freaked out. He was totally egging you on. It's like he wanted to get into a fight. Christ, that was so fucking bizarre." She bounced from one leg to the other and kept looking agitatedly up the path. "How is your dog?" she asked. "Is he okay?"

I called Rex over and, miraculously, he came. I felt his neck and shoulders, but there were no puncture wounds. He panted heavily. "He's fine," I said. "He doesn't even care. The blood must have come from the boxer." I hugged Rex, crying again. "Serves that awful dog right."

Then a police car drove up and an Officer Hagan stepped out. He seemed like a nice young man—Irish, freckled—and he shook his head in disgust as we told him the story. "You're lucky it wasn't worse," he said. "He coulda had a knife. That dog coulda had rabies. You coulda yourself gotten bit and had permanent nerve damage and lost use of your hands." He drove us around the park, to identify the man, but we did not find him. Rex acted subdued, like a perp on the way to the station. He kept his head out the window, a vengeful look on his face, hoping to track down and arrest our assailants, too. "That's a good-looking dog you got there. Very well trained." He asked me if I wanted to file a report. "Is it worth my while?" I asked, and he said no, not really. "To be honest, we don't have time. We got bigger fish to fry."

As we drove out of the park, along FDR Drive, I felt that I had failed at some essential component of living in New York. That I was not tough. That my dog had failed to protect me, even after I had protected him. Even after I had *saved his life*. Twice. Once at the shelter, and here, now. But suddenly I realized that I *was* tough. That I was brave. In fact, prying that boxer off Rex was the most heroic thing I had *ever* done. I felt proud in that moment. I never knew I had it in me.

"You should carry a cell phone at all times, young lady," Officer Hagan said as he dropped us in front of our building. "Especially a young woman out walking alone." But I just smiled at him with my newfound, unwavering confidence. They say that life-or-death situations bring out your true nature, your real self. You know at once whether you are a warrior or a coward. Afterward, you are never the same.

Ted went out the very next day to find the Boxer Man, and he did, and when he confronted the bully he got boxed, too, one swift jab to the lip. It turned out the man himself was an actual boxer, trained in the Bronx. Ted had to get stitches, but he said it was worth it, because the incident seemed to have brought out his true nature, too. He told me he realized he would do anything to protect me, and our dog; that it was his duty to keep us safe.

We moved in three days.

CHAPTER 13

Temp to Perm

It was Ted who found the apartment. I had been sitting at home, writing an essay about witnessing a dog attack for, I hoped, *The New York Times Magazine*. But I wasn't getting much done. Rex had been pawing at me all day while I sat at the computer. It was a new habit of his, to stand behind me and bark and paw and nudge, a clear indication that I wasn't doing a proper job of catering to him. To think this dog had once had no confidence! Now his sense of entitlement filled the room.

"Would you stop?!" I kept saying as he swatted me on the shoulder. "I'm writing about you. The least you could do is leave me alone!" He'd get an indignant look on his face, and swat me again, and make a little noise that sounded like frustration at not being able to communicate his exact needs. And frustration with me for not being able to read his mind. Then he nudged my hand with his snout—the hand that held the mouse. He was trying to coerce me into scratching the top of his head. "Stop!" I took my hand away.

The week before, I'd read an article in *The Atlantic* entitled "The Truth About Dogs." This article posited that dogs only pretend to like you to get what they want. They may *appear* to be loyal, loving, and devoted, but in reality they are "con artists of the first degree." Years of domestic evolution have taught dogs that if they *act* loyal they will get rewarded. They will get food, they will get shelter, they will get comfort. So dogs have perfected the act.

Next Rex tried to crawl onto my lap.

"Stop it! Do you know what comes right before Pets in the Yellow Pages? *Pests.* Now go away. Before I call an exterminator." He let out one last huff and curled himself under the desk.

It was then that the phone rang. "Hey!" Ted sounded excited. "I found an apartment! We're moving."

"Where? When?" I was still half-inside my writing world and had literally forgotten our intention to move.

"East Eightieth Street."

"Isn't that, like, the Upper East Side?"

"Kind of. It's technically on the border between the Upper East Side and Yorkville."

"The border," I said. "Story of our lives."

Rex pushed himself into the Sphinx position and lifted his ears, as if he detected some subtext in my words.

Ted sighed. "It was the only apartment I could find within our price range. You'll like it. Aren't you going to thank me for finding this for us?"

"Thank you," I said. "Is there a Starbucks?"

"I think there are eighteen of them on our block."

"Well, that's a plus."

"It's like that thing I read in *The Onion* a while back: 'New Chain of Starbucks Scheduled to Open Inside the Restrooms of Existing Starbucks.'"

"Oh, goodie. That'll save all us writers from having to pack up our computers and lose our tables every time we have to go to the bathroom."

"Pack up your computer soon," Ted said. "Because we're moving in three days."

"How can we possibly be ready in three days?"

"I'm going to take care of all of that. John and Chip already said they would help. If you can just take care of the dog and your own clothes, I'll take care of the rest."

After we'd hung up, I looked around the apartment, stunned. What caught my eye was the gold thong bikini on the wall, which was supposed to have inspired me to lose weight. And now we were moving, just like that. I felt panicked for a second and I couldn't say why. Was it because we'd never had a chance to eat at the Cuban place around the corner? Or visit the new gallery over on Clinton Street, or even the new doggie day care we hadn't had a chance to check out?

But wait. Was moving not the very thing I said I had always wanted? And was moving to the Upper East Side not the first single step, in that journey of a thousand miles, that would lead to the cabinets full of lemon curd?

I called Rex back into the room. He trotted in, tail held high, nails click-clicking across our shitty old linoleum floor. "We're moving!" I rubbed his head behind both ears. "We're movin' on up!" He wriggled with joy.

Ted, true to his word, did not ask me to help with any of the lifting when we moved three days later. He and his friends rented a moving van and took care of all the boxes. All I had to do was lift the dog's leash. And take him for one last walk around the block. Solemnly, deliberately, with that heightened awareness you have whenever you know you are doing something for the last time, Rex and I walked through the neighborhood. We walked past the abandoned bodegas and the poultry processing plant, past the community garden and the man who sold pickles out of a giant oak barrel, and I saw beauty in all of it, and also the grit. I saw how everything worked together, especially in New York. The sunflowers in the community garden drooped, their huge yellow heads sagging like weary laborers, ready to give in to the fall. This made me feel nostalgic again, because I hate endings, and by the time I returned to our apartment building I was teary eyed and the dog hadn't even peed. It was as if he knew he didn't need to mark this territory anymore. It was no longer his concern.

"I heard you were leaving," Waylon said outside the building. He wore a heavy black leather jacket and a turtleneck and jeans. It was almost winter. I guess you could say Waylon was fully clothed.

"Yes. Today, in fact. Believe it or not, I haven't even seen the place."

"Aren't you worried about that? What if you don't like it?"

"I didn't really like this place either. Well, I didn't love it. But that's New York, you know? Liking is good enough."

"I hear you," Waylon said. "How'd you find the place?"

"Ted found the apartment. And I'm fine with that. What matters is that someone finally made a decision. And it wasn't me. Which means if the apartment sucks, it's not my fault."

Rex paced around anxiously, sensing a major life change, looking for the comfort and safety of Ted. I bent down to stroke the dog, and soothe him, and tell him everything would be okay.

"Poor Leroy is worried," Waylon said. He bent down to pet the dog, too. "Leroy! Leroy my man! Who's going to be my main man if you ain't my man?"

Rex kissed him—his first non-Ted male kiss. I was about to explain this fact, but then I saw that Waylon had given himself a Mohawk, and it wasn't really that flattering, to tell you the truth.

As Ted and I drove away from Suffolk Street, I took one final look back at the streets we had walked for so many days. I spotted a used diaper in the gutter, and felt glad that we were leaving the edginess and the grit behind. Maybe we had outgrown it. Maybe it was impossible to keep your edge when you had a soft dog. Rex rode with his head out the window, smiling toward all the glorious buildings along Park Avenue, and wag-wag-wagging his tail.

Our new apartment, it turned out, was very much the same, in size and character, as the one we had just left behind. It was as if we had hauled the entire tenement building up eighty blocks. We were on the first floor of an old building with cracked tiles and soiled doors, and the two locks on the entry door were often broken, because our landlord, Bea Markowitz (whom we would soon call Bea Elzebub), did not give a shit. The light fixture in the foyer had no bulb—just a dangling wire—and it looked as though, if you pulled it, the whole ceiling would come down. And there were still bathrooms in the hallways, as we'd had in our old apartment building, but the big difference here was that these bathrooms were still in use.

The most important difference between this place and the last, however, was that we now had a 10021 zip code, and our living room faced the street. The first thing Rex did when we stepped into the new apartment was run up to the front windows, put his front paws on the sill, and wag his tail. He looked back at us with a smile on his face. *A view!* his look seemed to say. *A tree!* Then he sneezed, which made me worry about foxtails up his nose.

"He likes it here," Ted said.

"He likes everything," I said.

"No he doesn't," Ted said.

"Yes he does. Except the occasional dog."

"He likes other dogs."

"Not all of them. Not unneutered males."

"That doesn't count," Ted said. And on and on it went.

Suddenly I felt right at home.

When our friends got word of the move they were surprised and bemused, but mostly they expressed concern, as if we had joined a cult.

"Don't cry for me Loisaida," our friend John the Poet sang into our answering machine, to the tune of "Don't Cry for Me Argentina." Loisaida is what the original, mostly Latino residents of the Lower East Side called the neighborhood.

Don't cry for me Loisaida
The truth is, I never left you
I might have moved
To the Upper East Side
To shop at Barney's.

For the record, John the Poet lived on East Eighty-second Street, two blocks away, and would later, with his beautiful corporate wife, move to Greenwich, never to be heard from again. That's a risk you take, moving to the Upper East Side.

For days he left us new verses, reminding us of all that we had left behind.

Don't cry for me Loisaida
The truth is, I never left you
All through my wild days
My mad existence
I really yearned for
A Sherry-Lehmann
Within walking distance.

John and I had gone to graduate school together. "I'm glad you're making good use of your poetry degree," Ted would say to John when he returned the calls. "Is that why they call it an MFA? As in Master of Fucking Around?"

John's little jingles made me wonder. I mean, sure, there was a certain unalluring vacuity to our new neighborhood: the cookie-cutter high-rises east of Third Avenue, full of white people with office jobs, who shuffled en masse to the subways in the morning, clutching briefcases, the women wearing sneakers with their suits and socks over their nylons. And yes, you could find just about every superstore imaginable on Eighty-sixth Street—a Staples, a Barnes & Noble, a Petco, an Old Navy, and a Gap, but you could not find a grungy café or an out-of-print copy of John Fante's *Ask the Dust*. (In fact, none of the bookstores on the Upper East Side even had dust.) And, yes, at night, the rows and rows of restaurants—none of them any good, unless you leapt into the category of Café Boulud or Le Cirque—filled with all those bland people who demanded bland food. And, yes, the bars were lamentably similar to the ones I had prowled in college, full of frat boys who called beer "brewskies" and shouted "yeesssss!" every time the Yankees or the Knicks or the Rangers scored. And no, you could not find a single writer working on his laptop inside the Starbucks of Yorkville (or even inside the restrooms!). Instead, you found legions of stroller mothers, who sat in great circles like pagan ritualists, blocking every possible aisle and exit with their children and their shopping bags, talking about baby nurses and baby monitors and baby food and rock, rock, rocking the strollers nonstop. For a while there I thought of giving up caffeine, but I was going to visit my family at Thanksgiving, so I needed to be fortified.

And you can say, without really offending anyone above or below Fourteenth Street, that the UES had no soul, that it was not "downtown." There was the cleanliness, of course, and the stateliness, and the spectacular, multimillion-dollar mansions as you got closer to the park. There was the unsurpassable wealth and beauty you saw at every turn. The sidewalks here were cleaner than the city's public restrooms, which meant that there were no chicken bones, no Lower East Side rats. You could lie down on these sidewalks and lick up spilled ice cream, and not catch a disease. Every block had a manicurist and a dry cleaner and a florist with orchids in the windows in beautiful Italian pots. The apartment buildings all had awnings and elaborate topiaries, and doormen in white gloves, and polished brass doors. When we walked under these awnings they'd be heated, a great gust of wealth and warmth that somehow made me feel kept. In a good way. Rex, under these heat lamps, would always look up and around, startled, as if he sensed a poltergeist in our midst. And then he would pull us along, past the boutiques and antiques stores and the gourmet grocery stores where you could buy all the lemon curd you wanted, from every possible corner of the globe. Every building had fabulous window displays, the kind that made you want to press your face against the glass and drool—over the shoes, over the hand-bags, over the three-hundred-dollar bras. But of course you couldn't drool around here. For that you had to go below Fourteenth Street. Here, no one even blinked at the prices. Because we had moved to one of the richest square miles in the entire world.

But beyond all that, beyond this superficial elegance, I felt a subtle current of something I had never detected on the Lower East Side. It was permanence. Upliftedness. The Lower East Side was full of wan-nabes who had not yet found their place in the world. They hoped to find it, of course, and they pursued it madly every day. And while that mad pursuit gave the city—and that neighborhood in particular— a kind of manic energy you could ride on for days or even years, no one in Loisaida really planned to stay there. Whereas here, on the Uppereasaida, everyone had arrived.

"Finally," I said to Tara on the phone. "We're on the right side of the tracks."

"Are you west of Lexington?" Tara said.

I refused to answer.

"Then you're on the wrong side of the tracks."

🐾 🐾

The best thing about the Upper East Side was Central Park. Ted and Rex and I first encountered the glories of Central Park on a sunny morning in November, at a time when the oak trees surrounding the reservoir were at their peak. The whole city blazed in the last-ditch effort of fall, that final high note, and we felt, that first time we strolled along the Bridle Path, as if we were finally seeing the world in color. As if our life on the Lower East Side had played itself out in black-and-white.

The Bridle Path that morning was filled with the city's brightest and boldest movers and shakers, all of whom got there at seven A.M. You could tell these were the type of people who *really* seized the day, by the throat. They looked angry and determined, and they stampeded past us in Prada jogging outfits and Nikes in styles that weren't officially coming out until next year. Ted and the dog and I walked along the path slowly, taking it all in as they hurtled past us—two more people in this city they had to leave in the dust.

"Move it, asshole!" people shouted as they zoomed past. "Get that dog on a leash."

"He *is* on a leash, you idiot!" Ted shouted back.

"Get that dog the fuck off the Bridle Path!" another man shouted. This one was wearing a Price Waterhouse T-shirt and a platinum watch.

"Dogs on leash are *allowed* on the Bridle Path!" I'd shout.

"Get the fuck out of the way!" This came from an elegant old woman with silver-gray hair. She had Burberry jogging shoes—a phenomenon I did not know existed.

❧ ❧

"So you're walkin' the bridal path, eh?" Tara said. In person. We met at our old place downtown—Café Limbo. They had terrific iced coffee there—a strong French roast that sent you orbiting. The dude behind the counter wore a T-shirt that said DEATH BEFORE DECAF and the bathrooms were lit only with tiny night-lights, so that the junkies couldn't lock themselves in and shoot up. City girls never came here for dates, because you could never tell if you had spinach in your teeth in the bathroom mirror. But I knew I would always feel at home here, no matter what.

"The Bridle Path is a place where psycho Upper East Siders jog!" I said. "Not a metaphor." But still I blushed.

Tara stared at me, inspecting me like a work of art. "I almost forgot what you look like. I thought you'd be wearing gloves and pearls."

"And I thought *you'd* have hair," I said. She had shaved her black hair into a buzz cut and bleached it blond, like Eminem. "When did you do that?"

"About four months ago," she said.

I bent down to pet the dog. Who was sitting peacefully under the table like a true French café dog. Tara had not yet asked about him. "We can start meeting here every few weeks again," I said. "It only takes me forty-five minutes to get down on the train. I can come down all the time."

"Everyone says that when they first move uptown. Next thing you know, you're pregnant and moving to Greenwich."

A man walked by with a big American bulldog on a preposterously thick chain. One of those chains you'd use to lock a motorcycle to a telephone pole. He was a tough-looking, squat man with a pushed-in face. He wore a striped Yankees shirt with matching shorts and the dog wore a spiked metal collar. "My dog fights," he announced to all the passersby. He seemed proud of this: he walked with his chest pushed out. "My dog fights," he said to the couple whose golden retriever rose to say hello. The bulldog reared up at the golden and the man yanked him back. I placed a protective hand on Rex's flank and held his collar, but my dog merely growled without even lifting his head.

"It's true that all dogs look like their owners," I said as the man strutted past our table. "You'd never see a face like that on the Upper East Side. Do you think I should get an Irish setter, to match my hair?"

"Do you have a cigarette?" Tara said.

"No, I quit again."

"When did you re-quit?" Tara asked.

"About four months ago. About three weeks after I restarted. Once the dog calmed down I didn't need the psychological addiction anymore. Now he's such a great dog."

Tara gazed out onto the sidewalk as if to flag down someone who did have a cigarette. She did. She scored. She lit up and exhaled. "You really love him," she said.

"Yes," I said. "It's a perfect love."

"I'm proud of you," Tara said. "At the way you stuck it out. Even with your writing. I haven't written diddly since we graduated. But here you are, plugging away, against all odds."

I blushed. "Oh, you've been too busy fending off all the rock stars who hit on you every night at the club."

"Speaking of, let's meet next time at Moomba. You have to be able to tell your grandchildren you saw Leo before he went passé."

"Let's," I said. "And we also have to go to Bryant Park Café. You know, I think that's exactly halfway between uptown and downtown. And I think they allow dogs!"

Tara took her lipstick out—it was a deep red color called Vampire. She offered me the first swipe (we always shared lipstick), but I shook my head no. Then Tara smiled and shook her head, too. "Upper East Side," she said.

"I keep telling you, it's just a place!" I said. "Not a metaphor!"

But what Tara said was true: that everyone morphs into something unrecognizable when they move uptown. You tell yourself it's not going to change your lifestyle, or your personality, when you get to that new 'hood. But in New York, everything always boils down to five blocks—the ones closest to your apartment. Our five blocks had a Starbucks and a movie theater and enough restaurants to feed Taiwan. We had five—count 'em, five—high-end thrift stores, filled with last season's—or even last month's—Versace and Chanel, and we had four spectacular gourmet grocery stores. And oh, the grocery stores! Within four blocks in each direction we had an Eli's, a Citarella, Grace's Marketplace, and Agata & Valentina—all expensive über-markets with the best of everything: cheeses, olives, meats, fish. You could buy a five-dollar tomato imported that morning from Holland, cold-pressed olive oils from Spain. There were homemade sorbets packed into miniature pineapples in the freezer, and tiny crème brûlées in the bakery aisles. Downtown, the closest grocery store was a Key Foods in the East Village, where more than once Ted and I had seen mice in the cereal aisles, and they sold without compunction curdled milk and expired meats. Buying food there had become a sordid, entirely distasteful experience, and that is why more often than not we ate out. That and the fact that I didn't really cook.

Now Ted got prime cuts of beef, and imported cold cuts for lunch. Rex got big, succulent bones from the butcher's counter, and freshly ground turkey, and fingerling potatoes from France.

"Don't cry for me Loisaida," John sang into my answering machine as I walked in the door. "The truth is—"

I picked up. "*You* shop at Citarella!" I said.

I suppose Rex loved the perks of the grocery stores, but what he loved best about the new 'hood was Central Park. Here, he found a whole new encyclopedia of smells to sniff out with his excellent nose. Here, he found a whole new catalog of flora and fauna, including ducks, geese, horses, one pheasant, raccoons, and tourist-fattened squirrels. These squirrels were not as wily or fast as their Lower East Side counterparts. They had been reduced to laziness by all the popcorn and peanuts the tourists fed them, and they no longer knew how to forage for food. From day one, Rex tooled around the park with his nose to the ground, his tail wagging with a speed and exuberance we had not yet seen. It was like a windshield wiper set on its highest speed. And Rex's delight brought us delight. We felt certain that the move had been a good choice.

Rex certainly thought so. Dogs were allowed off-leash in Central Park, as in all the New York City parks, before nine A.M. and after nine P.M. And because Central was the city's biggest and best park, we beheld the city's biggest and best dog population. Every day, scores of them would arrive in the morning, led by their guardians, or their dog walkers, or their manicurists and personal trainers, and they would be released into the park's wide-open fields. Ted and I stared at this phenomenon our first morning, delighted and wide-eyed. These dogs were, forgive the pun, a breed apart from the mixes and rescues we encountered on the Lower East Side. There were Bernese mountain dogs and Belgian Malinois. There was even a Tibetan lion dog, a breed I thought had been eradicated by the Chinese. There were varieties of shepherds and sight hounds and scent hounds I had seen only at the Westminster Dog Show, and they were all gorgeous and shiny and happy to be alive.

For two hours in the morning they romped and frolicked, chased and were chased, played tug-of-war or catch, or swam in the lake. It was like Westminster on acid. Or more likely Veuve Clicquot.

At nine on the dot, we would all head back to our townhouses, or our tenements, or our deluxe apartments in the sky. We humans walked en masse, all of us attached by leashes to all these dogs, of all different sizes, shapes, and countries of origin. The dogs strained onward, pulling us, their varied tails a-wag-wag-wagging like the rows of flags outside the UN. Walking among those dogs and their people I had the sense that I was part of something larger, a group.

But to truly belong on the Upper East Side, you had to shell out some bucks. You had to join a charitable organization or club. This lends you clout in a city where most people have clout spilling out of their Fendi baguettes. And in the 10021 zip code, even the dogs belong to clubs. Spend an hour in Central Park, and you can behold the Weimaraner Club, the Border Collie Club, the French Bulldog Brigade. It seemed that the guardians of purebreds stuck together, like little high-school cliques, and met in certain parts of the park whose locations they wouldn't reveal. "I don't want it to get around," an anonymous member of the Pug Play Group told me. She wore giant Jackie O sunglasses and had her hair wrapped in a scarf. "Because then everyone will want to join, including the non-pugs."

"A non-pug?" I said. "Is that a breed?" She squinted at me in the sun and I squinted back. I didn't want her to know whether I was joking or not.

One man we met—the president of the Gentle Giant Club, a multicultural club that included Scottish deerhounds, Cane Corsos, and Great Danes among its members—kept three Russian wolfhounds in his apartment. "People make snide remarks all the time to me on the sidewalks," he said. "They tell me how cruel I am for having these dogs in the city. They tell me I should be put in jail. But look at them now." The two male wolfhounds tore after each other at lightning speed, covering the length of a football field in sixty seconds. The female, whom the man had rescued recently, seemed to be playing Mom with a Jack Russell terrier, who allowed the great wolfhound to carry him around by the scruff. She'd set him down in a sand pile, walk away, and the terrier would run back up to her again and bow down before her so that she could seize his scruff once more. "Chewy, put that down!" the man shouted. The guardian of the terrier laughed and said it was okay. "Her name is actually Anna Karenina," he told us, "but I started to call her Chewbacca and it just stuck. My wife still calls her Anna though. What's in a name?" He told us that this wolfhound had been rescued from a puppy mill and was so emaciated she had to be removed by stretcher when the rescue group came. "All she did, all her life, was lie in a cage and birth puppies. I don't know what happened to her puppies. But I can tell she still misses them terribly. Every night she arranges all her chew toys along her stomach and curls around them so that they can nurse."

"Our dog kills his toys," I said.

Ted added, "He eviscerates stuffed animals."

"What kind of dog is he?" the man asked. We all looked around for Rex, who was tearing across the Great Lawn in pursuit of a squirrel.

"A French spaniel," I said.

"An English setter," Ted said at the same time. If we ever got married and grew old together, I knew what would be on our headstones. "He's a French spaniel," mine would say. Ted's would say, "No, he's not. He's an English setter."

The man looked at us both. Ted held his eye contact longer.

"There's one man who has three setters," the man with the wolfhounds told us. "He usually walks around a stand of trees called the Pinetum at around eight. You should get together with him."

Ted smiled. "We will."

We set out to find the Setter Man that evening. Both of us, I suppose, had distinct missions in mind in finding him and joining his club. Ted wanted an expert to prove our dog was indeed an English setter, and I wanted to strike up a fast friendship with this country gentleman, who no doubt weekended in Millbrook and threw fabulous dinner parties full of hunt people in smart clothes. Finally—all those invitations to country houses that I had dreamed of last summer would come pouring in! It was easy to spot the Setter Club as we approached the Pinetum. Its one lone member wore an orange track suit and was busy doing deep-knee squats near a bench. Three gorgeous setters wove in and out among the trees, their noses to the ground, their coats shiny, their gaits smooth and quick. The man communicated with his dogs in a series of clicks, whistles, and heps. Two of the setters were tricolor (red, black, and brown) and the third was white with orange speckles—a belton setter, we later learned.

Their faces were focused, serious, and suddenly I understood the emotion behind the face of Rex. He wasn't mopey or depressed. He was a bird dog who needed to be in the presence of birds. "Look at how splendid they are!" I shouted. "Let's go say hi!"

But the thing about English setters, we quickly learned, is they don't seem to want to belong to any club that will have them as a member.

Those setters showed no interest in Rex, and vice versa. You'd think such gorgeous creatures would want to stand together and toss their gorgeous heads, the way the supermodels do at Moomba. But no. All four of them just wanted to sniff the ground and follow scent trails. And it wasn't wariness or fear or even aloofness that kept the dogs apart. They just all had better things to do.

"This explains a lot about his personality," I said to Ted. "The face, the behavior. All this time I thought he had been scarred for life by being taken away from his mother too young. But this is genetics. It's in his blood."

"Are you saying he's a setter?"

"No. Well, maybe half."

"Let's go talk to the setter guy," Ted said. "And join his gun club."

Thus we learned that people with setters don't want to join any clubs either. The man showed no interest in us. When we cornered him to express admiration for his setters, and introduce him to ours, he didn't even stop doing his knee bends. "Two males," he said between knee bends. "One female. Mother. Sons. Yours?"

"Male."

"Handsome. Llewellyn?

"Likely," said Ted.

"Inconclusive," I said. "Abandoned. Rescued. Formerly aggressive. Cured."

The man laughed a brisk German laugh: "Hah!"

We said our goodbyes and continued upon the winding paths. Rex did figure eights around the trees, his ears flopping backward, his lips stretched into that doggie smile. "Those hunting dogs are such loners," I said, kind of sadly.

"Like dog, like owner, I guess," Ted said.

I didn't know whether he was referring to himself or me. But seeing the setters made me think loner-ness wasn't something you had to cure.

On our way home from the park, we walked past the Metropolitan Museum of Art. It was only four blocks from our apartment and one of the greatest museums in the world. Seeing it each day made me feel lucky to be a New Yorker. Tonight, and every night, some high-powered charity held its benefit there, which meant that every night, as Ted and I walked past the Met on our Late Night Walk, we'd stop and watch the glitterati descending that grand staircase; we'd listen to the laughter and the gossip and the swish of the women's voluminous gowns. "Another party we weren't invited to," Ted always said, putting his arm around me. Within weeks, this became our favorite new joke on the Upper East Side. And sometimes it still mattered that I hadn't been invited to the Costume Institute Gala, that Oscar de la Renta had not telephoned to ask me to wear one of his gowns. Sometimes, I'd still feel that tiny sting of regret that told me I might never be rich or famous or even own a pair of Manolo Blahnik shoes. And then the dog would do something silly: grab the stick from Ted's hand and run away with it. Or seize the leash in his mouth and pull. And then I'd be running alongside the dog on the sidewalk, laughing, skipping, the Met on my right and Jackie O's former apartment on my left, and Ted would be saying, "No leash biting!" in his happy dog voice, and I'd be glad—positively, solidly, permanently glad—that most of the shoes in my closet were now Merrells and Nikes. Because now they allowed me to run and skip and play.

As I've said, no relationship ever remains on a plateau. The sidewalks may have been wider on the Upper East Side, but there were also more people with whom we had to share them. Tourists and residents alike. And dogs. The street dogs were different from their counterparts in the park. And I don't really mean street, I mean avenue. On Madison, most of the dogs were little pansy froufrou types, made up with lavender crocodile collars with matching leashes and brass hardware, and little barrettes. Here, the froufrous were walked by women you could tell had standing appointments for blowouts at

Brad Johns. I bet the dogs got blowouts, too. And manicures. Some of the dogs had highlights—from their summers in the Hamptons—and a second country house upstate. All of them lived in better apartments than we did, of course, and they had doormen who opened doors for them, and addressed them by their formal names. A lot of the dogs were named Madison. The Lower East Side had more creative names: a fluffy bichon named Cotton Mather, a silver standard poodle named Dorian Gray. One of the Marching Band Man's dogs was named Sheba, short for "She Who Must Be Obeyed." But on the UES, your dog revealed your status. Thus, Maddie, Mercedes, Fendi, Countess, Your Majesty, even Lloyd (as in Lloyd Neck).

On our own block we had an Afghan named Paris and a mastiff named Joy, after the most expensive perfume in the world. Whenever she saw Rex, Joy would lie down on the sidewalk and wriggle her big fat body onto her back. She'd wait there, belly up, while her human tried to get her to move on. "Joy, darling, up! Up! Let's go." But a woman in Manolos cannot budge a 120-pound dog. "Oh, go ahead and say hi then."

Rex would come up and sniff her privates, and somehow the transaction would be complete. "What a way to say hi," Ted said. Joy, ecstatic, would leap up to play, but Rex would already be looking onward, toward the park.

"Who's aloof?" Ted would say. "Who's a Loof Boy?"

Rex was hands-down the best-looking dog on the block. More classic than the Afghans, more elegant than the mastiff, and clearly superior to the little pansy froufrous, who always got gummy red streaks under their eyes no matter how many times they were bathed. "He's a French spaniel," I would say to anyone who asked, and I said it rather haughtily, although deep down I didn't want to be the type of person who would lie. But I couldn't help it. Daisy Buchanan's voice may have sounded like money; my dog *looked* like money. He *belonged*.

And when you belong, you start to want to keep out those who don't belong. When you share so little space with so many people, you start to get territorial.

Two dogs were already living in our building when we moved in. We had Floozy, who lived right next door, in an apartment that mirrored our own. Floozy was an old girl, an eighteen-year-old geriatric, and she may, at some point in her life, have been a wirehaired terrier, but now she looked like Yoda. She was incontinent, and toothless, and her poor arthritic body was moguled with tumors and the occasional patch of fur. Her guardians—two schoolteachers named Nick and Sarah—had to carry her up and down the stairs twice a day so that she could do her business, and the rest of the time Floozy wheezed or slept.

So, needless to say, Floozy did not give Rex any opposition in the territory department. Nor did our other dog-neighbor: a neutered male Rottweiler named Ziggy. The stereotypical reputation of Rottweilers is a fierce one—brave, loyal guard dogs with powerful jaws—so I was admittedly biased and wary when Rex first moved in. But Rex and Ziggy, from the very beginning, displayed a mutual tolerance of each other that surprised me. At their first meeting, in the foyer of our apartment building, they greeted each other with the defeated resignation of inmates being led to their cells.

What are you in here for, man? Ziggy's indifferent sniff seemed to say. Ziggy wore a silver leather collar with rhinestone studs.

Four attempted escapes, might have been Rex's answer.

I hear you, man. I'm in for scavenging trash cans. Sucks, man. But it beats the streets.

I was frankly stunned by the lack of incident. Rex, as we know, still did not like other dogs at this stage in his development and more often than not tried to attack them. So why did he not hate Ziggy? Perhaps Rex was too confused about the move to worry about such matters as territory; perhaps both he and Ziggy were humbled by the sight of Floozy-slash-Yoda and decided, like wise old Buddhists who contemplate the impermanence of life, to have compassion for all living creatures. I like to think that, deep down inside, the main reason the two dogs got along was that they had an empathy for each other that transcended borders. They were both formerly formidable creatures who had been neutered and fettered and forced to wear pansy collars. They both suffered the indignity of having to navigate their large bodies through narrow hallways, of constantly having soot and grit and tenement dust make its way up their nostrils, of having to be walked by teetering, easily overpowered women who insisted on wearing tight white jeans and high heels.

"No, Ziggy!" I could often hear Liv, my neighbor and Ziggy's guardian, shout. "Don't jump up on me, Ziggy, no! Aw, frig, Ziggy, you ruined another pair of pants." That last word always came out in two syllables: *pay-ants*. Liv was a Jersey girl.

Anyway, Rex and Ziggy managed to cohabit benignly, and Rex seemed proud of his new dominion. He made sure the hallways stayed free of burglars, Jehovah's Witnesses, and drug dealers, and Ted and I relaxed into the notion that the world was now a much safer place.

But then our neighbor Liv's boyfriend moved in, and he brought with him another huge Rottweiler named Tank. The boyfriend, Gregory, was a tall, bald, gorgeous African American who wore gold chains and silk shirts and delicate floral cologne. He worked as a personal trainer and his manly, oversized muscles gleamed like polished wood. Tank possessed the same sort of rippling glossiness as Gregory, and when the two of them walked together they parted crowds— what with the commanding scowls on their faces, and their muscles shifting and gleaming with every step. Rex, however, hated Tank from the very start. If they encountered each other in the hallways, a snarling match would ensue, both Rex and Tank straining on their prong collars, barking savagely, baring their teeth. Rex seemed to go into a trance of anger: his pupils would narrow to pinpoints and his voice would deepen to a primordial bellow, and when he barked it was as if the fury and injustices of all his ancestors were being channeled instantaneously through his throat. I did not know it was possible for a ten-month-old canine to have such deep-seated emotions, but there it was. I'm told there is something called Spaniel Rage, a syndrome in which inbred springers suddenly turn psycho and have to be put on drugs. I'd thought it was an urban myth. But now I thought I understood the meaning of Spaniel Rage.

And where did all this rage come from? What incited it? Did it come from having been abandoned as a puppy, and possibly abused? Was it simply a territory thing? Or was something much larger at work? It could be something that involved balls. Two of them, to be precise. Tank was unneutered.

According to the Monks of Steel, our dog suffered from something called "intermale aggression." "The problem is an inescapable canine situation related to testosterone secretion and the environment in which males are raised," the Monks said.

"Huh?" I said to Ted.

"To control this, defecation and urination by a male must be restricted to the dog's immediate area. This is so that he does not mark off the whole neighborhood as his private domain, which will easily lead to confrontations with other males who intersect his kingdom."

"I thought we were supposed to let him mark," I said. "To build his confidence." On the Lower East Side, Rex had marked all the blocks stretching from Ludlow Street to the East River. He had laid claim to some undesirable property, such as the Columbia projects and that noisy stretch of Delancey Street under the Williamsburg Bridge. But the real estate market had skyrocketed like one week after we'd left. (The old chicken factory on Pitt Street was going to be converted into condos that would start at $400K.) And Rex's holdings had increased even more dramatically now that he had marked off most of the Upper East Side. He had claimed, much to my delight, some of the most magnificent architecture in Manhattan, such as the George and Martha Whitney House (designed by Cross & Cross), and the Vincent and Helen Astor House (designed by Mott B. Schmidt). Rex peed on these, as well as the boundary lines of Gracie Mansion and the Met. Our dog was a wealthy landowner indeed. And now the Monks were saying this was a problem?

Oh, yes they were. We had seen the enemy and the enemy had scrota.

This enemy-among-us added a new dimension to our lives with Rex. Suddenly the battle zone was not far away, in the South Bronx for example (where we never went anyway, but where, ironically, my storage space was), but right outside our kitchen doorway. I had to press my ear against the door in the mornings to make sure the Rottweilers were not in the hallway (note the plural: Ziggy had, by his close association with the Mortal Enemy, become an enemy, too). Then, if the coast was clear, Rex, Ted, and I would scurry down the stairs like fugitives. I found, as we emerged into the sunlight, that I carried a new tension within me, a nervous energy stemming from the fact that a pair of balls could be lurking on any corner. My skin prickled at the sight of any approaching canine, and I learned to watch Rex's nose. He could detect an excess of testosterone ten blocks ahead, and the whole experience felt very *film noir*.

Whenever Rex saw Tank coming his whole body tensed up, his fur rose and bristled, and he would start in with the Spaniel Rage. Next to Tank, Rex looked puny, a little spaniel squirt, and I worried for his safety. I tried to sweet-talk him, give him treats, anything to make him back off, but nothing was stronger than his primal fury. "He thinks he owns this sidewalk," I'd say with desperate cheerfulness to the horror-stricken passersby, or to Liv if we got close enough. "Well, he doesn't," the well-dressed man who lived in the old Whitney mansion finally said. "*I* do. And you need to learn how to control that dog. This is a residential block," he said. "Not some dog-fighting ring."

The worst barking matches occurred when Tank, in sight of Rex, lifted his leg on Rex's trash cans. Rex raged so much I worried that his vocal cords might burst, as well as my eardrums. My heart rate increased so rapidly from all the nervous tension I realized I was getting a legitimate cardiovascular workout from a quick trip around the block.

"It's just a garbage can," I'd finally tell him with a little impatience. "It's not as if it's a villa in St. Tropez. Come. Let's go back inside. Rex, come!"

But Rex would not go back inside until he could place his final mark on the garbage cans with his own superior scent. Only then would he be willing to mount the stairs; only then would a balanced look return to his face. And we could retire for the evening, smug with the knowledge that we had maintained our positions in the world. At least until the next morning when it all began again. Good Lord! It really was as if I were in the middle of a genuine turf war with two rival gangs.

Inside, Ted and I were also having turf wars. Moving always brings out latent territorial issues with a couple, especially if you move to a slightly smaller apartment in New York. Eternal, existential questions arise: Who am I? Where am I going? Who gets the closet? Who gets the extra shelf in the tiny bathroom medicine cabinet? Should we get basic or premium cable? And how do you split something in two that is barely enough for one? You have to make yourself so small in a New York City apartment, and that is hard to do—it's almost counterproductive—in such an expansive city. So you start to feel like you are living inside a pressure cooker all the time. With an equally compressed boyfriend. And a dog.

Our turf wars began just two hours after we moved into the new apartment. "I see you've already claimed the bigger closet," Ted said as he took off his T-shirt, which was all sweaty from the just-completed move. He looked only half amused. "Where am I going to put my clothes?"

"I've been thinking about that," I said. I maneuvered between stacks of crates and cardboard boxes four feet high. "I was thinking we could buy a big oak armoire, and put it here?" I motioned to the front corner of the bedroom. "We could put it behind one of the French doors."

"That means we could only open one door."

"We'd only need one."

"Don't be ridiculous," Ted said. "Can't I just put some of my clothes in your closet, to make up for the fact that yours is bigger than mine? Or maybe I could at least put one of my guitars in there?"

"Well, I could try to make some room." I made an effort to smoosh my clothes to the left a few inches—against a united front of Armani knockoffs, feather boas, and metallic blouses—but nothing budged.

"Look at all the crap you have in there! Why don't you get rid of some of that stuff?"

I knew where this was going.

"You mean like this?" I brought out the leather miniskirt and held it toward him, close enough so that he could smell its leathery night-club smell.

Ted's eyes narrowed, as if he had just puffed from a joint. "No. I guess you can't get rid of that. You look good in that." His thoughts wandered off, I could tell, to one of our early dates, which had ended up with the two of us gyrating lewdly on some blues-club dance floor.

"Or this?" I held up the gold thong.

"We'll work something out," he said.

But space is an issue that is never entirely resolved in New York City. No matter how many times you take the shuttle bus to Ikea, no matter how creative you become in your storing methods (say, sus-pending bicycles from the ceiling, or storing pans in the oven), in the end there just isn't enough room. And there's no getting around it. Old space-related issues are automatically reactivated anytime you move, or think of moving, or try to introduce a new object into your apartment, say a spoon or a toaster oven. Or a large crate for the dog.

Which leads us to Rex again. When we moved to the new apartment, we decided to get a dog crate, in the hopes that we might travel with Rex someday, but the big question was where to put it. We lived, as I say repeatedly, for shock value if nothing else, in a two-hundred-and-ninety-nine-square-foot apartment. If you subtract our mass (twenty-four cubic feet of human), that of the dog (six cubic feet of canine), that of the furniture, the cabinetry, the milk crates, the space-saving shelving units from Ikea, the shoe storage units that doubled as end tables, the linen crate that doubled as a coffee table, etc., we were left with about nineteen square feet of space to actually move around in: nine in the living room, six in the adjoining bedroom/office/dog supply room, four in the "kitchen," and about six inches in the bathroom. Rex's dog crate would take up an additional twenty-six by thirty-six by twenty-eight inches. So something had to give. Some*one* had to give up some of his/her space. And neither Ted nor I was willing to do that.

"Why don't you get rid of some of your clothes?" Ted began to say over and over again. It was like all I had to do was press Play and go about my business, half listening, because I knew it all by heart. "Why don't you go through your closet and throw away anything you haven't worn in a year?"

"You have to understand—before I moved to New York I got rid of half my wardrobe. What you see here is the pared-down version of me—only the essentials."

"You consider a mermaid costume essential?" he said. "Or old *Playboy* magazines? What are you, someone's father?"

I laughed. "I won the *Playboy* College Fiction Contest a few years ago. They gave me a free subscription. And apparently it's for life."

"Give the magazines to me, then. But get rid of some of those clothes!"

"Here." I pulled that old pink linen dress out of the closet, still in its dry-cleaning bag. "I'll retire this. It will symbolize the end of my American Dream."

"Very funny," Ted said. "Well then, why don't you get rid of some of your books? You have fifty-two square feet of books."

"Why don't *you* get rid of some of your videotapes? You have twenty-four square feet of videotape, plus an additional twenty of television and video equipment."

"We both use the TV!"

"But I don't watch every single episode of *The Simpsons* ever recorded."

"I need those for work," he said, instinctively pulling episode Eight Hundred and Ninety-two to his chest.

"Well, *I* need my books for work, too."

"I haven't seen you read anything but a dog book since June. Put them under the bed, for Christ's sake."

I marched over to Ted's closet, threw the door open, and pointed hatefully at his guitar. "Look!" I said. His guitar was stored in his closet at a forty-five-degree angle to the wall, thereby creating three square feet of Wasted Space. "Look at this! You insist on storing this guitar at an angle. You insist it would be *bad for the guitar* to press it up against the wall. We could store a forty-pound bag of dog food in there! So don't talk to *me* about being frivolous."

Our argument then deteriorated into accusations about who wasn't appreciating whom, whose fault it was that we lived in such a small apartment, and who was being more selfish about not giving in, which led to proclamations that we shouldn't be together, and threats on both our parts to move out. "I don't want to live in this shithole anyway," I'd shout. "It sucks!"

"You go out and try to find something better then!" Ted shouted. "And see how far you get!"

And finally, after we had been shouting and snarling for ten minutes like a spaniel versus a Rott, Rex let out an exasperated moan. It was quite unlike any sound we had ever heard from him before. "What is it?" I said to the dog. "What?" Rex wagged his tail just once, like a judge bringing down his gavel. His face held a look of self-righteousness and worry. Then he started to verbalize something—a complex, earnest mumble that sounded like an attempt at human words. *Build some shelves in the bedroom,* he seemed to say. *Buy bookshelves that are twice the height. Put that wardrobe behind the French doors. And I don't need a crate. I just want us all to get along. Why can't we all get along?*

"He's talking to us," I said.

"He doesn't like it when we argue," Ted said.

And then, like that, we were focusing all our attention on the dog, petting him, talking baby talk, saying how cute he was, what a good boy he was. Rex soaked it all in: case closed, court adjourned. "Who's a referee?" Ted said. "Who's my little referee?" Then we were putting on our matching baseball caps to take the dog to the park. (Making sure of course that Tank wasn't in the hallway before we ventured out there.) End of argument. For now.

For days it went on like this: the turf war, the escalating arguments, Rex bringing down the gavel, the truce, and then the donning of the baseball caps and the trip to the park. And sometimes we'd see Tank, and sometimes we didn't. Sometimes there'd be Spaniel Rage, sometimes peace. After an argument about where to put the microwave, and whether Ted's gargantuan collection of matchbooks had to go into storage or deserved a place on the shelf, Ted and I actually didn't talk for two days. I'd come home to the apartment after work to find Ted with his jaw set, watching the television. Rex of course would come bounding over, and leap and spin as I took off my shoes, and practically knock me over with his kisses when I knelt down to say hello. "At least someone's happy to see me," I'd say loudly. "At least someone doesn't care about my clothes. Who's my love? Who's my handsome little love?"

"Are you going to get rid of some of those books?" Ted said.

There were twin cocker spaniels who lived on our block, and the man they belonged to told us they were named Mr. Nice and Mrs. Mean. Ted couldn't resist. He started to call me Mrs. Mean. Which was presented as a loving nickname, but still it had a sting. So I never called him Mr. Nice in return.

Rex, so unnerved by all that infighting, began to chew on the furniture. And hide in his crate. "Hey, he's crate-training himself," Ted said. Anything the dog did was cute. "He's getting used to his crate! What a good boy!"

"I don't know how you two do it," Ted's friend from rural Virginia would always say—he of the built-in pool and the landscaped yard. "Lolly and I would be divorced if we tried to live the way you live."

"We're not even married yet," Ted said. "It's like relationship boot camp."

"Well, any couple that can survive a two-hundred-ninety-nine-square-foot apartment is a sturdy couple indeed."

"Now I understand why there are eighteen Starbucks in our

neighborhood," I said to Tara. "And eighteen more franchises inside their restrooms. There are eighteen thousand couples stuffed into these high-rises, arguing about space. Starbucks is where they all come to escape."

As Tara and I were talking, I heard Tank outside our door, growling and scratching, trying to claw his way in. I could see his black nose through the one-inch space at the bottom of the door. "Hold on," I told Tara. "There's an impending crisis." And sure enough, Rex came scrambling from the back bedroom and dove toward the door, barking more loudly than Tank. I nudged Rex aside and brought out my spray bottle of Grannick's Bitter Apple, an all-natural dog repellent with an unpleasant taste. I crouched down and sprayed it straight into Tank's nostrils, which made him roar and snort like a bull.

"Is that Ted?" Tara said.

"No, it's a neighbor's dog. It's a long story."

I heard Gregory say, "Come on, old boy, give it a rest," and pull the snorting Tank away. Rex barked one last time in triumph: *And stay away!*

"We're having turf wars," I said. "And I'm resigned to the fact that it will never end."

But then I saw our new neighbor's apartment. Sarah, very kindly, had brought some gazpacho over to our apartment Sunday night, and the following evening, I knocked on her door, to present her with some garlic-dill pickles from the Essex Street Market and to return her bowl. She asked me in, of course, and there I beheld the Apartment That Mirrored Our Own. Everything was as we had it, but in reverse: the old kitchen as you walked in, the nonworking fireplace in the interim room; French doors leading to the bedroom in the back. And yet, and yet, their apartment seemed livable somehow. It had a vibe of ease, of calm. Everything seemed settled, as if the furniture had decided to stick around for a while. The door to the wardrobe could shut, meaning that it wasn't overstuffed with asinine party clothes.

Floozy waddled out, bumping blindly into the door frame as she entered, and then positioned her body between Sarah and me. The calm, brave, and unassuming way she guarded Sarah touched me. "She's like the rabbit in *Monty Python and the Holy Grail*," I said.

Sarah laughed. "She thinks she is, at least. She thinks she is a fierce and formidable creature." She picked the dog up. "Poor old girl. According to medical science, she should have been dead long ago." Then she offered to show me the sweater she was knitting for Floozy. "For when the weather gets cooler, of course." She explained that no one wanted to pet Floozy anymore—not since she lost all her fur. "And I hope this, you know, will change things." She held up the little pink garment, made of a delicate wool thread.

"Was Floozy ever territorial?" I asked.

"Nah, she's female. All she wants is love," Sarah said, picking up Floozy and kissing her. "Don't you, little Flooz?"

Sarah looked at me from over the top of the dog's head with something like pity. I could tell she had heard our arguments through the wall.

I left the apartment stunned. How had Sarah and Nick managed to be so normal in *their* two-hundred-and-ninety-nine-square-foot apartment? Why were they not at each other's throats?

Perhaps it was simply a difference between being a new couple and an established couple. Sarah and Nick had been living together seven years by the time we moved in, whereas Ted and I had only been there seven weeks. But I think something larger was at play—something that made all the difference. Nick and Sarah had pared their lives down to fit their apartment. They had compromised; they had merged.

Back inside my own apartment, I inspected it slowly, with new eyes. There were very clear delineations between my stuff and Ted's. Last week, thinking I'd appease Ted, I'd rearranged all the books on the shelves according to height and color, so that it wouldn't look like a jumbled mess, and when Ted came home he balked, and made me unarrange them again, because he couldn't tell which books were mine and which were his. There were milk crates stacked from floor to ceiling, stuffed with file folders and Ted's winter clothes. Things disappeared—they fell behind the refrigerator, or down into the space between the wall and the stove, but we would never go so far as to try to retrieve anything, because that stove was perhaps forty years old. And so was the dirt behind it. And because the floors weren't level we were constantly breaking water glasses and knocking things over. Nothing was fixed or solid; nothing seemed safe.

I looked over at Rex, who was curled up on the analyst's couch.

He opened one eye and acknowledged me, and then closed it again, as if to say: *This is not my doing.* Which made me laugh. I rushed over to kiss and coo over him. "You're so cute, you're such a cutie cute. Who's a sweetie sweet?" He kissed me. He smelled like comfort food. His eyes were all puffy from sleep.

Oh, how I loved this funny, complicated dog. I knew I would bend over backwards to make this dog's life good. I'd do *anything* for this dog, I realized. Shouldn't I at least attempt to do the same for Ted?

And so, at last, I decided to make more room for Ted in my life, and in my heart.

That evening, when Ted came home from a developing session at the darkroom, I told him I was ready to get rid of some of my books. "You were right," I said. "I don't need them all."

"We can put some into storage," Ted said. "Then as a reward I'll take you both to Krispy Kreme."

We spent a few hours packing and labeling boxes and then, triumphantly, we carried three stackable bookshelves out to the curb. As I wiped the final bit of bookshelf dust from my hands, I felt lighter somehow; cleansed. "Now there's room for a Rex crate," I said.

Ted, too, seemed pleased. In fact, the look on his face was that of Rex getting in that final pee on the garbage can—smug with the knowledge that he had maintained his position in the world.

"Look at you!" I said. "I think *you're* the one who suffered from intermale aggression. With me."

"Yes, yes," Ted said. "Very funny."

"Why don't we all go for a walk?" I said. "Before the sun goes down."

And in the time it took us to retrieve the dog and come back out onto the sidewalk with our matching baseball caps, another couple had claimed the bookshelves. This happens all the time in New York—one man's trash is another man's treasure. And this couple was having a familiar debate. "We don't have room for these," the woman was saying. "We don't have room for another box of Q-tips." And he countered by saying that they were too old to be using cinder blocks and planks. You could tell they were living together just because of the real estate market. "This will be a step up," the man said. "Trust me."

Ted and I looked at each other and laughed. Rex, however, didn't see the point in just standing there, so he inched toward the book-cases, prepared to lift his leg. I held back on his leash. "Those aren't yours anymore," I whispered. Rex continued to tug on his leash and, realizing I wasn't going to move with him, turned around and looked at me, perplexed. "Tank won't get them either," I said. "I promise. Now come on, let's go."

We went then, to the park, a pack of three. Rex raced off after squirrels, so happy to be tearing around off-leash he didn't even bother to mark any territory. He owned us, I realized. We were his place, and his space. And that's all the territory he was ever going to need. Things felt complete.

"Mrs. Nice," Ted said.

I teased: "Mr. Mean."

On the way home from the park, Ted and I stopped at an expensive pet store on Madison to pick up another forty-pound bag of California Natural organic lamb-rice-blend dog food. Ted hoisted the bag over his shoulder and handed me the leash. And as we walked home together, I watched the way Ted balanced the bag competently on one shoulder, like a provider, like a family man. I found myself filling with a sense of abundance and safety. Ted had always done all the lifting, because he worried I might injure my back. He would always shoulder the burdens without complaint. And as he set the bag down outside our building, I felt cared for in a way I had never known before. Rex leapt happily alongside. *Food! Food for me! Food! For me! I'm special! I'm special!*

"You'd make a good father," I told him.

"And you'd make a good mother."

"Do you think?"

Ted held the door for us. Inside, Rex ran into his crate and twisted around and faced us, safe in his little lair. It seemed we had all gotten used to our crates.

CHAPTER 14

A Bedtime Story

Until we moved to the Upper East Side, Rex had not been sleeping on our bed. The Monks of Steel had not allowed it. Therefore, neither did Ted. "If you allow a dog to sleep on the bed, they'll start to think they're human," Ted always said, quoting the Monks. "Rex will start to think he's an equal in the pack."

"Then maybe *I* should start sleeping on the floor, too," I said. Ted had not let me pick out the restaurant the night before.

"Who would satisfy my needs, then?" Ted said, grabbing me for a kiss.

"How flattering," I said.

So on the Lower East Side, I was allowed in the Master Bed, but Rex was not. He, the poor deprived thing, had to sleep in that little green polyester bed on the floor next to our bed. A dog should *by all means* be allowed to sleep in the bedroom, the Monks stressed. "This will build trust and confidence, and the dog will truly benefit from the extended period of contact with your scent." I always liked the idea of this—that simply lying around in our presence could soothe our dog, and calm him, and build a foundation of trust. It made raising a dog seem so easy and effortless. I once saw an art exhibit in London, which consisted of Tilda Swinton sleeping all day in a booth of glass, and I remember thinking: I wish I could get a job like that.

But when we moved to the Upper East Side we found ourselves

with a bedroom that was so small it could barely accommodate a bed. (My twin nieces, when they visited, called it "the hallway with the bed in it.") We couldn't fit the side table, or the bureau, or even the little wicker box in which we kept the condoms, inside that room. So of course we couldn't fit a dog bed either. But could we defy the Monks of Steel?

"My friend Annie keeps her dog in a crate in the bathroom," I said. "With the lights out. And a lot of people keep them gated off in the *kitchen*."

"How cruel," Ted said. "Rex would be on the phone to the ASPCA in a second if we tried to crate him overnight."

"And what about those people who make their dogs sleep in *dog-houses*? Out in the yard?"

"Criminal," Ted said.

See? We agreed on some things. So we had no choice but to allow Rex up on the bed with us. "But he has to stay at the foot," Ted said. "They stress that in all the books. We can't let him anywhere near that pillow. Dogs have to know their place."

"Maybe if we get a bed-within-the-bed," I said, "he'll have his own little bed that's separate from ours, like a raft."

"Good idea," Ted said.

"So this means I can buy a new bed!"

Shopping, in my book, is always a good idea. And the only time Ted didn't try to curb my spending was when I bought things for Rex. I spent the next several days poring over doggie catalogs, investigating fabrics, and even visiting the decorative arts section of the Met to see how the dog beds in the Louis Quinze room looked. And, in the end, I finally settled on a very sensible Snuggle Nest from Petco. I was partnered with a very sensible person, after all. Who would not have liked the fact that I had purchased a six-hundred-dollar blue velour floor pillow with spring green piping at New York's most exquisite furniture store: ABC Carpet & Home. But anyway, what sold me on the reasonably priced Snuggle Nest was the advertising photo—of a spanking-clean spaniel snoozing sweetly, with his cute little snoutie squished against the side of the bed. Who can resist such images? I also ordered, in the spirit of passive resistance, some plush toys, a peppermint-flavored tug-a-rope, more poultry-flavored dental rinse, and some Choo Hooves. Anyway, a few days later, the buzzer rang, which meant the giant dog bed and other amenities had arrived via UPS, and Rex danced around with excitement. He leapt up on the door and pawed at it, *a-woo-woo-wooing* with the zest of a trumpeter. He no longer felt compelled to attack large strange men who came to the door. In fact, now he knew they were always delivering the latest and greatest dog products directly to him.

"What's all this?" Ted said, as he unpacked the bed, and then the Choo Hooves, and the all-natural flea repellent, etc., from the box.

"Oh, some stuff he needed."

Ted raised his eyebrows in suspicion. "This cost how much?" But then he raised them in delight when Rex pulled out the tug-a-rope and brought it to Ted.

"Who has a rope-a?" Ted said. "Who has a new rope?"

"It's a minty rope," I said, speaking like a commercial spokeswoman. "To freshen his breath."

"Who's going to have fresh breath?" Ted asked Rex.

While they tugged, I brought the Snuggle Nest into the hallway-with-a-bed-in-it and put it on the bed. It didn't leave Ted and me much leg room, but I figured if we slept back-to-back, curling up our legs like stowaways, it might work.

"Come check this out," I said.

Ted came in, dragging the snarling minty-breathed dog behind him with the rope.

"Move it further toward the foot of the bed," Ted said.

"I don't want him to slide off."

Rex dropped his end of the rope and watched with interest.

"Where's he going to go?" Ted said. "Do you think he'll slide down those six inches between the bed and the wall?"

"*Okay.*"

We made a big show of positioning the Snuggle Nest, and then Ted told Rex he could do a test drive. "Hop up!" Ted said to the dog in his happy Rex voice. Rex cocked his head. "This is your bed!" Ted said. "Your new little bed. This is where Rex will sleep. Okay, now, hop up."

And Rex hopped up, with an air of self-righteousness that made me suspicious. He had been planning this for a long time, I realized. All that sitting when we told him to sit, the coming when we called him to come, was just a ruse, a ploy to trick us into giving him this privilege. They say that's the only reason men are truly nice to women: to get them to allow them to crawl into their beds.

"Look at him," I said to Ted. "He's acting like a king."

Rex turned a few circles on the mattress and settled in. Then he let out a grunt of satisfaction, a rather corporate grunt, as if a contract had just been signed—the hostile takeover he had been orchestrating for months. "What time would you like your wake-up call, sir?" I asked him. "And shall you be wanting breakfast in bed?"

Sensing that I was offering him something (even if it was in jest), Rex inched toward me. Ted shouted, "You stay at the foot of the bed!"

We found we loved having the dog down there at our feet, in his little doughnut-shaped bed. He was just so cute in his little Snuggle Nest, with his face pushed up against the sides. He slept so solidly, so peacefully—the kind of sleep, it seems, that God intended. A sleep without bad dreams, or the grinding of teeth. Now he dreamed dog dreams, and woofed lightly in his sleep and flexed his paws. He was dreaming of squirrels, of course, and butterflies, and perhaps even of us. Ted and I always stopped whatever we were doing to watch him woof like this. We'd stand over him with our arms around each other, smiling tenderly, as if he were a baby in a crib.

We started to invite him up for morning cuddles. Ted managed to track down an out-of-print dog-training book that said it was fine to have a dog sleep on the bed, as long as the owner issued the command. So the new rule became that Rex spent the night in the Snuggle Nest, and in the morning he would be allowed between us for a quick cuddle before we all went out for the Morning Walk. Both Ted and I loved these cuddle sessions. Rex liked to sleep in any number of positions, all of them equally cute: with his head hooked over my ankle and the rest of his body curled around my feet. With his head on my pelvis and one paw draped atop my thigh. Mostly he liked to sleep between the two of us, touching us both. Rex would hook his own neck over his father's, and his back legs over my legs, and sigh the sigh of one who has had all his worldly needs met, and then start to snore lightly. And if you have a shelter dog who spent the first ten months of his life in misery, this snore can be a very satisfying sound indeed.

The morning cuddles became morning and evening cuddles. Rex, in the still of the night, while we were sleeping, would creep out of his Snuggle Nest—like a soldier crawling through a foxhole—and when we woke up he'd be there, between us, an expectant dog-smile on his face.

"You get back down there," Ted would say, but then Rex would rest his head on Ted's chest, and Ted would say, "Aw, who's this little sleepyhead? Who snuck up here even though he knows he's not supposed to?"

Around this time Ted had taken on another documentary project that required him to leave early in the day. I liked to linger in bed after Ted got up in the morning. I liked to lie there as Ted made the coffee and started talking about the day. As soon as Ted left the bedroom Rex would scootch his body farther up toward the pillows, as if to claim the warm space Ted had just left behind. We'd cuddle. I liked the way Rex smelled in the mornings—a mixture of dog and laundry soap— and I liked the soft sound of breath moving into and out of his nose. I'd doze off for a while, then wake up to find Rex facing me, with his face so close to mine our noses almost touched, our nostrils aligned like a plug and a socket. I breathed in the air he breathed out, and vice versa, and the exchange—so soft and delicate—made me feel connected to this dog on levels that were beyond anything Ted and I shared. It was as if my prana were his prana; as if we flowed with the very same life force.

Now, whenever Ted and I wanted to, you know, we had to coerce Rex into getting off the bed. This involved first giving him the Off command, which he knew we knew he knew. But Rex seemed to feel he was the CEO in this mattress corporation, so he rarely deigned to obey. "Off!" Ted would say a few more times. "Rex, off!" Then would come a low growl of warning, then the corporate grunt, as if to remind us of the hostile takeover, and then Ted, naked, would throw the sheets off his legs and stand up and physically lift the dog onto the floor. "I said *Off*!" Ted would shout, right into the stubborn dog's ear. "Now you lay down. Down! And stay!"

Then Ted would turn to me, and dim the lights, or light a candle, and try to pick up where we left off (Off! Off!), but soon, inevitably, in the midst of something unmentionable, I'd glance over Ted's shoulder and see a dog head resting on the foot of the bed. Rex had broken his Down command and was now standing, waiting, his chin resting on the mattress, as if it were too much effort to hold his head up himself.

I always broke into peals of laughter at this point, and then Ted would yell at Rex to "lie down, dammit!" and the whole scenario would begin again. But never quite finish. It seemed we wouldn't be having children anytime soon.

The running joke, between me and myself, was that Rex was the only one getting off. I don't think Ted would have found that funny.

Eventually, inevitably, all the dog rules went out the window. The Monks of Steel, had they flown in through our windows with their brown sack capes, would have found chaos. No dogs on the bed? No playing in the bedroom? The bedroom is a peaceful place? Now, the first thing Ted did when he got home was grab the dog and invite him to have a wrestling match right on the bed. The two would growl at each other and try to snatch each other's legs—Rex using his mouth, Ted using his hands, and every once in a while I would hear the growling stop and Ted saying, in his dog voice, "Ow! Too hard, too hard!" And I'd come check to see if Ted was okay, and Rex would be sitting there with a startled look on his face, as if Ted had somehow cheated and changed the rules. "He never learned how to play-bite as a puppy," I said. "Now you're teaching him. It's so cute."

Or how about "No table scraps! The dog must stay in a Down/ Stay during mealtimes, preferably under the table!"? Now, everything I ate, he got a taste of. And why not? He liked food, and I liked to watch him enjoy his food. I liked to watch the way he chewed, seriously, with his mouth open, in a sort of smile.

"Do dogs have taste buds?" I said to Ted.

"I can't imagine," Ted said. "Think of all the garbage they eat."

"Here Cutie Boy," I said, "taste this coconut shrimp and tell me if you think it's good."

Rex would stand up to take the treat. "Don't give him that!" Ted said. "You're going to give him diarrhea. And you're not supposed to feed him from the table."

As a compensation, I always let him lick the plate. When Ted wasn't looking, of course. Soon Rex figured out that whatever I was eating would be shared with him. He sat next to me at the dining table. It eventually got to the point where he would try to eat right off my plate. Ted and I often ate with our plates on our laps in front of the TV, and rested our feet on the coffee table. And Rex had been known to crawl onto the coffee table, walk right over to my plate, and lick at my macaroni and cheese.

"Hey!" Ted said. "You can't do that."

I would giggle and kiss the dog on the head. "You have to wait until Alpha is not looking."

The next rule was "No dogs *on* the table during meals." And "No raw meat on the bed." Other than that the dog could do whatever he wanted.

And sure enough, Rex got less and less obedient. The Monks had been right all along. Outside, in the park in the mornings, he'd take his time returning to us when we called, stopping off to pee on this tree or that, then pinning his nose to the ground and veering off to follow the scent trail of a bygone squirrel. When Ted screeched at him to "Come! Now! Dammit!" Rex would lift his head in true surprise, as if this was the first he'd heard of such a request. And when Ted shouted another "Come! Here! Now!" Rex would tense up into that pre-sprint position, look at us one last time to see if we were watching, and then leap up and run away. "Damn dog!" Ted would say. "It's because he's sleeping in the bed. I'd like to sleep with just you once in a while."

It was around that time that the subject of a vacation came up.

"We should go to Paris," Ted suggested. "We can celebrate. We can spend a few days in Paris and drive to the south of France."

Ted was turning thirty that month, and I—drum roll please— had finally, finally, finally finished the novel. And had hand-delivered it to the hottest agent in town. So, indeed, we had much to celebrate.

Normally my heart would flutter at the sound of the word *Paris*. At the thought of strolling with a handsome, generous, French-speaking man along the Quai Voltaire. A few years earlier I had lived in Antibes, and I knew it was one of the most beautiful places on the planet. It would be fun, I realized, to visit my past. With my present.

But wait, we had a dog. So how could we take a vacation? We had never been away from him before. This is a dog that, if you tried to tie him to a parking meter while you ran into the deli to get *The New York Times*, would howl and scream so painfully that passersby (the same ones who would step over a freshly stabbed person to catch the M10) would stop and try to comfort him. I'd come out of the deli to find a doctor, on his knees, offering Rex his breakfast bagel; two nurses singing "How much is that doggie in the window?" and stroking his ears; and a schoolgirl or two looking self-righteous. "He was upset," the first schoolgirl would say, dangling a little stuffed gorilla key chain in front of Rex's nose. "He didn't even want my maple scone." "And his heart is *racing*," the doctor would say, holding a hand to Rex's chest. "This poor boy is terrified. *Terrified*."

I could only stare blankly at my accusers. We had moved to a neighborhood full of hospitals and private schools. "He has separation anxiety," I told them feebly. Rex pounced on me again and again, shouting *a-woo-woo-woo* and muddying up my skirt.

"He came from a shelter," I explained. "Before we rescued him, he was abandoned, I think. Sometimes I think he was one of those dogs who got left tied to a pole. But I'm trying to recondition him. I'm trying to teach him that *I'm* not abandoning him when I tie him to a pole."

One of the nurses nodded her head, and said "Uh-huh," in that way that suggested she didn't believe a word I said. It turns out she worked in the psychiatric ward at St. Luke's.

"People steal dogs, you know," another person said—a businessman in a Sean John suit who just happened to be walking by. "It happened to my wife's cousin. They steal them from parking meters and then sell them to labs." He began to talk of dogs being maimed, probed, and blinded by cruel laboratory technicians. He talked of the "brokers" who would comb the want ads looking for free puppies, and then sell them for a profit to the labs. He talked of the outright thieves, the scum, who patrolled the streets of this very city, looking for dogs to steal. The schoolgirls turned around to look at me accusingly. Rex and I fled the scene.

My heart was racing as we hurried away. Gosh! It was enough to make you want to have your *New York Times* delivered, but in my building, people stole that, too.

"Just because I tied you to that parking meter doesn't mean I was abandoning you," I told Rex on the way home. "You know that, right? I would never leave you. Sometimes I just like to read the paper, to find out what's going on in the human world."

Rex just gave me an uncertain look and continued to trot worriedly toward Third Avenue, back to our apartment, to the safety of his crate. He remained extra clingy for the rest of the day—following me from the desk to the refrigerator, to the bathroom, and back to the desk. He kept placing his body between me and the doorway and giving me an imploring look, as if to say: *You're not gonna do it, right? You're not gonna go, right? You won't forget me, will you?*

"I would never leave you!" I kept pulling his face toward mine and kissing him all over his head and snout. "You're my baby boy. You're my little love!" His sweet determination made me sad. And a little frustrated. What would it take to convince my dog that I would never leave him? That I was his for life? That Ted was too?

Maybe I just needed to resign myself, once and for all, to the fact that our dog, as the psychiatric nurse would say, had "issues." Issues that, because of their sheer mystery, we could never cure.

Meanwhile, Ted had issues, too. He was worried about our, um, intimate life. We were now sleeping with a large dog wedged between us, a dog who spooned with me while simultaneously pushing Ted away with all four paws. Rest on that image for a while, and you will see a bigger picture.

"Come on," Ted kept suggesting. "Let's go to France on my birthday. We deserve this."

"Can Rex come with us?" I said.

"No!" Ted said. "I would never fly him. It's not safe."

"Well, then why do we have a giant training crate in our living room?"

But Ted wasn't listening. He was already packing sensual body lotions and the *Frommer's* travel guide. "The whole point is to get away for a while, just the two of us, alone."

"Oh," I said. "Well, we'll have to find a really good dog-sitter."

The good dog-sitter came to us in the form of Donna—a cheerful, heavyset woman who sold advertising space at the pharmaceutical magazine where I used to temp. Her own dog, a sleek Italian greyhound, had died a few months earlier, and Donna still kept a giant studio portrait of Organza on her desk. Most of the people in the office had thought it was weird, even excessive, to spend five thousand dollars on a dog portrait, but I never did. I loved to hear stories about her dearly departed dog. I cried right along with her when she told me how Organza had died in her arms on the way to the vet's office. We had a bond that went beyond the normal office gossip.

So when I mentioned to Donna that Ted and I wanted to go away, and that we were looking for a dog-sitter, she immediately offered to do it. "I'd love to," she said. "I really miss the company of dogs." She wasn't ready to get another dog yet, she told me. "That's a big commitment, and I want to play this dog-dating game for a while." But she'd be happy to watch Rex while we were away. "Hell," she said laughing. "Maybe after that week I'll be ready to march right down to the pound and get me another hound."

I didn't tell her that Rex was the sort of client who made you *not* want to get a dog.

Now, my reference book, *The Hypochondriac's Guide to Overprotective Dog Care*, states that before you leave your dog for an extended period, you should do a trial sleepover, in which you leave the dog at the kennel or the dog-sitter's for a short overnight visit and make a big show of picking him up the next morning. That way, the book advised, your dog will know for certain that you're coming back.

"You want to what?" Donna said.

After I described, once again, the benefits of a trial sleepover, she said, "You don't need to do that. Organza used to stay at my ex-boyfriend's house all the time, and she would just walk right into his apartment when I brought her over. She'd hop right up on the sofa and wouldn't even look back at me. Trust me, Rex will be fine."

I realized Donna was using her sales-pitch voice. (Donna's job was to convince doctors that their patients had illnesses that didn't yet exist, and then present a new miracle drug that would cure them.) "It's not just for Rex's peace of mind," I said. "It's for mine and Ted's, too. Could you humor us and take him Friday night?"

She looked at me and nodded and said "Uh-huh," the same way that psychiatric nurse had. "I'll tell you what. You treat me to a facial at Bliss when you get back and it's a deal."

We brought Rex over for the trial sleepover that weekend. Donna had an apartment on Gramercy Park with multiple rooms. This amount of space was in itself a novelty to Rex (who had known only the concrete box of the shelter, and then the only slightly larger concrete box of our tenement apartment). He ran from room to room with the excitement of a prospective buyer. He'd dash off and then come clattering back into the living room all breathless, wagging his tail at us as if to say: *Look! It has a fireplace! Look! The bathroom has a Jacuzzi! Look! There are three beds on which to nap!*

"He likes it here!" said Donna. She had a tennis ball ready when we got there, and threw it down the hall for Rex to chase. Rex scrambled happily across the slippery hardwood floors, his four legs no longer working in concert. We laughed.

"It's a great apartment," I said. I couldn't disguise the jealousy in my voice. I wondered if Ted and I would ever live in such a place.

Ted wanted to walk with Donna and Rex through the neighborhood, to give her the lowdown on Rex on leash. But when he took out the prong collar, Donna shook her head. "I never use those things," she said. "They're inhumane. Organza had a choke collar. I still have it actually. We'll use that."

"But his hair only just grew back," I said. I hadn't meant for my statement to come out like a whine, but it did.

"The last choke collar we used pulled all his hair out," Ted said.

Donna looked at us. "Hair grows back. It always does. Try Rogaine. Or a new product we're marketing called Grocitan." Donna fastened the nylon choke collar around Rex's neck, and made a great ceremony of giving it a sharp tug. Rex twisted his head toward her, looking startled and a bit betrayed. I had promised Rex, after the Epilady days, never to use a choke on him again.

"See?" Donna said crisply. "That gets his attention. Now let's go, shall we? Rex, would you like to go for a walk?" The word *walk,* as always, set Rex into a tizzy of barking, leaping, and swirling. Then he pulled Donna through the doors in one great jerk. "That's why we use the prong," Ted called after her. "He pulls."

I raised my eyebrows at Ted and shrugged. One of the nicknames we had for Rex, that we used on the way to the park, was Pull McCartney. His nickname on the way back was Stubborn Boy.

Outside the building, Donna brought Rex to the curb and stood between two parked cars. "Okay, Rex," she said. "Now do your business, do your business." She put one hand on her hip and turned to us. "Organza always used to pee right here. She just went right to this spot, did her job, and turned around to go back inside. If she had keys she could have let herself in and out."

I looked at the building's awning, and then at Ted. He gave a shrug. I finally realized that other dog people expect all dogs to act like *their* dog.

There were two elaborate topiaries on either side of the awning posts that Rex might be tempted to piss on, but clearly Donna had never had a male dog. She hadn't experienced the one-hour pee session, released one teaspoon at a time at choice locations. Another nickname we had for Rex was the Prince of Pee.

"What's wrong with him?" Donna said. She continued to hover over him saying, "Do your business, do your business." Meanwhile Rex was looking at her with a mixture of impatience and dismay, as if to say he would do his business on his own time, thank you very much.

"Um, you might have to walk him around the neighborhood," I said. "He has this thing where he never poops in front of our own building. You have to take him at least a block and a half. Also, he never goes on a corner, but he does like to go in front of other dogs' buildings. I should have written this all down," I said to Ted.

"Give me another minute," Donna said. "It didn't take me long to train Organza to pee right here. Now, come on Rex, do your business. If you do your business I'll give you a treat."

Ted rolled his eyes. "We're going to be standing here for days," he said. "Come on, Rex!" he shouted. "Let's go for a walk!" He clapped his hands together and started walking. Rex hurried after Ted, dragging poor Donna behind him. Rex finally peed near the National Arts Club three blocks south. I'd always dreamed of giving a reading there.

We didn't know what to do with ourselves that night. The apartment felt empty, devoid of life. Rex's presence was huge; his absence huger. I called a few people to tell them Rex was having his first sleepover, but no one was home. It was Friday in New York. Ted suggested dinner, and we ordered a thin-crusted pizza at Totonno's, with a robust and fruity red wine, with hints of pepper and cherry, and we discussed this wine in detail—its vintage, its Italian provenance—but we both knew the conversation was fake. All through dinner we worried if Rex missed us as much as we missed him. I wondered if he felt he was being punished for some reason. If he felt abandoned or lost or alone. I remember how shocked I was years ago, when my sister told me she hadn't spent one full night away from her daughters—not one—for the first *six years*. Up until now I'd found that unfathomable. But now I think I got it. Eating that pizza that night was just not fun, because there was no dog around trying to convince you to give it away.

But all in all, the trial period went fine. Rex was exhausted when we picked him up and Donna had not suffered any puncture wounds. Rex slept on the way home in the cab. We had no idea whether this exhaustion came from frolicking or nervous tension, but we felt confident that we could safely leave Rex with Donna for a week. And so, we said goodbye to our Love Child, leaving him with some toys, his favorite blankie, and two rank T-shirts—one that smelled like me, and one that smelled like Ted. And then we rushed out Donna's door, not wanting to hear the old Roger Daltrey howl.

"I hope he doesn't yank Donna's arm out of her socket," I said, putting my head on Ted's shoulder as we sat on the plane. "Or try to bite her or anything. I wasn't very forthcoming about his past."

"They'll be fine," Ted said. But he wasn't even listening to me. He was reading a travel guide and circling all the restaurants he wanted to visit. Ted was the type who traveled with a full itinerary, whereas I just kind of floated along, letting myself be carried into any shop, restaurant, or museum that crossed my path. We suited each other in this regard, as Ted kept us tethered to the practical, but I led us on adventures we might otherwise not have had.

Ted made some notes in his little travel diary. "When we stop in Paris, we'll have to eat at that place near Montmartre, where you had the octopus salad and I had that steak. Remember the waiter brought me a bottle of ketchup, just to be funny, because we were American?"

"Do you think Rex misses us yet?" I said.

"He's fine," Ted said. "Donna is taking good care of him. You saw how she was. Now stop thinking about it. We're going to have a great time."

Being on vacation always softens a couple; being in France turns you into buttery croissant dough. All the issues and arguments you cling to so tightly in your hometown simply don't matter in France. What matters is wine, lingerie, beaches, shopping, and food. "This is going to be a dream vacation," I said.

But there was one problem about this particular vacation: I could not get out of my mind the image of Rex, lying in Donna's foyer with his head between his paws, staring at us with utter shock and betrayal, as he realized we were really going to leave him. All the dog people out there know that look. For centuries, it has been pulling on the heartstrings of all humankind.

And so, despite the fact that I was in Paris, for God's sake, the most beautiful city in all the world, the City of Light, the City of Love, I could not forget the Look. Even as Ted and I shopped for three days in the sixth arrondissement, all I could really see was that head between those paws, and I was filled with longing and guilt. Plus, there were Rex-like dogs everywhere. He may have been a one-of-a-kind dog in New York City, but here, in Paris, *épagneuls français* filled the city—you could spot them riding on the buses, dozing under café tables, poking through stores. They were delightfully French in their attitudes—crossing the streets in front of cars with a mixture of entitlement, arrogance, and disdain. And seeing them made me miss Rex even more.

Now, Ted and I both loved to travel. In fact, we had officially fallen in love on a trip to the Czech Republic when we discovered our mutual passions for museums, pilsner, fried food, and Egon Schiele. So why was I acting so distracted? From Paris we drove to the Riviera, the second-most beautiful place in the world, and booked ourselves into a quaint *auberge* with a four-star restaurant. But even as Ted and I swam in the aquamarine waters in Juan les Pins and hiked along its rocky beaches; even as, at night, we dined on *moules frites* and mainlined Côtes du Rhone, my mind kept coming back to the face of our poor neglected spaniel. Was it guilt that held me in this fickle mindset? Or did spending all my days with a dog mean I had finally lost the ability to have simple human fun? Maybe Rex had finally turned me into a domesticated animal, ready for the apartment on Gramercy and the kids. Was this the fate I was headed toward? Giving up my dreams of excitement and travel in order to stay home with my dog? For the next six years?

Ted missed Rex, too, but in a healthier sort of way. He kept promising me we'd call Donna and check in, but every time we headed for a phone booth he'd get distracted by all the sexy French mannequins in the lingerie shops, or by the food. Our *auberge* faced an open-air market, and every morning, starting at eight, vendors from throughout the region would set up tables of produce, olives, lavender products, and cured meats. "Look at these cheeses!" Ted would say, pointing toward miniature rounds of goat cheese, coated in curry powder, red pepper, black pepper, or basil leaves. Soon our whole day would be centered around this cheese. "We can get a skewer of that, and a baguette and some sausage, and that'll be our lunch." At the market, Ted always had a beady-eyed look on his face that reminded me of the crazed focus with which Rex beheld a squirrel.

"I thought we were going to call Rex this morning," I said. A lone Afghan hound sat at a café table as if waiting for his date.

"We'll do it after lunch," Ted said. "Let's find something to eat for breakfast first." And then he would lead me through the crowds of French people, following the scent of an apricot tart.

Days passed like this. Basically, I thought about Rex every twelve seconds. I'd read somewhere that this is how often a male human thinks about sex. I suddenly felt as if I had a new understanding of Ted's gender. "How do you get anything accomplished?" I said to him that night over dinner (lobster ravioli, followed by pressed duck and a green salad, then tiny pots of crème caramel). "I mean, if you're thinking about sex all the time, how can you complete a thought? How can men be *presidents* for God's sake?"

"What did you say?" Ted said. All the food and wine had hypnotized him and lulled him into a permanently hedonistic state. He was licking crème caramel off a spoon and staring at my breasts.

"Can we call Rex tonight?" I said.

"Let's go for a walk first," Ted said. The word *walk* hung between us for a second, and made us stare at each other, unsure of what to do. There was no Rex around to seize upon this word and dance and spin and bark at the door. Rex, I realized, was like an exclamation point. Could it be that without him our lives lacked punctuation? Even our bed felt emptier without him.

But this was our last night in France, so we went for a walk along the ramparts—the ancient, giant seawalls that had protected the city of Antibes from foreign invasion. I took Ted's hand and inhaled the scent of the Mediterranean as we picked our way along the cobblestones. I felt at peace. Two years earlier, when I lived in Antibes, I used to roam these streets at night, so full of loneliness and doom I was convinced that love and all its glories had eluded me entirely. I believed, back then, that I was meant to be alone. That something in me could never, had never, and would never reach out to another person, and that I should simply give up that quest. And yet here I was again, stepping across the very same cobblestones with Ted. The streetlights glowed a pale pink above us. A soft breeze carried the scent of orange blossoms and mimosa. The click of my heels echoed off the ancient walls.

Ted and I stopped and looked into an apartment window. From within came the low voices of a couple sharing dinner, accompanied by the tinkling of silverware and glass. Two years earlier, the beauty of this place had often been too much for me, because such beauty should be shared, and I could not bear to encounter it alone. But now I had the sense that I had traveled through time somehow. That at any moment we would turn the corner and greet the shadow of my former self, and I would be able to hug her and tell her: *Look. There was no need to worry. He is right here. He was there the whole time, waiting for us.*

Then we could all go out for an apéritif and I could show her pictures of our dog.

Ted took my arm as we walked past the Picasso Museum. I felt a tender gratitude rise within me—for the lonely person I was then; and to Ted for bringing me here. Perhaps now is the time to confess that my first novel was about this loneliness—the novel that I had just finished. And had released. And passed on. I didn't realize until that moment how freeing it is to bring something to its final conclusion, to let go.

I pulled Ted's arm around my waist. I kissed his cheek. Above us, lining a tall stone wall, stood rows and rows of bronze statues: tall, thin figures with their arms held stiffly across their midsections. We stopped to study them. They seemed to be guarding something; they seemed to be guarding themselves. "They're like four soccer players awaiting a penalty kick," I said. Then Ted turned to face me with a weird, almost manic look on his face. He took my hand and kissed it. "I can't believe you used to live here, in such a beautiful place. Why did you ever leave?"

"I ran out of money," I told him. "Plus, NYU had offered me that teaching job."

I did not say I had left to escape the loneliness. It had simply followed me back to New York anyway.

"Will you marry me?" Ted suddenly said. I looked at him wide eyed, and then away, shy with disbelief. Something had caught in my throat and I couldn't speak. So I threw my arms around Ted and held him, waiting for my mind to wrap around this moment so that I could form some words. A cat poked its head from underneath an archway, a deliberate look on its face as it prepared to stalk the night, but when it saw us it hesitated. And then withdrew.

"Yes," I finally said. "Yes." And then I started to cry.

Ted hugged me tightly, and kissed my neck, and then pulled away to see my face. "You look so beautiful out here in the moonlight. How'd I get so lucky?"

I smiled.

"I can't believe we're getting married. I'll give you the ring later," he said. "My mother has two old family rings she'd like to offer, and I told her I'd let you choose."

"You told your mother? And she's offering her ring? She's so nice!" I hugged him again and looked over his shoulder. Above us, the moonlight glittered on the Mediterranean, a wise old moon that seemed to wink at me in a grandfatherly way.

I pulled away from Ted again. "Let's skip," I said.

"What?"

I realized Ted was just as nervous about marriage as I was. But he was willing to take a chance.

"Let's skip, like Dorothy in *The Wizard of Oz.*"

And so we took each other's hands and skipped, past the statues, down along the cobblestones, toward the *auberge.* Corny, yes, but totally sincere.

"We need to call Rex!" I said.

At the airport the next morning, everything felt different. Announcements about our impending departure were made over and over again in English, and then in French. I kept looking at Ted and saying, "We're engaged!" And he would say: "Now we can make Rex a legitimate child." And when he mentioned Rex I'd get tears in my eyes, for all that he was, for all that he would be, and then I'd say again: "We're engaged!" We did this every twelve seconds, and continued to do so as we flew across the Atlantic, toward New York. Both of us seemed to be in a mild form of shock, and that was fine, because it helps to be in a state of shock when you get to New York City. That way you are never really surprised.

There was an infant sitting one row in front of us, who slept through the entire flight. And as we stood to deplane, I found myself facing him as the mother carried him off. He locked his eyes onto mine, in that way that babies do, and smiled a damp, gummy smile. I felt as if I knew this baby, I felt as if he knew me. The baby must have been nine months old. "He's cute, isn't he?" I said to Ted.

Ted squeezed my shoulder. "He is."

I always used to return from vacations with some sense of dread at having once again to face the reality of my mundane life. But as we pulled away in our cab from Kennedy airport, I couldn't contain my excitement. We were going to get Rex! In half an hour! Twenty minutes! Fifteen!

Finally, the cab pulled up in front of Donna's apartment building. We rang the buzzer. I bounced on my toes. I had a huge dumb smile on my face and so did Ted. Donna buzzed us into the building and then sent Rex down the hall. Through the glass doors we saw him running. Ted and I both sank to our knees. The door opened and Rex barreled into our arms. He was so excited he couldn't stay still: he wiggled and squirmed out of my arms and into Ted's, then back into mine again, covering us with kisses the whole time. "Look how happy he is," Donna said, laughing. She clapped her hands. "He was a good, good boy."

But we weren't really listening to Donna. The sounds that emerged from Rex's throat were unlike anything I had ever heard before. He was grunting and muttering and making little yelps that rose and fell as he squirmed between us. It sounded like he was trying to tell us something—the story of his week, the story of his life. I swear I heard, in his dog language, a complex range of emotions full of both pleasure and pain.

Later, I would find out from Donna that Rex had escaped twice from her choke collar, once up at her country house, and once right here on Gramercy Park. We would learn that he had attended his first sales meeting and had seen his first snow. But in this moment, I hugged Rex with tears in my eyes. Because it dawned on me that he was saying to us: *I thought I would never see you again. My first person left me and I never saw him again. So I thought you had left forever, too. I thought I would never see this day.* And I realized this was the very same sentiment that had caught in my throat outside the Picasso Museum. "It's okay," I told Rex, petting him and petting him. I reminded him we weren't anything like his First Person. We were his Second Person Plural. "We got engaged!" I told him.

"Hey, congratulations," Donna said.

Rex twisted out of my arms and kissed Ted full on the mouth. And then he kissed me again. It was as if he was sealing something between the three of us. As if he were saying: *I do, I do, I do.*

Acknowledgments

I have had the immense good fortune, throughout my life, of connecting with dozens of talented, inspiring, and truly generous people. The list below comprises those who helped bring this book (and me) to life.

Claudia Kawczynska and Cameron Woo of *The Bark* magazine were the first to publish my column, "Rex and the City," back in the summer of 2000. It was Claudia who told me, as I described to her my anecdotes about raising a rabid hunting dog with a rabid boyfriend in a tiny apartment in New York City, "You have a story here." I thank Claudia and Cameron and the whole *Bark* team for their unwavering generosity, encouragement, and support. They gave Rex a home, and me a start, and made this book possible. I also appreciate their dedication to quality dog writing, and to all causes that advocate the humane treatment of all animals (and the people who care for them). Their efforts are truly making this world a better place. I would also like to thank the readers of *The Bark* for their enthusiastic fan mail. Their compliments always made my day.

At Random House, I wish to thank Dan Menaker and Lee Boudreaux for having enough faith in me to acquire two unfinished books (the latter based on twelve pages of prose). I also wish to thank, thank, thank my editor, Laura Ford, whose kindness, patience, dedication, and editorial expertise really brought this book into a new dimension. I feel blessed that she and I connected and have been able to work together on this book. My copy editors, Holly Webber and Beth Pearson, deserve special recognition, since they took over at a point when both Laura and I were bleary-eyed from reading this manuscript. They and the proofreaders, Graham Maby and Melissa Pierson, picked up on every inconsistency and grammatical error, and they graciously allowed me to keep all my made-up words. I would also like to thank our publicists, Kate Blum and Megan Fishmann; our marketing wizard, Avideh Bashirrad; the photographers, Karen Ngo and Amanda Jones; our stellar book and jacket designers, Mercedes Everett and Allison Saltzman; and web designer Breton Hornblower.

Sue Synarksi, who did the cover illustration for this book, has been bringing Rex/Wallace to life (in her own twisted way) in the *Bark* series for six years. I appreciate her talent and humor, as well as her ability to capture, in her illustrations, the personality of a dog she never met.

At ICM, I wish to thank Lisa Bankoff—who has been my best friend and advocate in the publishing industry and beyond—and her assistant, Tina DuBois Wexler, who has always been gracious, attentive, quick to respond, and, above all, kind. That matters a lot.

I am grateful to all the members of my family, who pretend not to mind when I write about them, and who are willing to admit that I do it with love: Dad and Jane; Robbie, Melanie, Jessica, and little Mikey; Deb, John, and the twinsies, Sarah and Jen; Mary, Dale, Dee, Chelsea, and their dogs, Bailey and Cody; Marty and Michelle; David, Kenny, and Chrissie; Andy (my Irish twin and a talented poet); and of course, the Little One, Christine. Mary has mothered me, Andy has guided me toward goodness, and Christine—the miracle child—has been a shining light. May all her hidden talents continue to unfold. The Hills and Cabans always welcomed Wallace into their homes (thereby putting their children at risk). I thank them.

I am especially grateful to my surrogate mother, Judy McKelvey, who has been Rex's number one fan from the get-go (and who has probably set the world record for the number of *Bark* gift subscriptions purchased to date). Judy's abundant love, enthusiasm, support, and belief in me as a writer literally made this book possible. She will always be a mother in my heart.

And I have yet another surrogate family: the Friedmans. Karen,

Davi, David, Annie, and Debbi came into my life when I was ten, and lost, and they have been there ever since.

Many thanks to my friends for their love, companionship, and support: Courtney Baron, Liz Brody, Karen Blood, James Bond, Christine Brotherson, Adrienne Brodeur, Nina Burleigh, Henri and Lisa Cattier, Kristi and Jean-Marc DeFrasne, Abby Ellin (who gave me shelter from the storms), Alec Emerson, Jessica Erace, Ann and Ed F., David Frankel, Deborah Garrett, Janet Goddard, Patricia Graf, Teresa Hohl, Elizabeth and Louise Leborgne, Torie Ludwin, Jim McKelvey, Cindy Moeller and Dave Morgan, David Muller, Susan B. Naughton, Kelcey Nichols, Uma Parikh, Cathy Reily, Gay Salisbury, Shelly Santos, Jack Sinnott, Arbie Thalacker, Anne Tunno, Mary Kay Wieler, and Philip Weinberg.

A few extra-special friends read the manuscript and offered editorial suggestions: Bonnie Downing, Carol Ann Fitzgerald, Christine Harrington, Heather Long, and Samantha Schnee. I am lucky to have had the assistance of these smart and savvy ladies.

And then, of course, there are my two best friends: Karen E. F. Smart and Bethany Lyttle. They are, in a word, everything.

Dog kisses go to Wallace's favorite human friends: Joseph Walser, Radha Subramanyam, Eva Marie Cassanos, Simon at Biscuits & Bath, Mary Jacquelline Trussel, and Betsy Goldberg. More kisses go to Chloe's favorite dog friends, Lexi, Emma, Myrtle, and the Loo; and to their human counterparts, Scott, Jackie, Michael, and Chantay, who, as dog park acquaintances, spent an entire winter listening to me complain about how hard it was to write a book about the past while trying to live in the present.

I must thank Marta and Jasellynne at Antonio Prieto, who have also spent eighteen months listening to me complain about writing while they gussied up my hair. I pay them more than I pay a therapist, and it is worth every cent.

Thank you also to those friends and acquaintances who are portrayed, in disguised form, in these pages. Please trust that your portrayals are presented with good intentions and utmost fondness. (Let us hope you find them flattering.) An extra nod (and a wink) goes to those three girlfriends who appear as the fictional composite Tara. And long live the Monks of New Skete and the Marching Band Man.

I am blessed to have had the following teachers and mentors, healers and helpers: Edward Albee, Arthur Caliandro, Richard Brown, Elizabeth Carpenter, John Cheever, Francis Ford Coppola, Wayne Dyer, F. Scott Fitzgerald, Anne Goelitz, H.H. the Dalai Lama, Judy May, Rhea Nodell, Paul Hewson, Lisa Litt, Pamela Painter, Paramahansa Yogananda, Sharon Sageman, Satya Sai Baba, Sri Sri Ravi Shankar, Pete Townshend, Alice K. Turner, Oprah Winfrey, and the Women of Tuesday.

My childhood dogs—Nina, Tasha, Happy, and Stinky—brought love and happiness into my life and, in a way, brought me to where I am now: writing books about dogs. Who would have thought that dogs could change peoples' lives so profoundly? I thank them for setting this in motion.

And finally, magnanimously, I thank Ed, with whom I shared a life, a love, a soul, a golden ticket, and a dog. We also shared an entire glorious city—a city that never sleeps, and never dies.

About the Author

LEE HARRINGTON's series, "Rex and the City," has
been appearing in *The Bark* magazine since 2000.
She lives in New York City with her second dog,
Clothilde. Visit her website at www.rexandthecity.net.